A Prairie Home Companion®

PRETTY GOOD JOKE BOOK

D0029809

NEW 6TH EDITION

A Prairie Home Companion®

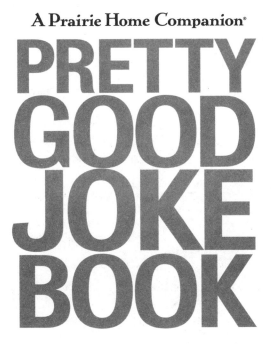

PRETTY GOOD JOKE BOOK

NEW 6TH EDITION

HIGHBRIDGE, A DIVISION OF RECORDED BOOKS

PRINCE FREDERICK, MARYLAND

Published by HighBridge
A Division of Recorded Books
270 Skipjack Road
Prince Frederick, MD 20678

3   4   5   6   7   8   9   10

Joke research by Jeff Alexander, Brian Becker, Joyce Besch, Theresa Burgess, Ellen
Burkhardt, Melissa Christensen, Mike Danforth, Alan Frechtman, Rachel Goettert,
Kay Gornick, Kate Gustafson, Tiffany Hanssen, Julie Jackson, Rob Knowles,
Theresa Larson, Stephen Lehman, Laura Levine, Kathy Mack, Andrea Murray,
David O'Neill, Olivia Pelham, Frank Randall, Katy Reckdahl, Hillary Rhodes, Russ
Ringsak, Dan Rowles, Ella Schovanec, Elena See, Kathryn Slusher, Vincent Voelz,
and the staff and friends of *A Prairie Home Companion*.

Graphic design by Christopher Marble; adapted by Sandy Ackerman and
Mark Lerner.
Cover design by Sandy Ackerman, adapted by Denise Barrs.
Cover images © Shutterstock.com.
Printed in the United States of America.

ISBN-13: 978-1-62231-863-6

The Library of Congress has cataloged a previous edition as follows:

A prairie home companion pretty good joke book.—New 4th ed.
   p.   cm.
   ISBN 1-56511-979-7 (pbk.)
  1. American wit and humor. I. Prairie home companion (Radio program)
   PN6165.P73 2005
   818'.60208—dc22

                                 2005020062

CONTENTS

INTRODUCTION

The New York Times came out with a big story in the spring of 2005 saying flatly that The Joke Is Dead. Naturally, this got my attention right away. And then, like a lot of what you read in newspapers, the big story petered out down around the third paragraph. It turned out that the reporter had talked to a few stand-up comedians and they do not tell jokes in their acts. From this slight evidence, the reporter naturally reasoned that nobody in America knows any knock-knock jokes and men aren't walking into bars and lightbulbs aren't getting changed and priests don't hang out with rabbis.

For all that the *Times* may know about the Middle East, the *Times* is not authoritative when it comes to humor. You will notice this from reading it. Looking to the *Times* for an assessment of American humor is like asking George W. Bush to review dance. In fact, people tell jokes just as much as they ever did, and maybe

more, and the Internet speeds the absorption of new jokes into the word-of-mouth joke culture. Janet Jackson had her blouse fall open accidentally and her breast fall out at the Super Bowl halftime show and in a couple days the e-mails were flying: "Did you hear that Janet Jackson was pulled over by the L.A.P.D.? Yeah, her right headlight was out." A week after the President confessed to canoodling with the intern, someone said to me, "They had a Presidents' Day Sale at Macy's and all men's pants were half off."

You go along thinking you've heard every knock-knock joke in Christendom and then along comes

Knock, knock.
Who's there?
Eskimo Christians.
Eskimo Christians who?
Eskimo Christians, and I'll tell you no lies.

The Eskimo Christian knock-knock does not displace the Sam

and Janet knock-knock in your affections or the Olive or the Amos, but you add it to your hard drive and from now on, if the dinner-table conversation should ever veer toward the Inuit people, you now have something interesting to offer.

Likewise, after years of men walking into the bar, and termites ("Is the bar tender here?") and horses and cheeseburgers and drunks of all sorts,

> *A dog walks into the bar and says, "Hey, my name is Bob and I'm a talking dog. Isn't that something? Ever heard a talking dog before? Not one as smart as me, I'll bet. How about a drink for a talking dog?" And the bartender says, "Sure, the toilet is right down the hall."*

What's dead is the practical joke. The tipping of outhouses, the use of whoopee cushions and dribble glasses, the placement of a Holstein cow in your uncle Earl's bedroom. Those boyish pranks seem to have ended back in the fifties somehow, at least among grown men. But the telling of jokes is a durable feature of small talk in America.

In the Chatterbox Cafe in Lake Wobegon, if you are new in town, the odd guy who married the farmer's daughter, you might sit with the group of gentlemen telling jokes and then, when the opportunity presents itself, you offer a joke and if it's new and you tell it well and don't flounder around in the setup but tell it cleanly and simply with not too much topspin, remembering this is Minnesota and we like it dry, and if you tell it gracefully, not overselling the joke, you'll be welcome here. No need for a résumé or testimonials. If you can tell a joke, you're okay.

Jokes are democratic. Telling one right has nothing to do with having money or being educated. It's a knack, like hammering a nail straight. Anyone can learn it, and it's useful in many situations. You can go through life and never need math or physics but the ability to tell a joke is often handy. Jokes are good for your health. At the Chatterbox, nobody says, "I don't know why, I just can't remember jokes," or "People sure don't tell as many jokes as they used to, do they," people simply sit and drink coffee and as the conversation hops around in a surrealistic way from hunting to dogs and cats, and then to elephants and Alzheimer's and old age, sex, Lutherans, someone leans back and says, "I read in the paper the other day that the nursing homes are giving out Viagra." And someone says, "Oh really?" "Yeah, they're giving it to the old guys to keep 'em from rolling out of bed." Your clothes may be disheveled and your life in chaos, you may be of the wrong religion and be hopeless when it comes to politics, you may walk around with the *New York Times* tucked under your arm, but if you can tell a joke well, you'll be okay.

—GARRISON KEILLOR

ONE-LINERS

Dyslexia! I went to a toga party dressed as a goat.

Apple has developed a new high-tech toilet. It's called the iPeed.

I called up SeaWorld. I got a recorded message that said, "Calls may be recorded for training porpoises."

I told my friend she drew her eyebrows too high. She looked surprised.

What do you get when you cross a joke with a rhetorical question?

The only time the word *incorrectly* isn't spelled incorrectly is when it's spelled incorrectly.

A magician was driving down the road, and then he turned into a driveway.

In the Miss Universe pageant, why are all of the winners from Earth?

Why didn't the lifeguard save the hippie?
   Because he was too far out, man!

One tectonic plate bumped into the other tectonic plate and said, "Sorry, my fault."

The worst time to have a heart attack is during a game of charades.

There are two types of people in the world: those who can extrapolate from incomplete data.

When I was a kid, my English teacher looked my way and said, "Name two pronouns."
     I said, "Who, me?"

If you can't be kind, at least be vague.

Light travels faster than sound. This is why some people seem bright until you hear them talk.

I wondered why the baseball was getting bigger, and then it hit me.

Before they invented golf balls, how did they measure hail?

If it's true that we are here to help others, then what exactly are the others here for?

Why do people point to their wrist when asking for the time, but when they ask where the bathroom is, they don't point to their pants?

Whose cruel idea was it for the word "lisp" to have an "s" in it?

If things get any worse, I'll have to ask you to stop helping me.

I longed for the pitter-patter of little feet, so I got a dog. It's cheaper, and you get more feet.

Rehab is for quitters.

If it's zero degrees outside today and it's supposed to be twice as cold tomorrow, how cold is it going to be?

If you don't go to other people's funerals, then they won't come to yours.

Did you hear about the dyslexic agnostic who stayed up all night debating the existence of Dog?

My best friend became addicted to line dancing. It got so bad he had to enter a two-step program.

On my computer are the two buttons representing the things I can never have: Control and Escape.

Did you hear about the paranoid dyslexic?
    He always thought he was following someone.

Last night I lay in bed looking up at the stars in the sky, and I thought to myself, "Where is the ceiling?"

The quarterback wanted to call his wife, but he couldn't find the receiver.

I've got two wonderful children. Two out of five isn't bad.

If you're not part of the solution, you're part of the precipitate.

If God had meant us to use the metric system, there would have been ten Apostles.

Borrow money from pessimists. They don't expect it back.

Do you know how to live to a ripe old age?
    Eat a meatball a day for a hundred years.

What do you call thirteen witches in a hot tub?
    A self-cleaning coven.

Two flies fly into the kitchen. Which one is the cowboy?
    The one on the range.

Build a man a fire and he'll be warm for a day, but set a man on fire and he'll be warm for the rest of his life.

The main reason Santa is so jolly is because he knows where all the bad girls live.

My name's Pavlov. Ring a bell?

The trouble with being a leader today is that you can't be sure whether people are following you or chasing you.

I'm a vegetarian and when I'm feeling wild, I eat animal crackers.

I don't do drugs anymore because I find I get the same effect just standing up really fast.

Incontinence Hotline—can you hold, please?

As long as there are tests, there will be prayer in public schools.

Always remember to pillage before you burn.

The trouble with doing something right the first time is that nobody appreciates how difficult it was.

Always remember you're unique, just like everyone else.

The lottery is a tax on people who are bad at math.

When guns are outlawed, only outlaws will accidentally shoot their kids.

Friends help you move. Real friends help you move bodies.

Be nice to your kids. They're the ones who will be choosing your nursing home.

Xerox and Wurlitzer are merging. They're going to manufacture a reproductive organ.

A clear conscience is the sign of a bad memory.

For every action, there is an equal and opposite criticism.

He who hesitates is probably right.

Depression is merely anger without enthusiasm.

Eagles may soar, but weasels don't get sucked into jet engines.

I went to buy some camouflage clothing, but I couldn't find it.

"Veni, Vidi, Velcro"—I came, I saw, I stuck around.

My wife went to a self-help group for compulsive talkers. It's called On & On Anon.

I'm reading a terrifically interesting book about anti-gravity—I just can't put it down.

I always wanted to be somebody, but I guess I should have been more specific.

If you are what you eat, I'm dead meat.

Middle age is having a choice of two temptations and choosing the one that will get you home earlier.

Seen it all, done it all, can't remember most of it.

It's a cruel choice: work or daytime television.

Lead me not into temptation—I can find the way myself.

The sooner you fall behind, the more time you'll have to catch up.

I intend to live forever—so far, so good.

I have seen the truth and it makes no sense.

Just when I was getting used to yesterday, along came today.

The best part about owning a restaurant for cats is that your customers don't complain when they get hair in their food.

The best part about fighting your way to the top of the food chain is that you can choose to be a vegetarian or not.

The best part about computers is that they make very fast, accurate mistakes.

My software never has bugs—it just develops random features.

According to my calculations the problem doesn't exist.

A Freudian slip is when you say one thing but you mean your mother.

Everyone has a photographic memory. Some people just never insert the memory card.

Sometimes I think I understand everything—then I regain consciousness.

Save the whales! Trade them for valuable prizes.

I said no to drugs, but they just wouldn't listen.

Age doesn't always bring wisdom. Sometimes age comes alone.

A bus station is where a bus stops. A train station is where a train stops. Now you know why they call it a workstation.

I'd rather have this bottle in front of me than a frontal lobotomy.

God grant me the senility to forget the people I never liked, the good fortune to run into the ones I do, and the eyesight to tell the difference.

The difference between capitalism and communism is that under communism man exploits man, whereas under capitalism it's the other way around.

My pig learned karate. Now he's doing pork chops.

Politicians and diapers should both be changed regularly—and for the same reason.

Someday we'll look back on all this and plow into a parked car.

Everybody is somebody else's weirdo.

Alcohol and calculus don't mix. Never drink and derive.

Don't sweat the petty things and don't pet the sweaty things.

If at first you don't succeed, skydiving is definitely not for you.

Some days you're the dog, some days you're the hydrant.

Some days you're the bug, some days you're the windshield.

Health is merely the slowest possible rate at which one can die.

Those who live by the sword get shot by those who don't.

It's not the pace of life that concerns me; it's the sudden stop at the end.

The only reason I'd take up jogging is so I could hear heavy breathing again.

Sometimes I feel like a man trapped in a woman's body. But luckily that man is gay, so nobody seems to notice.

If you're going to try cross-country skiing, start with a small country.

Never say anything bad about a man until you've walked a mile in his shoes. By then he's a mile away, you've got his shoes, and you can say whatever you want to.

Time may be a great healer, but it's a lousy beautician.

The early bird gets the worm, but it's the second mouse who gets the cheese.

The early bird gets the worm, but look what happens to the early worm.

When I'm not in my right mind, my left mind gets pretty crowded.

Why is it called a building when it has already been built?

He is not quiet; he is a conversational minimalist.

He does not get lost; he discovers alternative destinations.

Why isn't "phonetic" spelled the way it sounds?

He was the number-one laxative salesman in the whole United States, but he was just a regular guy.

He does not have a beer belly; he has developed a liquid grain-storage facility.

He is not short and wide; he is anatomically compact.

He does not eat like a pig; he suffers from reverse bulimia.

Twenty-four hours in a day, twenty-four beers in a case. Coincidence?

Do Roman nurses refer to IVs as 4s?

Why is the alphabet in that order? Is it because of the song?

Have you ever imagined a world with no hypothetical situations?

You go to the ballet and you see girls dancing on their tiptoes. Why don't they just get taller girls?

If corn oil comes from corn, where does baby oil come from?

Why is "abbreviation" such a long word?

What's another word for "thesaurus"?

Why do they put Braille dots on the keypad of the drive-up ATM?

Do they sterilize the needles for lethal injections?

If a cow laughed, would milk come out of her nose?

Why is "brassiere" singular and "panties" plural?

If you ate pasta and antipasta, would you still be hungry?

If the black box survives a plane crash, why isn't the whole airplane made out of the stuff?

Why do they report power outages on TV?

Why is it called tourist season if we can't shoot them?

Is there another word for "synonym"?

Why is there an expiration date on sour cream?

Why are builders afraid to have a 13th floor, but book publishers aren't afraid to have a Chapter 11?

Shouldn't there be a shorter word for "monosyllabic"?

If we aren't supposed to eat animals, why are they made of meat?

As you grow older, do you miss the innocence and idealism of your youth, or do you mostly miss cherry bombs?

Did you hear about the blind man who picked up a hammer and saw?

Did you know that half of all people are below average?

Birth-control pills are tax deductible, but only if they don't work.

Two goldfish are in a tank and one says to the other, "Do you know how to drive this thing?"

Lawyers get disbarred and clergymen defrocked. So doesn't it make sense that ballplayers would be debased, politicians devoted, and cowboys deranged, models deposed, Calvin Klein models debriefed, organ donors delivered, and dry cleaners depressed, decreased, and depleted?

Did you hear that Ford announced a huge recall of late-model Mercurys?
They found traces of tuna in them.

A man walks up to a blind man and hands him a piece of matzo. The blind man says, "Who wrote this nonsense?"

What is the difference between ignorance, apathy, and ambivalence?
I don't know and I don't care one way or the other.

Did you hear about the home brewer who entered his first brewing contest?
The report he got back read: "Dear Sir, your horse has diabetes."

How do you get an elephant out of the theater?
You can't. It's in their blood.

PUNS

What did Salvador Dali like to eat for breakfast?
  Surreal.

Sherlock Holmes comes in carrying a box of lemons. Watson asks, "Where did you get those?"
  "A lemon tree, Dear Watson. A lemon tree."

A Native American chief has three wives. The first lived in a teepee made out of bear skin, and she bore him a son. The second lived under a buffalo skin, and she also had a son. The third lived in a teepee made out of hippo skin, and she gave birth to twin sons. Therefore, the squaw of the hippopotamus is equal to the sons of the squaws of the other two hides.

Maybe PMS should just be called ovary-acting.

Why do demons and ghouls hang out?
  Because demons are a ghoul's best friend.

What is a hippie's wife called?
  Mississippi.

Why did the Canadian DJ turn down the gig at the local Y?
  Because, why emcee, eh?

How do you split Rome in half?
  With a pair of Caesars.

Why do melons get married in church?
Because they cantaloupe.

There once was a butterfly who fell in love with a bumble bee. Said the bumble bee to the butterfly, "Will thou marry me?" "Nay, nay," said the butterfly. "For I am the daughter of a monarch, and you are just a son of a bee."

The plane came in for a hard landing, but it wasn't the pilot's fault. It was the asphalt.

Two brooms were hanging in the closet and after a while they got to know each other so well, they decided to get married. One was the bride broom, the other the groom broom. The bride broom looked very beautiful in her white dress. The groom broom was handsome and suave in his tuxedo. The wedding was lovely. After the wedding, at the wedding dinner, the bride broom leaned over and said to the groom broom, "I think I am going to have a little whisk broom!" "Impossible!" said the groom broom. "We haven't even swept together!"

Two Mexican detectives were investigating the murder of Juan Gonzalez.
"How was he killed?" asked one detective.
"With a golf gun," the other replied.
"A golf gun? What's a golf gun?"
"I don't know, but it sure made a hole in Juan."

Have you heard about the new existentialist breakfast cereal?
It's called Raisins D'etre.

A man has a son who was born without a body, only a head. When the head turned 21, his father decided they would go and have some beers. So they go to the local pub and the boy gets his first beer. After drinking just a sip he instantly grows a body. Then with another drink he grows a set of arms. In excitement, he drinks the rest and grows legs and feet. He jumps up and down with elation, runs out of the bar and directly into the street, where he is hit and killed by a semi. The moral of this story is that sometimes you should quit while you're a head.

Have you heard of the new chainsaw? It uses only a single double A battery and two cups of salt to run all of its electrical systems. It is charged with a salt and battery.

What do you get when you throw a hand grenade into a French kitchen?
   Linoleum Blown-Apart!

Why did ancient Romans close down the Coliseum?
   The lions were eating up the prophets.

A woman walks into the kitchen and finds her husband using tiny strips of gauze to tie a pair of toothpicks to each pea in a bag of frozen peas. "What do you think you're doing?" she asks. He looks up from his work and says, "What does it look like I'm doing? I'm making splint pea soup." A few days later she finds him in the kitchen again, this time stabbing potatoes repeatedly with a pencil. "Now what do you think you're doing?" she asks. "What else?" he answers. "I'm making potato leak soup."

A recent newsworthy item stated that there was a murder at the local fish market. A woman killed a gentleman just for the halibut. He was hard of herring, it was later found.

I'm nice to both of my wives. Isn't that bigamy?

A school teacher was arrested at the airport for trying to go through security with a slide rule and a calculator. He was charged with carrying weapons of math instruction.

A couple attended a Japanese Noh play. Afterward the wife said, "I didn't get it." And the husband said, "What part of Noh don't you understand?"

What did the DNA say to the other DNA?
   Do these genes make me look fat?

Did you hear about the new restaurant that opened in India?
   It's a New Delhicatessen.

Once upon a time, a beautiful young antelope had a wild date in the forest, so she was getting all gussied up—new dress, makeup, everything. Suddenly, as she was just about ready, she was stampeded by a herd of wildebeests, becoming the world's first self-dressed, stamped antelope.

A woman got free airplane tickets for her five babies under the airline's free quint flier program.

My cousin is a transvestite. He likes to eat, drink and be Mary.

The waters receded and the ark settled and Noah told the animals to go forth and multiply. He was cleaning out the ark, and he saw a couple of snakes still there. He said, "Didn't I tell you to go forth and multiply?" They said, "We can't multiply. We're adders."

There was once a horse who was a genius. It mastered math and physics and history, but it couldn't master philosophy, which proves you can't put Descartes before the horse!

Did you hear a guy was murdered in town last night? Police found the victim face down in his bathtub, which was filled with milk and cornflakes. They think it was a cereal killer.

The family of potatoes sits down to dinner, the daddy potato, and mommy potato, and three daughter potatoes. The eldest daughter says that she has an announcement to make—she's getting married to an Idaho potato. And the potato parents say, "Oh my, how nice, getting married! We are so happy." The second daughter says that she too has an announcement, that she is engaged to marry a Russet potato. "Oooh! A Russet potato, that's so nice. Congratulations, we are very happy for you." And then the youngest daughter says that she has an announcement to make, that she is getting married to NBC's Scott Pelley. And the mommy potato bursts into tears and says, "Oh honey, you could do so much better than him. He's just a common tater."

Why is it great to be a test-tube baby?
    You get a womb with a view.

28

I would like to go to Holland someday. Wooden Shoe?

There once were identical twins—born in Greece and separated at birth—put up for adoption. One was sent off to Saudi Arabia, and he was named Amal. The other one was sent off to Spain, and he was named Juan. Many years later, their relatives arranged for a reunion. It was a big event, and everyone showed up at the airport in Greece to greet the twins. The plane from Spain landed, and off came Juan, to the delight of the crowd. Then they waited for the plane from Saudi Arabia. Soon it arrived, but Amal wasn't on it— he'd missed the plane. One relative said to the other, "Well, they are identical twins. And if you've seen Juan, you've seen Amal."

A young snail bought a new sports car with a big red "S" painted on the side. He wanted to drive around town and hear people say, "Look at that little 'S' car go!"

Leif Erickson returned home from a voyage and found his name missing from the town register. His wife insisted on complaining to the local civic official, who apologized profusely, saying, "I'm sorry, Mrs. Erickson, I must have taken Leif off my census."

A farmer is milking his cow and as he is milking, a fly comes along and flies into the cow's ear. A little bit later, the farmer notices the fly in the milk. The farmer says, "Hmph. In one ear, out the udder."

Did you hear that NASA has launched several Holsteins into Earth orbit?

It was the herd shot around the world.

So, these two vultures decided to fly to Florida on an airline. They got on board carrying six dead raccoons, and the flight attendant said, "I'm sorry, but there's a limit of two carrion per passenger."

Did you hear about the frog who wanted to get out of the construction business, but sadly, all he could do was rivet, rivet, rivet…

What do you call the cabs lined up at the Dallas airport?

The yellow rows of taxis.

This duck walks into a drugstore and he says, "Gimme some Chapstick and put it on my bill."

"I was in Mercy, Australia, and I was served tea made from the hair of a koala."

"Made from the hair of a koala? You're kidding! How was it?"

"Oh, it was awful. It was filled with koala hair!"

"Well, you know, the koala tea of Mercy is not strained."

A doctor liked to stop at a bar after work and have an almond daiquiri. One day, Dick the bartender ran out of almonds and used hickory nuts instead. The doctor took a sip and said, "Is this an almond daiquiri, Dick?" And Dick said, "No, it's a hickory daiquiri, Doc."

There's a nudist colony for communists. Two old men are sitting on the front porch. One turns to the other and says, "I say, old boy, have you read Marx?" And the other says, "Yes. I believe it's these wicker chairs."

Recently, a Frenchman in Paris nearly got away with stealing several paintings from the Musée d'Orsay. However, after planning the crime and getting in and out and past security, he was captured only two blocks away when his Econoline ran out of gas. When asked how he could mastermind such a crime and then make such an obvious error, he replied, "I had no Monet to buy Degas to make the Van Gogh."

Early one spring morning, Papa Mole decided to check out the sounds and smells of the new season. He traveled along his burrow until he could stick his head out and survey the area. It was such a beautiful morning, he quickly called to Mama Mole to come join him. Papa Mole said, "It is such a beautiful spring morning. I hear the birds singing and I smell…bacon…yes, someone is frying! It smells so good." Mama Mole said, "It is indeed a beautiful morning and…why, yes…I think I smell someone cooking pancakes. Yes, delicious buckwheat pancakes! Come quick, Baby Mole, you must experience these delectable sounds and smells!" Baby Mole raced along the burrow but could not squeeze past his parents. Mama said, "Do you smell those delicious smells of breakfast, Baby Mole? Doesn't it make you hungry and happy that spring is here?" Baby Mole replied, somewhat disgruntled, his voice a bit muffled as he tried to squeeze past his parents again, "I wouldn't know. All I can smell is molasses!"

There was a fire at a Basque movie theater. Unfortunately there was only a single emergency exit door, so several people were trampled. Which goes to show that you shouldn't put all your Basques in one exit.

Mahatma Gandhi walked barefoot everywhere, to the point that the soles of his feet became quite thick and hard. Being a very spiritual person, he ate very little and often fasted. As a result, he was quite thin and frail. Furthermore, due to his diet, he ended up with very bad breath. Therefore, he came to be known as a super callused, fragile mystic plagued with halitosis.

Out in the Pacific Ocean, Sam and his wife Sue, two clams, owned a restaurant that had live disco music every Saturday night. Their diner was known for its great musicians, the shrimp quartet. Bob played guitar, Chuck played the drums, Sally sang, and Harry played the harp. One day while crossing the street, Harry the shrimp was involved in an accident and was trampled to death by an urchin driving an out-of-control sea horse. Everyone at Sam's disco was devastated. Without old Harry playing his harp, the disco just wouldn't be the same. Even Harry, now in heaven, was sad. He asked St. Peter if he could go back just once more and play with the shrimp quartet on a hopping Saturday disco night. St. Peter said yes and allowed him to leave heaven for one night. Harry joined the shrimp in their disco frenzy and had a great time catching up with all his old crustacean friends. When the night was over, he sadly returned to heaven. St. Peter looked at him and asked, "Harry, where is your harp?" Harry sighed, "I guess," he paused, "I left my harp in Sam Clam's disco."

What is the difference between a joist and a girder?
The first wrote "Ulysses," and the other wrote "Faust."

Two boll weevils grew up in South Carolina. One went to Hollywood and became a famous actor. The other stayed behind in the cotton fields and never amounted to much. The second one naturally became known as the lesser of two weevils.

There was a horse trainer who raised a filly, and when he raced her in the evening she always won, but when she raced during the day she lost. She was a fine horse, but she was a real night mare.

An elephant and a giraffe come down to the watering hole for a drink. They see a turtle fast asleep, basking in the sun. The elephant goes over and kicks the turtle—whack—to the other shore. "Boy, that was cruel," said the giraffe. "Why did you do that?" The elephant said, "That turtle bit a big chunk out of my trunk fifty years ago." "Fifty years ago! Wow, what a great memory," said the giraffe. "Yes," said the elephant, "I have turtle recall."

This guy goes into a restaurant for a Christmas breakfast while in his hometown for the holidays. After looking over the menu he says, "I'll just have the eggs Benedict." His order comes a while later, and it's served on a big, shiny hubcap. He asks the waiter, "What's with the hubcap?"
    The waiter sings, "O, there's no plate like chrome for the hollandaise!"

There was a man who entered a pun contest. He sent in ten different puns, in the hope that at least one of the puns would win. Unfortunately, no pun in ten did.

A group of chess enthusiasts checked into a hotel and were standing in the lobby discussing their recent tournament victories. After about an hour the manager came out of the office and asked them to disperse. "But why?" they asked, as they moved off. "Because," he said, "I can't stand chess nuts boasting in an open foyer."

A man who lived in a block of apartments thought it was raining and put his hand out the window to check. Just as he did this, a glass eye fell into his hand. He looked up to see where it came from and saw a young woman looking down from an upstairs window.

"Is this yours?" he asked.

She said, "Yes, could you bring it up?"

When he got up to her apartment, he found she was extremely attractive, and she offered him a drink. After they'd finished their drinks, she said, "I'm about to have dinner. There's plenty; would you like to join me?"

He readily accepted her offer, and they both enjoyed a lovely meal. After dinner, she said, "I've had a marvelous evening. Would you…like to stay the night?"

The man hesitated, then said, "Wow, do you act like this with every man you meet?"

"No," she replied, "only those who catch my eye."

Why did Jesus go to a Japanese restaurant?

Because he loved miso.

Did you hear that Miss Muffet and Saddam Hussein once got together for a meeting to discuss their common problem?
They both had Kurds in their way.

Did you hear about the Buddhist who refused novocaine during his root canal?
He wanted to transcend dental medication.

One day, a Russian couple was walking down the street, and they got into an argument over whether it was raining or sleeting. So they asked a communist party official, Comrade Rudolph, if it was officially raining or sleeting. "Today it is officially raining, Comrades," said the official, and walked away. The wife said, "I still think it's sleeting." The man said, "Rudolph the Red knows rain, dear."

Darth Vader: Luke Skywalker, I know what you're getting for Christmas.
Luke: How do you know?
Vader: I felt your presents.

LIGHTBULB JOKES

How many bureaucrats does it take to screw in a lightbulb?

Two. One to assure everyone that everything possible is being done while the other screws the bulb into the water faucet.

How many terrorists does it take to change a lightbulb?

One hundred. One to change the lightbulb and ninety-nine to take the house hostage.

How many musicians does it take to change a lightbulb?

Five. One to change the bulb and four to get in free because they know the guy who owns the socket.

How many Methodists does it take to change a lightbulb?

Whether your light is bright or not, you are loved—you can be a lightbulb, fennel bulb, or tulip bulb. A church-wide lighting service is planned for Sunday.

How many Jewish Renewal rabbis does it take to change a lightbulb?

Four. One to change it, one to do a Buddhist mindfulness practice during the change, one to document the paradigm shift in a best-selling book called "The Jew in the Light Bulb," and one to lead a retreat weekend on the experience.

How many conservatives does it take to change a lightbulb?

None. Darkness is an Intelligent Design.

How many production assistants does it take to screw in a lightbulb?

Three. Onc to screw in the lightbulb, and two to wish they had been asked instead.

How many Apple employees does it take to change a lightbulb?

Seven. One to change the bulb, and six to design the T-shirt.

How many computer engineers does it take to change a lightbulb?

Why bother? The socket will be obsolete in six months anyway.

How many magicians does it take to change a lightbulb?

Depends on what you want it to change to.

How many Christians does it take to change a lightbulb?

Three, but they're really one.

How many Catholics does it take to change a lightbulb?

CHANGE?! Did you say "change"?

How many Einsteins does it take to change a lightbulb?

That depends on the speed of the changer, and the mass of the bulb. It just might be easier to leave the bulb alone and change the room. It's all relative.

How many Floridians does it take to change a lightbulb?

Don't know for sure, they're still counting.

How many sound men does it take to change a lightbulb?
One, two, three; testing, one, two, three.

How many supply-side economists does it take to change a lightbulb?
None. If the government would just leave it alone, it would screw itself in.

How many actors does it take to screw in a lightbulb?
Only one. They don't like to share the spotlight.

How many mystery writers does it take to screw in a lightbulb?
Two. One to screw it almost all the way in and the other to give it a surprise twist at the end.

How many consultants does it take to change a lightbulb?
I'll have an estimate for you a week from Monday.

How many therapists does it take to change a lightbulb?
How many therapists do you think it takes to change a lightbulb?

How many liberal arts professors does it take to screw in a lightbulb?
Interesting question. I just wonder if what we think of as a "darkness" is actually the absence of light, or a state of being—a "-ness"—such that the lack of a lightbulb—a thing—creates its counterpart—this thing we call "darkness."

How many choir directors does it take to change a lightbulb?
No one knows, because no one watches the director!

How many TV reporters does it take to change a lightbulb?
More at 11...

How many HMO administrators does it take to change a lightbulb?
None. Before they commit to a new lightbulb, they suggest you try doing more things during daytime hours.

How many liberals does it take to screw in a lightbulb?
None. They don't want to offend the lightbulb for not working.

How many Zen masters does it take to screw in a lightbulb?
None. The Zen master is the light bulb.

How many mediators does it take to change a lightbulb?
So what I hear you saying is that you want more light.

How many dyslexics does it take to screw in a lightbulb?
Never enough. They screw 'em in backwards.

How many male chauvinist pigs does it take to screw in a lightbulb?
Oh, let her cook in the dark.

How many middle managers does it take to screw in a lightbulb?
Let me get back to you on that.

How many sado-masochists does it take to change a lightbulb?

Two. One to hold it and one to kick the chair out from under him.

How many firemen does it take to change a lightbulb?

Four. One to change it and three to cut a hole in the ceiling.

How many Canadians does it take to change a lightbulb?

Four. One to go across the border to buy the bulb at the factory outlet, one to screw it in, one to translate everything into French, and one to drop the puck.

How many paranoids does it take to change a lightbulb?

Who wants to know?

How many Freudian analysts does it take to change a lightbulb?

Two. One to change the bulb and one to hold the penis—I mean, the ladder.

How many feminists does it take to change a lightbulb?

Ten. One to change it and nine to form a Survivors of Darkness support group.

How many Zen Buddhists does it take to change a lightbulb?

A tree in a golden forest.

How many cops does it take to screw in a lightbulb?
Six to sit and hope that it turns itself in.

How many gay rights activists does it take to change a lightbulb?
None. The bulb shouldn't have to change for society to accept it.

How many lesbians does it take to screw in a lightbulb?
Three. One to screw it in and two to write a song about it.

How many kids with ADHD does it take to screw in a lightbulb?
Let's go ride our bikes!

How many reed players does it take to change a lightbulb?
Only one, but he'll go through a whole box of a hundred bulbs before he finds just the right one.

How many Tech Support folks does it take to change a lightbulb?
We have the same lightbulb here, and it's working fine. Can you tell me what kind of system you have? Okay. Now, exactly how dark is it? Okay, there could be four or five things wrong…have you tried the light switch?

How many Microsoft engineers does it take to change a lightbulb?
One. But you are going to be downloading patches for years after he does.

41

How many pessimists does it take to change a lightbulb?
Never mind. Nobody would get the joke anyway.

How many optimists does it take to screw in a lightbulb?
None, they're convinced that the power will come back on soon.

How many babysitters does it take to change a lightbulb?
None, diapers don't come that small.

How many 16-year-olds does it take to change a lightbulb?
What-EVER.

How many procrastinators does it take to screw in a lightbulb?
One, but he has to wait until the light is better.

How many women with PMS does it take to change a lightbulb?
Six.
Why?
It just does, okay?

How many advertising execs does it take to change a lightbulb?
Interesting question. What do you think?

How many art directors does it take to change a lightbulb?
Does it have to be a lightbulb?

How many copy editors does it take to screw in a lightbulb?
The last time this question was asked it involved art directors. Is the difference intentional? Should one or the other instance be changed? It seems inconsistent.

How many art students does it take to change a lightbulb?
One, but he gets two credits.

How many grad students does it take to change a lightbulb?
One, but it takes ten years.

How many University of Iowa freshmen does it take to screw in a lightbulb?
None. That's a sophomore course.

How many Yale students does it take to change a lightbulb?
None. New Haven looks better in the dark.

How many Minnesotans does it take to change a lightbulb?
Ten. One to change the bulb and nine to apologize for it being out.

How many Californians does it take to change a lightbulb?
Six. One to turn the bulb, one for support, and four to relate to the experience.

How many narcissists does it take to change a lightbulb?
One. He holds the bulb while the world revolves around him.

How many reference librarians does it take to screw in a lightbulb?

I don't know, I'll have to check on that and get back to you.

How many existentialists does it take to screw in a lightbulb?

Two. One to screw it in, and one to observe how the lightbulb itself symbolizes a single incandescent beacon of subjective reality in a netherworld of endless absurdity reaching out toward a maudlin cosmos of nothingness.

How many psychiatrists does it take to change a lightbulb?

One, but only if the lightbulb wants to change.

How many conservative economists does it take to change a lightbulb?

None. The darkness will cause the lightbulb to change by itself.

How many psychoanalysts does it take to screw in a lightbulb?

How long have you been having this fantasy?

How many philosophers does it take to change a lightbulb?

Define lightbulb.

How many surgeons does it take to change a lightbulb?

None. You don't need it out today, but if it continues to give you trouble in the future, you should consider removing it.

How many surgeons does it take to change a lightbulb?

One, except there's a good chance he'll remove the socket, pull out the wiring, and then give you a flashlight.

How many telemarketers does it take to change a lightbulb?

Only one, but she has to do it while you're eating dinner.

How many chiropractors does it take to change a lightbulb?

One, but it takes him three visits.

How many Zen masters does it take to change a lightbulb?

Two. One to change it and one not to change it.

How many real estate agents does it take to change a lightbulb?

Ten, but we'll accept eight.

How many used car salesmen does it take to screw in a lightbulb?

I'm working out the figure on my calculator, and I think you'll be pleasantly surprised.

How many auto mechanics does it take to change a lightbulb?

We don't know yet, they're still waiting on a part.

How many auto mechanics does it take to change a lightbulb?

Three. One to look at the bulb, one to go get the wrong one, and one to tell you it won't be done until Tuesday.

How many statisticians does it take to change a lightbulb?
1.67.

How many IRS agents does it take to screw in a lightbulb?
Only one, but it really gets screwed.

How many real men does it take to change a lightbulb?
None. Real men aren't afraid of the dark.

How many lonely guys does it take to change a lightbulb?
One, but he wishes it were two.

How many humorless people does it take to change a lightbulb?
One.

How many college football players does it take to change a lightbulb?
The entire team. And they all get a semester's credit for it.

How many Irishmen does it take to change a lightbulb?
Fifteen. One to hold the bulb and the rest to drink whiskey until the room spins.

How many brewers does it take to change a lightbulb?
About one-third less than for a regular bulb.

How many evolutionists does it take to change a lightbulb?
Thousands, and it takes eight million years.

How many pro-lifers does it take to change a lightbulb?

Six. Two to screw in the bulb and four to testify that it was lit from the moment they began screwing.

How many computer programmers does it take to change a lightbulb?

None. That's a hardware problem.

How many computer programmers does it take to change a lightbulb?

Five. Two to write the specification program, one to screw it in, and two to explain why the project was late.

How many database people does it take to change a lightbulb?

Three: One to write the lightbulb removal program, one to write the lightbulb insertion program, and one to act as a lightbulb administrator to make sure nobody else tries to change the lightbulb at the same time.

How many Microsoft technicians does it take to change a lightbulb?

Three. Two to hold the ladder, and one to screw the lightbulb into a faucet.

How many tech guys does it take to change a lightbulb?

We have received your request concerning your hardware problem, and have assigned your request Service Number 39712. Please use this number for any future reference to this lightbulb issue. As soon as a technician becomes available, you will be contacted.

How many Internet mail-list subscribers does it take to change a lightbulb?

155. One to change the lightbulb and to post to the mail list that the lightbulb has been changed, 11 to share similar experiences of changing lightbulbs, 109 to post that this list is not about lightbulbs, 27 to post URLs where one can see examples of different lightbulbs, three to post about links they found from the URLs that are relevant to this list, and four to suggest that posters read the lightbulb FAQ.

How many software developers does it take to change a lightbulb?

None. The lightbulbs are working fine in all the other offices, so yours must be all right, too.

How many IBM engineers does it take to change a burnt-out lightbulb?

None. They merely change the standard to darkness and upgrade the customers.

How many IBM PC owners does it take to screw in a lightbulb?

Only one, but he'll have to go out and buy the lightbulb adapter card first, which is extra.

How many accountants does it take to screw in a lightbulb?

What kind of answer did you have in mind?

How many doctors does it take to change a lightbulb?

What kind of insurance do you have?

How many Lutherans does it take to change a lightbulb?
Five. One to screw in the new bulb and four to talk about how much they'll miss the old one.

How many Amish does it take to change a lightbulb?
What's a lightbulb?

How many Catholics does it take to change a lightbulb?
None. They use candles.

What do Catholics say when they change a lightbulb?
Glory be unto the Father and unto the Son and into the hole he goes.

How many charismatic Pentecostals does it take to change a lightbulb?
Hard to tell. All their hands are in the air already.

How many Christian Scientists does it take to screw in a lightbulb?
One. He prays for the old bulb to come back on.

How many Baptists does it take to change a lightbulb?
Two, one to screw in the lightbulb, and one to make sure he doesn't say "nipple."

How many dyslexics does it take to change a lightbulb?
Two. One to ladder the hold, the other to bulb in the screw.

How many surrealists does it take to change a lightbulb?
To get to the other side.

How many Unitarians does it take to change a lightbulb?

We believe that incandescent, fluorescent, tinted, or three-way are equally valid paths to light, and if, in your journey, you have felt the need to change your lightbulb, we are holding a lightbulb service on Sunday at which you're welcome to recite a poem or perform a dance about luminescence.

How many Unitarians does it take to replace a lightbulb?

You can't replace a lightbulb with a Unitarian—they don't give light, they discuss light.

How many surrealists does it take to screw in a lightbulb?

Two. One to hold the giraffe and one to put the clocks in the bathtub.

How many performance artists does it take to change a lightbulb?

I don't know, I left at intermission.

How many post-modernists does it take to change a lightbulb?

What makes you think it's not?

How many hipsters does it take to screw in a lightbulb?

It's a really obscure number. You've probably never heard of it.

How many sopranos does it take to change a lightbulb?

Two. One to hold the diet cola and the other to get her accompanist to do it.

How many sopranos does it take to change a lightbulb?
Four. One to change the bulb and three to pull the chair out from under her.

How many French horn players does it take to change a lightbulb?
Just one, but he'll spend two hours checking it to make sure it doesn't leak.

How many lead guitarists does it take to change a lightbulb?
None—they just steal somebody else's light.

How many drummers does it take to change a lightbulb?
Just one, so long as the roadie gets the ladder, sets it up and puts the bulb in the socket for him.

How many Deadheads does it take to change a lightbulb?
One to change it, 2,000 to take pictures of it, and 10,000 to follow it around until it burns out.

How many sound men does it take to change a lightbulb?
One. Upon finding no replacement, he takes the original apart, repairs it with a chewing gum wrapper and duct tape, changes the screw mount to bayonet mount, finds an appropriate patch cable, and re-installs the bulb fifty feet from where it should have been, to the satisfaction of the rest of the band.

How many singers does it take to screw in a lightbulb?
Eighteen. One to do it, and seventeen to be on the guest list.

How many bluegrass musicians does it take to change a lightbulb?

Four. One to change it and three to complain that it's electric.

How many drummers does it take to change a lightbulb?

None: they have a machine to do that now.

How many jazz musicians does it take to change a lightbulb?

Don't worry about the changes. We'll fake it!

How many punk rockers does it take to change a lightbulb?

Two. One to change it and the other to eat the old one.

How many skateboarders does it take to change a lightbulb?

One, dude.

How many communists does it take to screw in a lightbulb?

The lightbulb contains the seeds of its own revolution.

How many Republicans does it take to change a lightbulb?

Eighty-six. Twelve to investigate Obama's involvement in the failure of the old bulb, twenty-thee to deregulate the lightbulb industry, and fifty-one to pass a tax credit for lightbulb changes.

How many Republicans does it take to change a lightbulb?

Two. One to mix the martinis and one to call the electrician.

How many Democrats does it take to change a lightbulb?

Seventeen. One to change the bulb, six to talk about how wonderful it's going to be when the new bulb is screwed in, and ten to argue for increased funding for solar lighting research.

How many liberals does it take to screw in a lightbulb?
Five. One to screw it in, and four to screw it up.

How many gay men does it take to screw in a lightbulb?
Two, but they would probably put in track lighting instead.

How many cockroaches does it take to change a lightbulb?
No one knows; when the light comes on they all scatter.

How many managers does it take to change a lightbulb?
None. They like to keep employees in the dark.

How many assistant managers does it take to change a lightbulb?
Three. Two to find out if it needs changing, and one to tell an employee to change it.

How many poets does it take to change a lightbulb?
Two. One to look at the bulb and think of his mother and one to stand at the window and watch the rain.

How many symbolist poets does it take to change a lightbulb?
The bicycle is broken and the clocks are in the bathtub.

How many writers does it take to change a lightbulb?

Ten. One to change it and nine to say, "I could've done that."

How many editors does it take to change a lightbulb?

None. It's not a lightbulb. It's a lamp.

How many monkeys does it take to change a lightbulb?

Two. One to screw it in, and one to scratch his butt.

How many Americans does it take to screw in a lightbulb in Afghanistan?

Only one, but he does it from thirty miles away using laser targeting.

How many Bush administration officials did it take to change a lightbulb?

None. There was no need to change anything. They made the right decision to stick with that lightbulb. People who said that it was burned out were giving aid and encouragement to the Forces of Darkness.

How many directors does it take to change a lightbulb?

Three. No, make that four…on second thought three…well, better make it five, just to be safe.

How many old ladies does it take to change a lightbulb?

Two. One to do it and another to say, "Look, she's changing the lightbulb."

How many public radio personalities does it take to change a lightbulb?

We'll have that answer right after this pledge break.

How many public radio people does it take to change a lightbulb?

Three. One to change the bulb, and two to do the pledging around it.

How many public radio hosts does it take to change a lightbulb?

Who needs lightbulbs? It's radio.

KNOCK, KNOCK JOKES

Knock, knock.
> Who's there?
> Michael.
> Michael who?
> Michael-esterol is high these days.

Knock, knock.
> Who's there?
> Oscar.
> Oscar who?
> Oscar if she has a sister, I'm a little lonely right now.

Knock, knock.
> Who's there?
> Nadia Comaneci.
> Nadia Comaneci who?
> Nadia Comaneci your dinner is getting cold.

Knock, knock.
> Who's there?
> Sonia.
> Sonia who?
> Sonia paper moon sailing over the...

Knock, knock.
> Who's there?
> Dyslexic.
> Dyslexic how?

Knock, knock.
Who's there?
 Owen.
 Owen who?
 Owen the saints come marching in...

Knock, knock.
 Who's there?
 Minnesota.
 Minnesota who?
 Minnesota bad mood these days.

Knock, knock.
 Who's there?
 Boke.
 Boke who?
 Sorry, I don't speak French.

Knock, knock.
 Who's there?
 Doris.
 Doris who?
 Doris locked that's why I'm knocking.

Knock, knock.
 Who's there?
 Butcher.
 Butcher who?
 Butcher arms around me and gimme a kiss.

Knock, knock.
> Who's there?
> Don Imus.
> Don Imus who?
> Don, Imus have said something offensive.

Knock, knock.
> Who's there?
> Danielle.
> Danielle who?
> Danielle so loud, I heard you the first time.

Knock, knock.
> Who's there?
> Elvis.
> Elvis who?
> How soon they forget.

Knock, knock.
> Who's there?
> Obama.
> Obama who?
> Obama self, don't wanna be…

Knock, knock.
> Who's there?
> Illinois.
> Illinois who?
> Illinois me no end when those telemarketers call.

Knock, knock.
  Who's there?
  Arizona.
  Arizona who?
  Arizona one way to skin a cat, I don't care what they say.

Knock, knock.
  Who's there?
  Arkansas.
  Arkansas who?
  Arkansas this log in half in 30 seconds flat.

Knock, knock.
  Who's there?
  Dakota.
  Dakota who?
  Dakota comes at the end of the piece.

Knock, knock.
  Who's there?
  Connecticut.
  Connecticut who?
  The hip is Connecticut the thigh bone…

Knock, knock.
  Who's there?
  Sherwood.
  Sherwood who?
  Sherwood like to come in, if you'd only open the door!

Knock, knock.
Who's there?
Sincerely.
Sincerely who?
Sincerely this morning I've been waiting for you to open the door!

Knock, knock.
Who's there?
Stopwatch.
Stopwatch who?
Stopwatcha doing and open the door!

Knock, knock.
Who's there?
Consumption.
Consumption who?
Consumption be done about these knock-knock jokes?

Knock, knock.
Who's there?
Harmony.
Harmony who?
Harmony knock-knock jokes do you need me to do here?

Knock, knock.
Who's there?
Absentminded.
Absentminded who?
I'm sorry, what?

Knock, knock.
  Who's there?
  Sam and Janet.
  Sam and Janet who?
  Sam and Janet evening...

Knock, knock
  Who's there?
  Keith.
  Keith who?
  Keith me, thweetheart.

Knock, knock
  Who's there?
  Noah.
  Noah who?
  Noah good place to eat around here?

Knock, knock
  Who's there?
  Señor.
  Señor who?
  Señor underwear when you bent over.

Knock, knock.
  Who's there?
  Frankfurter.
  Frankfurter who?
  Frankfurter lovely evening.

Knock, knock.
    Who's there?
    Dexter.
    Dexter who?
    Dexter halls with boughs of holly.

Knock, knock.
    Who's there?
    Fortification.
    Fortification who?
    Fortification, we're going to Miami.

Knock, knock.
    Who's there?
    Mr. Walter.
    Mr. Walter who?
    You don't Mr. Walter until the well runs dry.

Knock, knock.
    Who's there?
    Itzhak.
    Itzhak who?
    Itzhak sin to tell a lie.

Knock, knock.
    Who's there?
    Earl.
    Earl who?
    Earl-y bird gets the worm.

Knock, knock.
  Who's there?
  Amos.
  Amos who?
  Amos behavin', savin' all my love for you…

Knock, knock.
  Who's there?
  Isabel.
  Isabel who?
  Isabel not working?

Knock, knock.
  Who's there?
  Carl.
  Carl who?
  Carl get you there faster than a bike.

Knock, knock.
  Who's there?
  Fornication.
  Fornication who?
  Fornication like this, you should wear a black tie.

Knock, knock.
  Who's there?
  Amarillo.
  Amarillo who?
  Amarillo-fashioned cowboy.

Knock, knock.
   Who's there?
   Euripides.
   Euripides who?
   Euripides pants, I breaka your face.

Knock, knock.
   Who's there?
   Justin.
   Justin who?
   Justin time for supper.

Knock, knock.
   Who's there?
   Diploma.
   Diploma who?
   Diploma is here to fix the sink.

Knock, knock.
   Who's there?
   Ida.
   Ida who?
   Ida called first, but the phone's not working.

Knock, knock.
   Who's there?
   Tarzan.
   Tarzan who?
   Tarzan Stripes Forever!

Knock, knock.
Who's there?
Knock, knock.
Who's there?
Knock, knock.
Who's there?
Knock, knock.
Who's there?
Knock, knock.
Who's there?
Philip Glass.

Knock, knock.
Who's there?
Repeat.
Repeat who?
Okay. Who, who, who, who, who.

Knock, knock.
Who's there?
Debussy.
Debussy who?
Debussy Fields!

Knock, knock.
Who's there?
Wilbur Wright.
Wilbur Wright who?
Wilbur Wright back after this guitar solo!

Knock, knock.
  Who's there?
  Dewey.
  Dewey who?
  Dewey have to do these jokes all night?

Knock, knock.
  Who's there?
  Agatha.
  Agatha who?
  Agatha blues in the night!

Knock, knock.
  Who's there?
  Luke.
  Luke who?
  Luke for the silver lining…

Knock, knock.
  Who's there?
  Toreador.
  Toreador who?
  Open up or I'll toreador down!

Knock, knock.
  Who's there?
  Aardvark.
  Aardvark who?
  Aardvark a million miles for one of your smiles!

Knock, knock.
　Who's there?
　The German border patrol.
　The German border patrol who?
　Don't ask qvestions!

Knock, knock.
　Who's there?
　Omelet.
　Omelet who?
　Omelet smarter than I look.

Knock, knock.
　Who's there?
　Panther.
　Panther who?
　Panther no panth, I'm going thwimming!

Knock, knock.
　Who's there?
　Bisquick.
　Bisquick who?
　Bisquick! Your pants are on fire.

Knock, knock.
　Who's there?
　Radio.
　Radio who?
　Radio not, here I come.

Knock, knock.
Who's there?
Eskimo Christians.
Eskimo Christians who?
Eskimo Christians, I tell you no lies.

Knock, knock.
Who's there?
Grace.
Grace who?
Grace skies are gonna clear up, put on a happy face.

Knock, knock.
Who's there?
Ammonia.
Ammonia who?
Ammonia bird in a gilded cage.

Knock, knock.
Who's there?
Olive.
Olive who?
Olive me, why not take olive me.

Knock, knock.
Who's there?
Ketchup.
Ketchup who?
Ketchup falling star and put it in your pocket…

Knock, knock.
  Who's there?
  Osbourne.
  Osbourne who?
  Osbourne under a bad sign.

Knock, knock.
  Who's there?
  Alex.
  Alex who?
  Alexplain it later.

Knock, knock.
  Who's there?
  Control freak. Now you say, "Control freak who?"

Knock, knock.
  Who's there?
  Charlotta.
  Charlotta who?
  Charlotta bad jokes around here!

Knock, knock.
  Who's there?
  Thesis.
  Thesis who?
  Thesis ridiculous.

Knock, knock.
    Who's there?
    Antithesis.
    Antithesis who?
    Antithesis finished I can't think of anything else.

Knock, knock.
    Who's there?
    Synthesis.
    Synthesis who?
    Synthesis going nowhere I think I better bail.

Knock, Knock.
    Who's there?
    To.
    To who?
    No, to *whom*.

An angel is talking to God. The angel says, "Look, God. I know that you're all-seeing and all-knowing, but for the knock-knock joke to work, you HAVE to say 'Who's there?'"

Knock, knock.
    Who's there?
    Saul.
    Saul who?
    Saul there is; there ain't no more.

CHICKEN JOKES

Why did the chicken cross the road?
To get to the other side.

Why did the fried chicken cross the road?
She saw a fork up ahead.

Why did the turkey cross the road?
It was the chicken's day off.

Why did the egg cross the road?
It had an inclination.

Why did the baby cross the road?
It was stapled to the chicken.

Why did the chicken cross the road?
To prove to the frogs that it could be done.

Why did the chicken cross the road?
She heard the mayor was going to lay a cornerstone, and she wanted to see him try.

Why did the one-eyed chicken cross the road?
To get to the Birdseye shop.

What happened when the chicken slept under the car?
She woke up oily next morning.

A chicken goes into the library, walks up to the librarian, and says, "Book."

The librarian says, "You want a book?"

"Book."

"Any book?"

"Book."

So the librarian gives the chicken a novel and off it goes. An hour later the chicken comes back and says, "Book-book."

The librarian says, "Now you want two books?"

"Book-book."

So she gives the chicken two more novels. The chicken leaves but again comes back later.

"Book-book-book."

"Three books?"

"Book-book-book."

So the librarian gives the chicken three books, but she decides she'll follow the chicken and find out what's going on. And the chicken goes down the alley, out of town and toward the woods, into the woods and down to the river, down to the swamp, and there is a bullfrog. The chicken sets the books down by him. The bullfrog looks at the books and says, "Reddit, reddit, reddit…"

Ham and eggs: a day's work for a chicken, a lifetime commitment for a pig.

Did you hear about the chicken poet who won the pullet surprise?

Why did the chicken cross the basketball court?
Because the ref was calling fowls.

Why did the chicken cross the road?
To show the deer how to do it.

When the rooster saw all the colored Easter eggs, he got jealous and killed the peacock.

Why did the lollipop cross the road?
It was stuck to the chicken.

A man walks into a restaurant and says, "How do you prepare your chickens?"
The cook says, "Nothing special. We just tell 'em they're gonna die."

What did the chick say when it saw an orange in the nest?
"Look at the orange mama laid."

How do chickens dance?
Chick to chick.

Why do hens lay eggs?
If they dropped them, they'd break.

Why do chicken coops have two doors?
Because if they had four, they'd be chicken sedans.

The chicken and the egg are lying in bed. The chicken is smiling and smoking a cigarette, but the egg is upset. She mutters to herself, "Well, I guess we answered that question."

How cold was it?

It was so cold I saw a chicken with a capon.

One day a traveling salesman was driving down a country road when he was passed by a three-legged chicken. He stepped on the gas, but at fifty miles per hour the chicken was still ahead. After a few miles, the chicken ran up a driveway and into a barn behind an old farmhouse. The salesman drove up to the house and knocked at the door. When he told the farmer what he'd just seen, the farmer said that his son was a geneticist and had developed this breed of chicken so that he, his wife, and his son could each get a drumstick. The salesman said, "That's fantastic. How do they taste?" The farmer said, "I don't know. We can't catch 'em."

How windy was it?

It was so windy that the chicken turned her back to the wind and laid the same egg six times.

Why did the chicken cross the road?

The New York City policeman said, "You give me five minutes with the chicken and I'll find out."

The Bible says, "And God said unto the chicken, 'Thou shalt cross the road.' And the chicken crossed the road, and there was much rejoicing."

Hemingway said, "He crossed the road. To die. In the rain."

Martin Luther King Jr. said, "I see a world where all chickens will be free to cross roads and no one will ask why."

Einstein said, "Did the chicken cross the road or was the road moved to the other side of the chicken?"

President Clinton said, "To the best of my recollection, that chicken did not engage in what I would call road-crossing behavior."

THIRD-GRADER JOKES

How did the tree get on the computer?
  It logged in.

What did the pirate say on his 80th birthday?
  Aye Matey!

Why do ghosts like health food?
  Because it's super natural.

The elevator didn't feel well. It felt it was coming down with something.

The Cyclops shut down his school because he only had one pupil.

What do you call a man with magical pee? A wizard.

What rock group has four men that don't sing?
  Mount Rushmore.

The ancient Egyptian children were confused when their daddies became mummies.

So the night before Christmas, Adam turned to his wife and said, "It's Christmas, Eve."

What's red and bad for your teeth?
  A brick.

Why is there a gate around cemeteries?
Because people are dying to get in.

Somebody said you look like an owl.
Who?

A baby mosquito came back from his first time out flying.
His dad asked, "How did you feel?" He replied, "It was
wonderful, everyone was clapping for me."

What did the big tomato say to the little tomato who was
falling behind?
Ketchup.

Why did the possum cross the road?
To show his girlfriend he had guts.

How do you make an egg roll?
Push it.

What do you call a sheep with no legs?
A cloud.

How do you get your grandma to swear?
Get someone else's grandma to say, "Bingo!"

Is it true that an alligator won't attack you if you carry a
flashlight?
Depends on how fast you carry the flashlight.

Two kangaroos were talking to each other and one said, "I hope it doesn't rain today. I just hate it when the children play inside."

What has four legs, is big, green, fuzzy, and if it fell out of a tree would kill you?
  A pool table.

Wow, that's a cool-looking cow!
  It's a Jersey.
  Is it? I thought that was its skin.

Hey, do you know the capital of Alaska?
  Juneau.
  Yeah, but I asked you.

What did the nuclear physicist have for lunch?
  Fission chips.

What's green, leafy and sings the blues?
  Elvis Parsley.

Did you hear about the cat that swallowed a ball of yarn?
  A few months later she gave birth to a litter of mittens.

Why don't they allow elephants on the beach?
  Because their trunks keep falling down.

What does the Little Mermaid wear?
  An algebra.

What do you get if you divide the circumference of a pumpkin by its diameter?
    Pumpkin pi.

What did one fly say to the other fly?
    Hey, fly, your dude is open.

Why did the dolphin kill himself?
    His life had no porpoise.

I was asking what the difference was between mime and pantomime and no one would say.

What happens if you don't pay your exorcist?
    You get repossessed.

What do you call a woodpecker without a bill?
    A headbanger.

Why didn't the oyster give up her pearl?
    She was shellfish!

A man went to a friend's costume party with nothing but a girl on his back. "What have you come as?" asked his friend. "A snail." "How can you be a snail when all you've got is a girl on your back?" "That's Michelle."

Where do boats go when they're sick?
    The Dock.

What do you do when you see a space man?
  You park in it, man.

What did the Earth say after the earthquake?
  Sorry, my fault.

Do you know why one side of the V formation of migrating geese is longer than the other?
  Because there are more geese on that side.

What is brown, shriveled and carries a machine gun in its hand?
  Al Caprune.

Guess what.
  What?
  That's what.
  What's what?

What do you get when you make a sandwich out of a pig's nose?
  A ham-booger.

What do you get if you cross a pit bull with a rabbit?
  A very happy pit bull.

  What do you do if you break your arm in two places?
  Don't go back to those two places.

Two ducks were swimming along, and one of them said, "Quack!"
The other duck said, "Oh, my gosh! I was just about to say the same thing!"

Did you hear about the butcher who backed into his meat grinder?
He got a little behind in his work.

Did you hear the Kleenex factory workers went on strike?
Now everyone will have to picket.

What did one burp say to the other?
Let's be stinkers and go out the other end.

How do you tell an elephant from an Italian grandmother?
It's the black dress.

Why do cherry trees smell?
Because George Washington cut one.

Why were all the ink spots crying?
Their father was in the pen.

Why did the mushroom go to the party?
Cuz he was a fungi!
Why did the fungi leave the party?
Cuz there wasn't mushroom!

Lady, this vacuum cleaner will cut your work in half.
Good. I'll take two of them.

Why do they put bells on cows?
  Because their horns don't work.

Excuse me, does this bus go to Duluth?
  No, this bus goes beep beep.

Why did the scientist install a knocker on his door?
  To win the no-bell prize.

What's brown and lives in the bell tower?
  The lunch bag of Notre Dame.

What's brown and sounds like a bell?
  Dung!

What's brown and sticky?
  A stick.

What do you call a boomerang that doesn't work?
  A stick.

Why are there so many Johnsons in the phone book?
  They all have phones.

Why do seagulls fly over the sea?
  Because if they flew over the bay, they'd be bagels.

How do you keep a bagel from getting away?
  Put lox on it!

What kind of bees give milk?
  Boobies.

What did the bee say to the flower?
  "Hey Bud, when do you open?"

Why did the man with one hand cross the road?
  To get to the secondhand store.

What's large, gray, and doesn't matter?
  An irrelephant.

I saw Ronald McDonald naked. He has sesame seed buns.

Why did the turtle cross the road?
  To get to the Shell station.

What kind of coffee was served on the *Titanic*?
  Sanka.

How can you tell a boy tuna from a girl tuna?
  Watch to see which "can" they use.

There were two fish in a tank and one turns to the other and
says, "Do you know how to drive this thing?"

How do you fix a broken pumpkin?
  With a pumpkin patch.

Why do ducks have webbed feet?
  To stamp out fires.

Why do elephants have flat feet?
  To stamp out burning ducks.

What do you call a fish with no eye?
  Fsh.

Two caterpillars are sitting on a branch and a butterfly flies overhead. One caterpillar says to the other, "You'll never get me up in one of those."

How did Dracula come to America?
  He sailed in a blood vessel.

What's gray?
  A melted penguin.

What do you get when you cross the Atlantic Ocean with the *Titanic*?
  Halfway.

Why did the pilgrims' pants fall down?
  Because they wore their belt buckles on their hats.

What goes ha, ha, ha, plop?
  Someone laughing his head off.

How do you catch a unique rabbit?
  Unique up on it.

How do you catch a tame rabbit?
  Tame way, unique up on it.

How do crazy people go catch a rabbit?
  You wait until it comes down the psycho path and unique up on it.

What did Mrs. Bullet say to Mr. Bullet?
  We're going to have a beebee.

Why was the tomato red?
  Because it saw the salad dressing.

Hear about the ship that ran aground carrying a cargo of red paint and black paint?
  The whole crew was marooned.

What lies at the bottom of the ocean and twitches?
  A nervous wreck!

What did the fish say when he hit a concrete wall?
  Dam.

Why is a giraffe's neck so long?
  Because its feet smell.

What's green and hangs from trees?
  Giraffe snot.

What's green and skates?
  Peggy Phlegm.

What's green and slimy and marches through Europe killing people?
  Snazis.

How do you get down from an elephant?
  You don't get down from an elephant, you get down from a goose.

Why shouldn't you have two elephants in your swimming pool at the same time?
  Because they'd only have one pair of trunks.

What should you do if you're eaten by an elephant?
  Run around and around till you're all pooped out.

Why is an elephant big, gray, and wrinkled?
  Because if he was small, white, and round he'd be an aspirin.

What do you get when you cross a fly with an elephant?
  A zipper that never forgets.

How do you make an elephant fly?
  You start with a 48-inch zipper…

Can an elephant jump higher than a lamppost?
  Yes. Lampposts can't jump.

Why do elephants paint their toenails red?
  So they can hide in cherry trees.

What do you do with an elephant with three balls?
Walk him and pitch to the rhino.

What's the worst part about hunting elephants?
Carrying the decoys.

Why do elephants have trunks?
Because they would look silly with glove compartments.

What is large, gray, and wears glass slippers?
Cinderelephant.

Why was Cinderella so lousy at baseball?
She ran away from the ball, and she had a pumpkin for a coach.

Why should you never fly with Peter Pan?
Because you'll never, never land.

Why did the banker break up with his girlfriend?
He lost interest.

Why did the Indian have a hard time getting into the hotel?
He didn't have a reservation.

Why did the atoms cross the road?
It was time to split!

Why was the baby ant so confused?
Because all his uncles were ants.

Why did Humpty Dumpty have a great fall?
　　He wanted to make up for a lousy summer.

Where did the king keep his little armies?
　　Up his little sleevies.

Did you hear about the corduroy pillows?
　　They're making headlines, aren't they?

What is the last thing that goes through a bug's mind as it hits a windshield?
　　His butt.

Why do gorillas have large nostrils?
　　Because they have big fingers.

"Dad, I'm going to a party. Would you do my homework for me?"
　　"I'm sorry, kid, but it just wouldn't be right."
　　"Well, maybe not. Give it a try anyway."

Where do otters come from?
　　Otter Space.

How does the man on the moon get his hair cut?
　　Eclipse it.

Did you hear about the restaurant on the moon?
　　The food is terrific, but there's no atmosphere.

Why is a moon rock tastier than an earth rock?
  Because it's a little meteor.

What did the number 0 say to the number 8?
  "Nice belt!"

Why was the math book sad?
  Because it had so many problems.

Why did the cookie visit the doctor?
  He felt crummy.

What did the hot dog say when he crossed the finish line?
  "I'm the wiener!"

What did one hot dog say to another?
  "Hi, Frank."
Why do hummingbirds hum?
  Because they can't remember the words.

What is bright orange and sounds like a parrot?
  A carrot.

Why do birds fly south for the winter?
  Because it's too far to walk.

Did you hear about the skunk who went to church?
  He had his own pew.

Why couldn't the pony talk?
  He was a little horse.

What has four legs and one arm?
A Rottweiler.

What do you get when you cross a pit bull with a collie?
A dog that rips your leg off, then goes for help.

What do you get when you cross a cantaloupe with a Border collie?
Melancholy babies.

What does a dog do that a man steps into?
Pants.

What do you call a dog that is left-handed?
A southpaw.

Where do you find a no-legged dog?
Right where you left him.

Whatdaya call a dog with no legs?
Don't matter, he ain't gonna come anyway.

Bert asked Ernie if he wanted ice cream, and Ernie said, "Sure, Bert."

So the male flea said to the female flea, "How about we go to the movies?"
And the female flea said, "Sure. Shall we walk or take the dog?"

If H2O is on the inside of a fire hydrant, what is on the outside?
K9P.

Did you hear that in New York the Stop and Shop grocery chain merged with the A&P?
Now it's called the Stop&P.

Did you hear about the snail that got beat up by two turtles?
He went to the police and they asked him, "Did you get a good look at the turtles who did this?"
He said, "No, it all happened so fast."

Did you hear about the two silkworms in a race?
They wound up in a tie.

Who yelled, "Coming are the British"?
Paul Reverse.

What did the mother buffalo say to her little boy when he went off to school?
Bison.

What's a metaphor?
So that livestock can graze.

What do you get when you eat onions and beans?
Tear gas.

Why did the man stop farting?
He ran out of gas.

What do you use to fix a broken tomato?
Tomato paste.

Why do golfers wear two pairs of pants?
In case they get a hole in one.

What did the tie say to the hat?
You go on a head, I'll just hang around.

Why didn't Noah fish very often?
He only had two worms.

How much do pirates pay for their earrings?
A buccaneer.

If Mr. and Mrs. Bigger had a baby, who would be the biggest of the three?
The baby, because he's a little Bigger.

Did you hear about the two antennas that got married?
The wedding was terrible, but the reception was great.

What do you say to a hitchhiker with one leg?
"Hop in."

What did one ocean say to the other ocean?
Nothing, they just waved.

What's a chimney sweep's most common ailment?
The flue.

Where does satisfaction come from?
A satisfactory.

Why can't a woman ask her brother for help?
Because he can't be a brother and assist her too.

What do you get when you pour boiling water down a rabbit hole?
Hot cross bunnies.

Why did the bunnies go on strike?
They wanted a raise in celery.

What do you give a deer with an upset stomach?
Elkaseltzer.

What do you call a deer with no eyes?
No ideer.

How did the mouse feel after the cat chased it through a screen door?
Strained.

What do you call cheese that doesn't belong to you?
Nacho cheese.

What do Eskimos get from sitting on the ice too long?
Polaroids.

What do prisoners use to call each other?
Cell phones.

Why do bicycles fall over?
  Because they are two-tired.

What's Irish and sits outside?
  Patio Furniture.

What is Mary short for?
  She's just got little legs, I guess.

How do you fix a broken tuba?
  With a tuba glue.

Why did the composer only compose in bed?
  He was writing sheet music.

Why did the toilet paper roll down the hill?
  Because it wanted to get to the bottom.

What do Alexander the Great and Winnie the Pooh have
in common?
  They have the same middle name.

What's the difference between roast beef and pea soup?
  Anyone can roast beef, but not many people can pee soup.

What do you call a guy who never farts in public?
  A private tooter.

Say lettuce and spell cup.
  Lettuce c-u-p.

A guy yells across the river, "Hey, how do you get to the other side of this river?"

A guy on the other side yells back, "You are on the other side!"

Did you hear about the giant that threw up?
  No, how'd you know?
  It's all over town.

What does a one-legged ballerina wear?
  A one-one.

Why are you scratching yourself?
  I'm the only one who knows where it itches.

Do you know how to make your own anti-freeze?
  Take away her fur coat.

Why do fire departments have Dalmatians?
  To help them find the hydrants.

"Okay, class. If anyone has to go to the bathroom, just hold up two fingers."
  "How will that help?"

INSULTS

My driver's license photo doesn't do me justice.
    You don't need justice, you need mercy.

My only sin is vanity. I look in the mirror each morning
and think how beautiful I am.
    That's not a sin—that's a mistake.

I'm desperate. I haven't written anything good in months.
Months!
    That's because your standards are improving.

I'd say he's about one Froot Loop shy of a full box.

The wheel's spinning, but the hamster's asleep.

I'd explain it to you, but your brain would explode.

I like your approach. Now let's see your departure.

I'd say he doesn't have all his dogs on the same leash.

He forgot to pay his brain bill.

His antenna doesn't pick up all the channels.

I like you, but I don't want to see you working with
subatomic particles.

Not the sharpest knife in the drawer, is he?

Doesn't have his belt through all the loops.

Where other people have a brain, he's got resonance.

Got an IQ that's about room temperature.

Got the IQ of garden tools.

Doesn't have the brainpower to toast a crouton.

He's so dense, light bends around him.

The gates are down, the lights are flashing, but the train just isn't coming.

I don't think his URL allows outside access.

A flash of light, a cloud of dust, and what was the question?

Looks like he played goalie for the darts team.

Definitely has a bad brains-to-testosterone ratio.

All booster, no payload.

I think he rode the Tilt-a-Whirl too long.

Hard to believe that he beat out a million other sperm.

He keeps a coat hanger in the backseat in case he locks the keys in his car.

I like long walks, especially when they're taken by people who annoy me.

Never underestimate the power of stupid people in large groups.

Here's a drum. Now beat it.

YO' MAMA JOKES

Yo' mama is so fat, she doesn't have a tailor, she has a contractor.

Yo' mama is so fat, she measures 36-24-36, and the other arm is just as big.

Yo' mama is so fat, she was in the Macy's Thanksgiving Day Parade—wearing ropes.

Yo' mama is so fat, she went on a light diet. As soon as it's light she starts eating.

Yo' mama is so fat, she's half Italian, half Irish, and half American.

Yo' mama is so fat, when her beeper goes off, people think she's backing up.

Yo' mama is so fat, when she goes to the movies, she sits next to everyone.

Yo' mama is so fat, when she goes in a restaurant she looks at the menu and says, "Okay."

Yo' mama is so fat, she puts her lipstick on with a paint roller.

Yo' mama is so fat, she has to pull down her pants to get in her pocket.

Yo' mama is so fat, you have to take a train and two buses just to get on her good side.

Yo' mama is so fat, she has to wake up in sections.

Yo' mama is so fat, she sat on a quarter and a booger popped out of George Washington's nose.

Yo' mama is so fat, she walked into the Gap and filled it.

Yo' mama is so fat, she has to put her belt on with a boomerang.

Yo' mama is so fat, she comes at you from all directions.

Yo' mama is so fat, when she was growing up she didn't play with dolls, she played with midgets.

Yo' mama is so fat, she uses two buses for roller-blades.

Yo' mama is so fat, when she goes to a buffet, she gets the group rate.

Yo' mama is so fat, she doesn't eat with a fork, she eats with a forklift.

Yo' mama is so fat, Weight Watchers won't look at her.

Yo' mama is so fat, the last time the landlord saw her, he doubled the rent.

Yo' mama is so fat, she put on some BVDs and by the time she got them on, they spelled "boulevard."

Yo' mama is so fat, I ran around her twice and got lost.

Yo' mama is so fat, the shadow of her butt weighs 100 pounds.

Yo' mama is so fat, the National Weather Service names each one of her farts.

Yo' mama is so fat, when she's standing on the corner, police drive by and say, "Hey! Break it up!"

Yo' mama is so fat, she's been declared a natural habitat for condors.

Yo' mama is so fat, she sets off car alarms when she runs.

Yo' mama is so fat, when she goes to the zoo, the elephants throw her peanuts.

Yo' mama is so fat, her blood type is Ragu.

Yo' mama is so fat, they had to let out the shower curtain.

Yo' mama is so fat that when she runs the fifty-yard dash, she needs an overnight bag.

Yo' mama is so fat, she can't even fit in the chat room.

Yo' mama is so fat, she gets her toenails painted at Lucky's Auto Body.

Yo' mama is so fat, when she wears a yellow raincoat people holler, "Taxi!"

Yo' mama is so fat, when she gets in an elevator, it has to go down!

Yo' mama is so fat, she could sell shade.

Yo' mama is so fat, people jog around her for exercise.

Yo' mama is so fat, she gets runs in her jeans.

Yo' mama is so fat, when she wears a Malcolm X T-shirt, helicopters try to land on her back.

Yo' mama is so fat, she eats Wheat Thicks.

Yo' mama is so fat, she can't even jump to a conclusion.

Yo' mama is so fat that when she was born, she gave the hospital stretch marks.

Yo' mama is so fat, her graduation picture was an aerial photograph!

Yo' mama is so fat, her job title is spoon and fork operator!

Yo' mama is so fat, she left the house in high heels and when she came back, she had on flip-flops.

Yo' mama is so fat, when she turns around, people throw her a welcome back party.

Yo' mama is so fat, her belly button doesn't have lint, it has sweaters.

Yo' mama is so fat, the last time she saw 90210 was on a scale.

Yo' mama is so fat, a picture of her would fall off the wall!

Yo' mama is so fat, when she gets on the scale, it says "To be continued."

Yo' mama is so fat, she sat on a dollar, and when she got up there were four quarters.

Yo' mama is so fat, she fell in love and broke it.

Yo' mama is so fat, when she takes a shower, her feet don't get wet!

Yo' mama is so fat, you have to grease the door frame and hold a Twinkie on the other side just to get her through.

Yo' mama is so fat, when she goes to an all-you-can-eat buffet, they have to install speed bumps.

Yo' mama is so fat, the sign outside one restaurant says, "Maximum occupancy, 512, or Yo' mama!"

Yo' mama is so fat, she puts mayonnaise on aspirin.

Yo' mama is so fat, the back of her neck looks like a pack of hot dogs.

Yo' mama is so fat, her cereal bowl came with a lifeguard.

Yo' mama is so fat, she has to iron her pants on the driveway.

Yo' mama is so fat, when she goes to a restaurant, she doesn't get a menu, she gets an estimate.

Yo' mama is so fat, when she ran away, they had to use all four sides of the milk carton.

Yo' mama is so fat, she was zoned for commercial development.

Yo' mama is so fat, when she sings, it's over for everybody.

Yo' mama is so fat, she looks like she's smuggling a Volkswagen.

Yo' mama is so fat, when she was walking down the street and I swerved to miss her, I ran out of gas.

Yo' mama is so fat, when she dances, she makes the band skip.

Yo' mama is so fat, when she got her shoes shined, she had to take the guy's word for it.

Yo' mama is so fat, she gets group insurance!

Yo' mama is so fat, she's on both sides of the family!

Yo' mama is so fat, she can't reach her back pocket.

Yo' mama is so fat, she was born with a silver shovel in her mouth!

Yo' mama is so fat, when she fell over, she rocked herself to sleep trying to get up again.

Yo' mama is so fat, when she hauls ass, she has to make two trips!

Yo' mama is so fat, when she was diagnosed with a flesh-eating disease, the doctor gave her ten years to live!

Yo' mama is so fat, we're in her right now!

Yo' mama is so fat, when she sits around the house, she sits around the house!

Yo' mama is so fat, her belly button's got an echo!

Yo' mama is so fat, her belly button gets home fifteen minutes before she does!

Yo' mama is so fat, she had to go to SeaWorld to get baptized.

Yo' mama is so fat, when she tripped over on Fourth Avenue, she landed on Twelfth.

Yo' mama is so fat, she's got her own area code!

Yo' mama is so fat, when she talks to herself, it's a long distance call!

Yo' mama is so fat, she's got smaller fat women orbiting around her!

Yo' mama is so fat, whenever she goes to the beach, the tide comes in!

Yo' mama is so fat, she was born on the fourth, fifth, and sixth of March.

Yo' mama is so fat, she was floating in the ocean and Spain claimed her for the new world.

Yo' mama's so fat, she wears aluminum siding.

Yo' mama's so fat, she could fall down and wouldn't even know it.

Yo' mama's so fat, she got hit by a VW and had to go to the hospital to have it removed.

Yo' mama is so dumb, she thought Meow Mix was a record for cats.

Yo' mama is so dumb, she asked for a price check at the dollar store.

Yo' mama is so dumb, when she heard that 90 percent of all crimes occur in the home, she moved.

Yo' mama is so dumb, she stole a car and kept up the payments.

Yo' mama is so dumb, she called Dan Quayle for a spell check.

Yo' mama is so dumb, she thought that Tupac Shakur was a Jewish holiday.

Yo' mama's so dumb, she got locked in a grocery store and starved to death.

Yo' mama is so dumb, when she saw the sign that said, "Airport Left," she turned around and went home.

Yo' mama is so dumb, she thought Boyz II Men was a day-care center.

Yo' mama is so dumb, she sold the car for gas money.

Yo' mama is so dumb, when she went to the movies and they said, "Under 17 not admitted," she went home and got sixteen friends.

Yo' mama is so dumb, when she missed the 44 bus, she took the 22 bus twice instead.

Yo' mama is so dumb, she went up on your roof because they said drinks were on the house!

Yo' mama is so dumb, she got fired from the M&M factory for throwing out the W's!

Yo' mama is so dumb, she only changed your diapers once a month because it said on the box "Good for up to 20 pounds"!

Yo' mama is so dumb, she thinks Johnny Cash is a pay toilet!

Yo' mama is so dumb, she sent me a fax with a stamp on it.

Yo' mama is so dumb, she bought a solar-powered flashlight.

Yo' mama is so dumb, she watches *The Three Stooges* and takes notes.

Yo' mama is so dumb, it took her two hours to watch *60 Minutes.*

Yo' mama is so dumb, she sits on the TV and watches the couch!

Yo' mama is so dumb, she stepped on a crack and broke her own back.

Yo' mama is so dumb, it takes her an hour to cook Minute Rice.

Yo' mama is so dumb, she cooked her own complimentary breakfast.

Yo' mama is so dumb, when your dad said it was chilly outside, she ran out with a spoon.

Yo' mama is so dumb, she sold the house to pay the mortgage!

Yo' mama is so dumb, she had to call the operator to get the number for 911!

Yo' mama is so dumb, they had to burn down the school to get her out of second grade.

Yo' mama is so dumb, when you stand next to her, you hear the ocean!

Yo' mama is so poor, she went to McDonald's and put a milk shake on layaway.

Yo' mama is so poor, she waves around a Popsicle and calls it air conditioning.

Yo' mama is so poor, when I saw her kicking a can down the street, I asked her what she was doing, and she said, "Moving."

Yo' mama is so poor, when she goes to Kentucky Fried Chicken, she has to lick other people's fingers!

Yo' mama is so poor, when I ring the doorbell she says, "Ding!"

Yo' mama is so poor, they ask for her I.D. when she pays cash.

Yo' mama is so ugly, the psychiatrist makes her lie face down.

Yo' mama is so ugly, for Halloween she can trick-or-treat over the telephone!

Yo' mama is so ugly, if my dog looked like that, I'd shave his butt and walk him backwards.

Yo' mama is so ugly, your father takes her to work with him so he doesn't have to kiss her goodbye.

Yo' mama is so ugly, they're going to move Halloween to her birthday.

Yo' mama is so ugly, all her neighbors chipped in for curtains.

Yo' mama is so ugly, she makes onions cry.

Yo' mama is so ugly, she went to the beauty shop and it took three hours—for an estimate.

Yo' mama is so ugly, the Red Cross talked her out of being an organ donor.

Yo' mama is so ugly, when she was a baby, her incubator had tinted windows.

Yo' mama is so ugly, she'd scare a buzzard off a gut wagon.

Yo' mama is so ugly, she looks like she's been bobbing for french fries!

Yo' mama is so ugly, when she walks into a bank, they turn off the cameras.

Yo' mama is so ugly that when she sits on the beach, cats try to bury her.

Yo' mama's so ugly, when she entered an ugly contest, they said, "Sorry, no professionals."

Yo' mama is so ugly, she could scare the moss off a rock!

Yo' mama's so ugly, the only thing attracted to her is gravity.

Yo' mama is so ugly, when she looks in the mirror, the reflection ducks!

Yo' mama is so ugly, her face is closed on weekends!

Yo' mama is so ugly, when she was born, the doctor slapped your grandma!

Yo' mama is so ugly, they know what time she was born, because her face stopped all the clocks!

Yo' mama is so ugly, when she cries, the tears run up her face.

Yo' mama is so ugly, her mother had to feed her with a slingshot.

Yo' mama is so ugly, she could scare the chrome off a bumper!

Yo' mama is so ugly, when she talks, hairs fall out of my nose.

Yo' mama is so ugly, your father kisses her with a stuntman.

Yo' mama's so ugly, at her wedding everyone kissed the groom.

Yo' mama's so ugly she needs two tickets when she goes to the zoo, one to get in and one to get out.

Yo' mama's so ugly that whenever she walks past a bathroom the toilet flushes.

Yo' mama is so skinny, her eyes are single file.

Yo' mama is so skinny, her pajamas have only one stripe.

Yo' mama is so slow, her ancestors arrived on the *June Flower*.

Yo' mama is so old, she farts dust!

Yo' mama is so old, she walked into an antiques store and they kept her.

Yo' mama is so old, her driver's license has hieroglyphics on it!

Yo' mama is so old, she still owes Moses a quarter!

Yo' mama is so old, when she was young, rainbows were black and white!

Yo' mama is so old, when she was born, the Dead Sea was just getting sick!

Yo' mama is so old, she was a waitress at the Last Supper.

Yo' mama is so old, when she was in school, they didn't have history.

Yo' mama is so old, when I told her to act her own age, she died.

Yo' mama is so old, she has a picture of Moses in her yearbook.

Yo' mama is so old, her birth certificate says "expired" on it.

Yo' mama is so old, she knew Burger King when he was still a prince.

Yo' mama is so old, she sat behind Jesus in the third grade.

Yo' mama is so short, she poses for trophies!

Yo' mama is so short, when she pulls up her stockings, she can't see where she's going.

Yo' mama's so short, you can see her feet on her driver's license!

Yo' mama's arms are so short, she has to tilt her head to scratch her ear.

Yo' mama's head is so small, she got her ear pierced and died.

Yo' mama's nose is so big, you can go bowling with her boogers!

Yo' mama's lips are so big, ChapStick had to invent a spray.

Yo' mama is so lazy, I've seen her step into a revolving door and wait.

Yo' mama's house is so dirty, roaches ride around on dune buggies!

Yo' mama's house is so dirty, she has to wipe her feet before she goes outside.

Yo' mama is so dirty, she brushes her teeth with chewing tobacco.

Yo' mama is so nasty, she joined the Four Horsemen: war, pestilence, death, famine, and yo' mama!

Yo' mama's underarms are so hairy, she looks like she has somebody in a headlock.

Yo' mama's armpits stink so bad, she made Right Guard turn left.

Yo' mama's teeth are so yellow, when she smiles, cars slow down.

Yo' mama is so cross-eyed, she dropped a dime and picked up two nickels.

Yo' mama's glasses are so thick, when she looks at a map she can see people waving.

Yo' mama is so cheap, when she takes out a dollar, George Washington blinks at the light.

Yo' mama is so tough, when carpenters buy a box of nails, they say, "Hand me some of those mamas."

DEATH/HEAVEN JOKES

St. Peter is at the pearly gates of Heaven greeting newcomers when a group of people from Wall Street arrive. St. Peter has never seen anyone from Wall Street at the pearly gates before, so he goes to ask God what to do. God tells him, "Go let them in." A few minutes later St. Peter returns and tells God, "They're gone!" God says, "Who, the people from Wall Street?" And St. Peter says, "No, the pearly gates!"

"What does your daddy do for a living?"
  "My daddy's dead."
  "What did he do before he died?"
  "He sort of clutched at his chest and fell over."

James Brown went to the pearly gates and met St. Peter who took him to a room where Jerry Garcia was playing with Jimi Hendrix and Jim Morrison and Janis Joplin. James Brown said, "I was worried maybe I was going to hell, but I guess not." Jerry Garcia said, "You think this is heaven?" Just then Lawrence Welk walked in and said, "All right, one more time. 'The Anniversary Waltz.' And a one and a two and a one, two, three…"

A man dies and goes to hell. He wakes up in a cheap little motel room. After looking around for a little bit, he discovers that it's not so bad. It has clean sheets, a decent shower, and basic cable. When he goes outside, he sees that Satan is outside in a golf cart. He says, "Oh, you're the new guy. I'm here to give you the tour." So Satan drives him around hell showing him all the sights, a pool, a family-style Italian restaurant. The guy says, "Hey, this isn't so bad." And Satan says, "Yeah, we like it here. Heaven is better, though. They've got premium cable, fancy restaurants, and a private lagoon, but we like it here." Then the golf cart turns the corner and the guy sees a flaming pit of naked souls in agony under an apocalyptic sky. "What is that!?" he asks. "Oh, that's for the Catholics," says Satan. "They insisted on it."

When Einstein died and went to heaven, St. Peter met him and said, "Can you prove that you really are Albert Einstein?" and Einstein wrote out a whole page of equations. St. Peter said, "Okay, I see." Picasso died and St. Peter said, "You look like Picasso, but how can I know for sure?" So Picasso drew his masterpieces one after the other. St. Peter said, "All right, that's fine." When George W. Bush died and went to heaven, St. Peter said, "I'm sorry, I need to ask you to prove who you are. I mean, Albert Einstein proved who he was, and Picasso, and so I have to ask you." George W. Bush said, "Who is Einstein? Who is Picasso?" St. Peter said, "Okay, come on in. I know it's you."

An engineer dies and goes to hell. He immediately fixes the toilets so they flush properly. Then he gives hell computers and TVs. Finally, he fixes the thermostat. God is horrified by the growing comfort level in hell and says to Satan, "If you don't reduce the comfort levels and get rid of that engineer, I'll sue!" to which Satan says, "Uh-huh. And just where are you going to get a lawyer?"

Both Dolly Parton and the Queen die and go to heaven. St. Peter meets them at the pearly gates and looks in his big book and says, "Sorry, ladies, but there is only room for one of you." Without hesitation, Dolly lifts up her sweater and says, "These should get me in!" A bit taken aback, St. Peter turns to the Queen, and without a word she goes to the commode at the pearly gates, lifts her skirt and does a pee and pulls the handle. Still flashing her bare chest, Dolly says, "These should still get me in." St. Peter shakes his head sadly and says, "Sorry, Dolly, but a Royal flush will always beat a pair."

A man dies and finds himself in a small room furnished with a couch and a TV. There's another guy sitting on the couch watching the TV. "So, is this heaven or hell?" the newly deceased asks the man on the couch. "Well, there are no windows or doors and no apparent way out," the man answers. "So this is hell?" the newcomer responds. "I don't know," says the other guy without looking up, "They did give us this big-screen TV!" "So maybe this is heaven?" the guy replies. "Maybe, but the TV only gets one channel." "Okay, so maybe this *is* hell?" "I'm not sure. The only station the TV gets is PBS." "So maybe this is heaven after all!" the newcomer exclaims. "Yeah, except for one thing," the other guy retorts, "It's always pledge week."

Once there was a rich man who wanted badly to take some of his fortune with him when he died. He prayed and finally God said, "Okay, you can bring some." So he found a large suitcase and packed it with gold bars, and soon afterward he died and showed up at the pearly gates. St. Peter said, "Hey, you can't bring that in here!" The man explained that God had allowed him one carry-on and St. Peter opened the suitcase and said, "You brought pavement?"

Bill Gates died and went to heaven and was given a little cottage in the woods and next door was a mansion on a hill with a golf course and tennis courts, and there lived the captain of the *Titanic*. "Why does he deserve better?" Bill asked God. "Because the *Titanic* only crashed once."

A man went to heaven and St. Peter was showing him around. The man saw a group of people milling around and asked who they were. St. Peter said, "Oh, those are the Unitarians—they are arguing about whether or not they are here!"

Three friends die in a car accident, and they go to an orientation in heaven. They are all asked, "When you are in your casket and friends and family are mourning you, what would you like to hear them say about you?"

The first guy says, "I would like to hear them say that I was a great doctor in my time and a great family man."

The second guy says, "I would like to hear that I was a wonderful husband and a school teacher who made a huge difference in our children of tomorrow."

The last guy replies, "I would like to hear them say... 'Look, he's moving'!"

A woman dies and goes to heaven, and St. Peter takes her on a tour of heaven. They pass a pit where there are people gnashing their teeth and wailing, and the woman says, "Who's down there?"

St. Peter says, "Oh, those are the Catholics who ate meat on Fridays."

They walk a little farther and there is another pit with more groaning and wailing, and she says, "Okay, who's down there?"

St. Peter answers, "Those are the Baptists who went to dances."

And a little farther along, there is another pit and people down there gnashing their teeth and crying and ripping their garments, and she says, "And those people?"

And St. Peter says, "Those are the Episcopalians who ate their salads with their dessert forks."

"Madame fortune teller, tell me: Are there golf courses in heaven?"

"I have good news, and I have bad news."

"What's the good news?"

"The good news is that the golf courses in heaven are beautiful beyond anything you could imagine!"

"That's wonderful."

"And you'll be teeing off at 8:30 tomorrow morning."

A man went on vacation and arranged for his mother to stay at his house and take care of his cat. And, just to be sure, he asked his next-door neighbor if he would look in on them every day and make sure they were all right. "No problem," said the neighbor. The man flew off to Mexico and after a couple of days, he called the neighbor and asked how things were going.

"Well," the neighbor said, "your cat died." "Geez," the guy said. "You have to come right out and tell me like that? Couldn't you have a little more consideration? I'm on vacation. Couldn't you have broken it to me a little more gently? Like first telling me that the cat was on the roof, then that the cat fell off the roof, then maybe the next day telling me you had taken the cat to the vet—like that, not boom all at once! By the way, how's my mom doing?"

"Well," said the neighbor, "she went up on the roof…"

Aaron Rodgers and Teddy Bridgewater die and go to heaven. After Aaron Rodgers enters the pearly gates, God takes him on a tour. He shows him a little two-bedroom house with a faded Packers banner hanging from the front porch and says, "This is your house, Aaron. You know, most people don't get their own houses up here."

Rodgers looks at the house, then turns around and looks at the one sitting on top of the hill. It's a huge two-story mansion with Minnesota flags lining both sides of the sidewalk and a huge Vikings banner hanging between the marble columns.

Rodgers says, "Hey! How come I get this little two-bedroom house, and Teddy Bridgewater gets a huge mansion?"

God says, "That's not Bridgewater's house, it's mine."

Three souls appeared before St. Peter at the pearly gates. St. Peter asked the first one, "What was your last annual salary?" The soul replied, "$200,000; I was a trial lawyer." St. Peter asked the second one the same question. The soul answered, "$95,000; I was a realtor." St. Peter then asked the third soul the same question. The answer was "$8,000." St. Peter immediately said, "Cool! What instrument did you play?"

A husband and his wife were driving home one night and ran into a bridge abutment and both were killed. They arrived in heaven and found it was a beautiful golf course with a lovely clubhouse and fabulous greens. It was free and only for them, and the husband said, "You want to play a round?"

She said, "Sure." They teed off on the first hole, and she said, "What's wrong?"

He said, "You know, if it hadn't been for your stupid oat bran, we could have been here years ago."

A minister dies and is waiting in line at the pearly gates. Ahead of him is a guy dressed in sunglasses, a loud shirt, a leather jacket, and jeans. St. Peter addresses this guy, "Who are you, so that I may know whether or not to admit you to the kingdom of heaven?"

The guy replies, "I am Joe Choen, taxi driver, of Las Vegas."

St. Peter consults his list. He smiles and says to the taxi driver, "Take this silken robe and golden staff and enter the kingdom of heaven." The taxi driver goes into heaven with his robe and staff, and it is the minister's turn.

He stands erect and booms out, "I am Joseph Snow, pastor of St. Mary's for the last forty-five years."

St. Peter consults his list. He says to the minister, "Take this cotton robe and wooden staff and enter the kingdom of heaven."

"Just a minute," says the minister. "That man was a taxi driver, and he gets a silken robe and golden staff. How can this be?"

"Up here, we work by results," says St. Peter. "While you preached, people slept; while he drove, people prayed."

This guy's father dies, and he tells the undertaker he wants to give his dad the very best. So they have the funeral, and the undertaker sends him a bill for $16,000. He pays it. A month later he gets a bill for $85, which he pays. The next month there's another $85 bill, and the next month there's another. Finally the guy calls up the undertaker. The undertaker says, "Well, you said you wanted the best for your dad, so I rented him a tux."

A man died one day and found himself waiting in the long line of judgment. As he stood there he noticed that some souls were allowed to march right through the gates of heaven. Others were led over to Satan, who threw them into the burning pit. But every so often, instead of hurling a poor soul into the fire, Satan would toss a soul off to one side into a small pile.

After watching Satan do this several times, the fellow's curiosity got the best of him. So he strolled over and asked Satan, "Excuse me, prince of darkness. I'm waiting in line for judgment, and I couldn't help wondering why you're tossing those people aside instead of flinging them into the fires of hell with the others?"

"Ah, those," Satan said with a groan. "They're all from Seattle. They're too wet to burn yet."

This couple is killed the night before their wedding. They go to heaven, and they ask St. Peter if they can be married.

St. Peter says, "Okay. I'll come and get you when we can do that."

Ten years later, he tells the couple, "Okay. We can have your wedding now."

So they get married, and there's a minister and flowers and nice music and all, but pretty soon they realize they made a mistake.

They go to St. Peter and say they want a divorce. St. Peter says, "Okay. I'll come and tell you when we can do that."

The couple asks how long it will take. And St. Peter says, "It took ten years to get a preacher up here. Who knows how long it's going to be before a lawyer shows up!"

Bill Gates died in a car accident. He found himself in purgatory being sized up by God. "Well, Bill, I'm going to let you decide where you want to go." Bill replied, "Well, thanks, God. What's the difference between the two?" God said, "I'm willing to let you visit both places briefly to help you make a decision." Bill said, "Okay, then, let's try hell first."

So Bill went to hell. It was a beautiful, clean, sandy beach with clear waters. There were thousands of beautiful women running around, playing in the water, laughing and frolicking about. The sun was shining and the temperature was perfect. "This is great!" he told God. "If this is hell, I really want to see heaven!" "Fine," said God, and off they went.

Heaven was a high place in the clouds, with angels drifting about playing harps and singing. It was nice but not as enticing as hell. Bill thought for a moment and then said, "Hmm, I think I prefer hell." "Fine," replied God, "as you desire." So Bill Gates went to hell. Two weeks later, God decided to check up on him.

When God arrived in hell, he found Bill shackled to a wall, screaming amongst the hot flames in a dark cave. He was being burned and tortured by demons. "How's everything going, Bill?" God asked. Bill responded, his

124

voice full of anguish and disappointment, "This is awful. This is not what I expected. I can't believe this happened. What happened to that other place with the beaches and the beautiful women playing in the water?"

God said, "That was the screen saver."

Three nurses die and go up to heaven. And St. Peter says, "So, tell me—what did you do with your life?" The first nurse says, "Well, I worked in an emergency room, and it was really challenging. But we were able to help some people and I think that's worthwhile." St. Peter says, "That's fabulous—come on in. I hope you enjoy heaven."

And St. Peter turns to the second nurse and says, "So, what did you do with your life?" And the nurse says, "I worked in a hospice, and it was a little depressing, since everyone dies. But we were kind to people and I think that's worthwhile." St. Peter says, "That's great. Come on in—I hope you enjoy heaven."

Then he faces the remaining nurse and says, "So, what did you do with your life?" And the nurse says, "For the last years of my life, I worked as a managed-care nurse for an HMO." St. Peter wrinkles his brow and pulls out a calculator, a whole set of manuals, and a pencil. He spends time writing and scrunching up pieces of paper, and then looks up and says, "I can approve you for a five-day stay."

Man: Is this the mortuary? Listen. You better make arrangements for a funeral. My wife passed away.

Funeral director: What?! Your wife died two years ago.

Man: I got married again.

Funeral director: Oh! Congratulations!

A bunch of salesmen went to the funeral of another salesman. They looked down at him in his coffin.

"Gosh, he looks terrible. What did he have?"

"North Dakota, South Dakota, western Minnesota…"

A young woman saw a funeral procession going by. There was a black hearse, followed by an older woman leading a pit bull on a leash, and after that was another hearse, and behind that was a line of two hundred women walking single file. The young woman walked up to the older woman and said, "I'm sorry to intrude on your moment of grief, but I can't help asking, whose funeral is this?"

The woman said, "Well, my husband is in that hearse up there. The pit bull killed him when it discovered him with his girlfriend. She's in that hearse back there."

The young woman said, "Can I borrow that dog?"

The old woman replied, "Get in line."

So this guy dies and goes to heaven and St. Peter takes him down the hall past a number of doors and then St. Peter stops and says, "You have to be very, very quiet going past that door. That's where the Mormons are, and they think they're the only ones here."

RELIGION JOKES

Four clergymen went on a hunting trip together and one night, in the hunting cabin, they decided to confess their worst sins to each other. The Catholic priest said, "My sin is lust; once a month I go to a burlesque show." The Episcopal priest said, "My sin is greed. I only put a nickel in the collection basket." The Lutheran pastor said, "My sin is gluttony. Once in a while, I get in my car and go to a faraway town and go through the drive-up window and order four half-pounders and a bucket of fries." And the Baptist minister said, "My sin is gossip, and I can't wait to get back from this trip."

What car would Jesus drive?
  A Christler.

An elderly woman walked into the local country church. The friendly usher greeted her at the door and helped her up the flight of steps. "Where would you like to sit?" he asked. "The front row, please," she said. "You really don't want to do that," the usher said. "The pastor is really boring." "Do you happen to know who I am?" the woman inquired. "No," he said. "I'm the pastor's mother." "Do you know who I am?" he asked. "No," she said. "Good."

So these four rabbis were arguing theology together, and it was three against one, so the odd rabbi cried out to heaven: "O, God! I know in my heart that I am right and they are wrong! Send a sign to prove it to them!"
  Suddenly there was a big black storm cloud in the sky above the four rabbis. The dissenting rabbi said, "A sign from

God! See, I'm right, I knew it!" But the other three said that one storm cloud meant nothing.

So the rabbi prayed for a bigger sign. This time there appeared four storm clouds and a bolt of lightning.

"SEE?" cried the rabbi, but the other rabbis said, "So? Eh? Lightning schmightning." Just then the sky turned pitch black, the earth shook, and a deep voice said, "HEEEE'S RIIIIGHT!"

The rabbi said, "Well?"

"So?" said the other rabbis. "Now it's three to two."

An atheist was telling the Christian how there was no God, no life after death, and the Christian said, "Well, let me ask you this? A horse, a cow, and a deer all eat grass. Yet a deer excretes little pellets, while a cow turns out a flat patty, but a horse produces clumps. Why do you suppose that is?" The atheist said, "I have no idea." The Christian said, "How can you talk about God when you don't know poop?"

How many angels can fit in a Honda?

All of them. For it is written: "All of my angels shall sing my praises in one Accord."

Michelangelo was bored as he was lying on the scaffolding high in the air painting the ceiling of the Sistine Chapel when a woman came into the chapel to pray.

He whispered, "I am Jesus Christ," and his voice echoed in the room. The woman kept praying. Michelangelo said again, "I am Jesus Christ," and the woman said, "Be quiet. I'm talking to your mother."

What did God say when He first saw Niagara Falls?
"Oh, my Self!"

Unitarians believe in, at most, one god.

A Unitarian Universalist prayed: "Dear God, if there is a God, please save my soul, if I have a soul."

A Unitarian meeting may seem strange to outsiders. Everybody sings "Praise Be to Whom It May Concern" and then somebody speaks and nobody listens, and then everybody disagrees. And if you disagree, then you'll fit right in.

A young Unitarian was visiting a Christian church when the pastor asked if she was saved. She said, "In my church, we try not to get lost."

A Unitarian is just a Quaker with Attention Deficit Disorder.

Why is a Unitarian Universalist congregation like granola?
When you take away all the fruits and all the nuts, all you have left are flakes!

A group of school children were trying to decide whether the pet rabbit was a boy or a girl. The Unitarian child said, "Let's take a vote on it."

A Catholic church, a synagogue and a Unitarian society all caught fire. Before the fire trucks got there, the priest dashed in and saved the consecrated Host, the rabbi dashed in to save the Torah scrolls, and the Rev. Nancy Smith dashed in to save the coffeemaker and the photocopier.

Why did the Unitarian cross the road?
    To support the chicken in its search for its own path.

The children in the Unitarian church school were drawing pictures. One girl said, "I'm going to draw a picture of God." The teacher said, "But nobody knows what God looks like." "They will when I get done with my picture."

A woman went into a fabric store and asked the clerk for nine yards of material to make a nightgown. The clerk said, "Nine yards is way too much material for a nightgown." The woman said, "I know, but my husband is Unitarian and he would rather seek than find."

The young minister was asked by a funeral director to conduct a graveside service for a homeless man with no family or friends. The cemetery was way back in the country, and the minister got lost. Finally, he saw the backhoe in the field and the gravediggers standing by, but no hearse was in sight. He dashed over to the grave and saw the vault lid was already in place. He opened up his Bible and began to preach. He preached about God's mercy and the parable of the Prodigal Son and the hope of the Resurrection, and then he bowed his head in prayer. And one of the workers said, "I ain't never seen anything like this before…and I've been putting in septic tanks for twenty years."

So the three skunks went to church. The priest made them sit in their own pew.

One Sunday morning, a mother went in to wake her son and tell him it was time to get ready for church, to which he replied, "I'm not going." "Why not?" she asked. "I'll give you two good reasons," he said. "One, they don't like me, and two, I don't like them." His mother replied, "I'll give you two good reasons why you should go to church. One, you're 59 years old, and two, you're the pastor!"

Jesus and his disciples were walking around one day, when Jesus said, "The Kingdom of Heaven is like 3x squared plus 8x minus 9." The disciples looked very puzzled, and finally asked Peter, "What on earth does Jesus mean—the Kingdom of Heaven is like 3x squared plus 8x minus 9?" Peter said, "Don't worry. It's just another one of his parabolas."

An old man was dying. He sent for his accountant and his lawyer to come and sit by his bed as he died. Jesus had died between two thieves, and that's how he wanted to go, too.

A Jesuit priest, a Dominican priest, and a Trappist monk were marooned on a deserted island. They found a magic lamp and rubbed it. And poof, a genie appeared and offered them three wishes, one for each of them. The Jesuit said he wanted to teach at a great university, and poof, he was gone! The Dominican wished to preach at St. Peter's in Rome, and poof, he was gone! And the Trappist said, "Gee, I already got my wish!"

Did you hear about the New Age Catholic Church? They've got an organic Communion wafer called I Can't Believe It's Not Jesus.

I saw a nun with her clothes on inside out. I asked her about it, and she said, "It's just a bad habit of mine."

Two nuns were shopping in a food store and happened to be passing the beer and liquor section. One asked the other if she would like a beer. The other nun answered that would be good, but that she would be uneasy about purchasing it. The first nun said that she would handle it and picked up a six-pack and took it to the cashier. The cashier had a surprised look and the first nun said, "The beer is used for washing our hair." The cashier, without blinking an eye, reached under the counter and put a package of pretzels in the bag with the beer, saying, "Here, don't forget the curlers."

A priest, a Pentecostal preacher, and a rabbi challenged each other to a preaching contest. They would all go out into the woods, find a bear, preach to it, and try to convert it. Two days later, they got together to discuss the experience. Father Flannery said, "Well, I read to him from the Catechism and then I sprinkled him with holy water and Holy Mary Mother of God he was gentle as a lamb. The bishop is coming out next week to give him first communion and confirmation." Reverend Billy Bob said, "Well, I read to my bear from God's HOLY WORD! And I took HOLD of him and wrestled him down to the creek. And I DUNKED him and BAPTIZED him and he became as gentle as a lamb. We spent the rest of the day praising Jesus." They both looked down at the rabbi, who was in a body cast. The rabbi said, "Looking back on it, circumcision may not have been the best way to start."

Abe and his friend Sol are out for a walk. They pass a Catholic church with a sign out front that reads "$1,000 to Anyone Who Converts." Sol decides to go inside and see what it's all about. Abe waits outside. Hours go by. Finally, Sol emerges. "So?" says Abe. "What happened?" "I converted," says Sol. "No kidding!" says Abe. "Did you get the thousand bucks?" Sol says, "Is that all you people think about?"

Did you hear about the pastor who used to be a dairy farmer? Before he heard the call, he used to call the herd.

Why was there only bread and wine at the Last Supper?
    It was a potluck and only men were invited.

At 50 below, your spit freezes before it hits the ground, and at 65 below, Jehovah's Witnesses stick to your screen door.

What is the definition of Unitarian diversity?
    Three colors of Subarus in the parking lot.

In a Unitarian church, the only time you hear the words, "Jesus Christ," is when the janitor falls down the steps.

Arguing with a Unitarian is like wrestling in the mud with a pig. After a while, you realize that they enjoy it!

Have you heard of the Unitarian Universalism?
That's where all your answers are questioned.

The preacher went to the bedside of a man who was seriously ill in the hospital. He said to the family, "Take a break. I'll sit here with Brother Jones." He went over close to the bed, and the family went out to take a much-needed break. Suddenly, he saw that the man was rapidly fading. He couldn't talk and was trying to make signals and wave his arms, so the preacher gave him a pencil and paper, and the man scribbled something down, and then he died. The family came back in, and the preacher said, "Well, I'm sorry to tell you that he's gone. It's a good thing I was here to comfort him in his last moments. Let's grieve together." And they did for a while. Finally the preacher said, "And one more thing. He wrote a note. It was something, obviously, that he really wanted you to know in the last moment of his life." He opens the note and reads: "Please get off my oxygen tube!"

If a Jewish boy marries a Catholic girl, what music do they play at the wedding?
Oy Vey Maria.

The preacher said to his congregation, "I want everybody who wants to go to heaven to stand up." Everyone stood up, except for one old man in the front. So he said, "I said, I want everyone who wants to go to heaven to stand up!" The old man in the front row remained seated. Finally, the preacher said, "Brother Williams, I said, everybody who wants to go to heaven, stand up!"

And the old man said, "Oh, I'm sorry. I thought you were getting together a group to go now."

What do you call Jews who adopt Minnesota culture?
Jewtherans. They have a lot of angst, but they can't talk about it.

The minister raises his hands and says, "We are but dust..." The little girl turns to her mother and says, "Mother, what is butt dust?"

So the Zen master said to the hot dog vendor, "Make me one with everything." So the hot dog vendor fixes a hot dog and hands it to the Zen master, who pays with a $20 bill. The hot dog vendor puts the bill in the cash drawer and closes the drawer. "Where's my change?" asks the Zen master. And the hot dog vendor says, "Change must come from within."

What's a transistor?
A priest who wears nun's clothes.

Jesus needed a new robe, so he went to Finkelstein, the Tailor, who made him a beautiful robe. Perfect fit. Jesus asked how much He owed but Finkelstein said, "No, no, no, for the Son of God? There's no charge. But when you give a sermon, perhaps you could mention that your nice new robe was made by Finkelstein, the Tailor." So Jesus did, and hundreds of people went to Finkelstein for their new robes, and so he offered Jesus a partnership. They thought of calling it Jesus & Finkelstein, but then they decided on Lord & Taylor.

Three men went to their seats at the football game and there were a couple of nuns sitting ahead of them. The men wanted to drink beer and swear at the referees and not be scolded by nuns, so they decided to badger the nuns and get them to move. One guy said, "I think I'm going to move to Utah. There are only 100 Catholics living there." The second said, "I want to go to Montana. There are only 50 Catholics there." The third guy said, "I want to go to Idaho. There are only 25 Catholics living there."

One of the nuns turned around and said, "Why don't you go to hell? There aren't any Catholics there."

Why is it dangerous to upset a Unitarian?
He might burn a question mark in your front lawn.

Why are Unitarians such bad singers?
Because they're always reading ahead in the hymnal to see if they agree with it.

In the Unitarian church there are only four commandments. The other six are suggestions.

What do you get when you cross a Unitarian with a Jehovah's Witness?
Someone out knocking on doors for no apparent reason.

What do you call a schizophrenic Zen Buddhist?
A person who is at two with the universe.

The Pope is visiting town and all the residents are dressed up in their best Sunday clothes. Everyone lines up on Main Street hoping for a personal blessing from the Pope.

One local man has put on his best suit and he's sure the Pope will stop and talk to him. He is standing next to an exceptionally downtrodden-looking bum who doesn't smell very good. As the Pope comes walking by he leans over and says something to the bum and then walks right by the local man.

He can't believe it, then it hits him. The Pope won't talk to him because he's concerned for the unfortunate people: the poor and feeble ones. Thinking fast, he gives the bum $20 to trade clothes with him. He puts on the bum's clothing and runs down the street to line up for another chance for the Pope to stop and talk to him. Sure enough, the Pope walks right up to him this time, leans over close and says, "I thought I told you to get the hell out of here."

The drunk went into the Catholic church to do the Stations of the Cross, but he did them backwards and the priest found him looking at the first one and crying. The man said, "I'm just so happy that he survived and he's getting his strength back."

Jesus and Satan were at their computers, writing reports and doing spreadsheets, and suddenly lightning flashed, thunder rolled, and the power went off. When it came back on, Satan bowed his head and wept because he'd lost everything, but Jesus had no problem because Jesus saves.

Mother Teresa died and went to heaven. God met her and asked if she was hungry. Mother Teresa said, "I could eat," so God opened a can of tuna and some rye bread and they shared it. As she ate, Mother Teresa looked down into hell and saw the people there eating huge steaks, lobsters, expensive wine, and flaming desserts. Mother Teresa said, "I'm really glad to be in heaven, God, but why do we just eat tuna and rye bread while down in hell they're eating like kings?" God said, "Well, for just two people, why bother to cook?"

A Jewish student was doing well in school in all subjects except for math. So his parents decide to send him to a private Catholic school.

While there, the boy came home from school and studied every day. At the end of the term, the boy got straight As. So his parents asked him, "What motivated you to do so well in school?"

He replied, "When I saw that guy nailed to a plus sign I knew they weren't fooling around!"

Did you hear about the married Amish woman who also had a lover?

She liked two Mennonite.

Did you hear about the Talking Jewish Mother Doll?

You pull the string and it says, "Again with the string!"

There's a lot of talk about when a fetus is viable. The Jewish conception of when a fetus is viable is when it graduates from medical school.

Why do Jewish mothers make great parole officers?
They never let anyone finish a sentence.

A Jewish mother sent a telegram: "Start worrying. Details to follow..."

An elderly Jewish man is brought to the local hospital. A pretty nurse tucks him into bed and says, "Are you comfortable?" He replies, "I make a nice living..."

Going into church one day, a man looking for a place to sit asked a lady: "Is the seat next to you saved?" To which she replied, "No, but I'm praying for it."

The first Jewish President is elected. He calls his mother: "Mama, I've won the election. You've got to come to the Inauguration."
    "I don't know, what would I wear?"
    "Don't worry, I'll send you a dressmaker."
    "But I only eat kosher food!"
    "Mama, I am going to be President. I can get you kosher food."
    "But how will I get there?"
    "I'll send a limo. Just come, Mama!"
    "Okay, okay, if it makes you happy."
    The great day comes and Mama is seated between a Supreme Court Justice and the former Vice President. She nudges them and says, "You see that boy, the one with his hand on the Bible? His brother's a doctor!"

So the little old Jewish woman is walking down the street in the garment district, and a flasher comes toward her and he whips open his raincoat and she looks over and says, "You call that a lining?"

We know Jesus was Jewish because he went into his father's business, he lived at home until he was 33, and his mother thought he was God. On the other hand, he could've been Irish because he never got married, he never held a steady job, and his last request was for something to drink. On the other hand, he had a Puerto Rican name.

What do you call ultra-orthodox Jewish farmers?
Hayseedim.

A sign at the Unitarian Church said: "Bible study at 7:00—bring your Bible and a pair of scissors."

The Episcopal priest stands up to start the Sunday services and his microphone falls apart. He says, "There's something wrong with this mike…" And the people respond, "And also with you…"

Why can't Episcopalians play chess?
They can't tell the difference between a bishop and a queen.

Why are we quiet in church?
Because people are sleeping.

Why don't Lutherans smoke?
Their butts can't fit in the ashtray.

How do you join the choir?

You go into the church looking for the AA meeting and you go into the wrong room by mistake and they're so happy to see you that you don't dare leave.

How do we know that Adam was a Lutheran?

Who else could stand beside a naked woman and be tempted by a piece of fruit?

Lutherans get rid of squirrels by baptizing them and making them members. That way, they only see them on Christmas and Easter.

After the christening of his baby brother in church, Jason sobbed all the way home in the back seat of the car. His father asked him three times what was wrong. Finally, the boy replied, "That preacher said he wanted us brought up in a Christian home, and I wanted to stay with you guys."

In Orthodox families, the man makes the coffee because in Scripture it says, "Hebrews."

A mother was preparing pancakes for her sons. The boys began to argue over who would get the first pancake. Their mother saw the opportunity for a moral lesson. "If Jesus were sitting here, He would say, 'Let my brother have the first pancake. I can wait.'" One of them turned to the other and said, "You be Jesus!"

God was talking to one of his angels. He said, "Boy, I just figured out how to rotate Earth so it creates this really incredible twenty-four-hour period of alternating light and darkness." The angel said, "What are you going to do now?" God said, "Call it a day."

So Moses was talking with God, and Moses said, "Wait a minute. Let me get this straight. They get to keep the oil, and we cut off the tip of our what?"

What do you get when you cross a Lutheran and a Buddhist?
   Someone who sits up all night worrying about nothing.

God calls up the Pope. "I've got some good news and some bad news," God says. "I've decided that there should be one church and one religion. No more confusion."
   The Pope says, "That's wonderful."
   God says, "The bad news is, I'm calling from Mecca."

Eve, in the Garden of Eden, said, "God, I have a problem. It's a beautiful garden, but I'm lonely and I'm sick of eating apples."
   "Okay," God said. "I'll create a man for you."
   Eve said, "What's a man?"
   "He's a creature with aggressive tendencies and an enormous ego who doesn't listen and gets lost a lot, but he's big and strong, he can open jars and hunt animals, and he's fun in bed."
   "Sounds great!" said Eve.
   "There's just one other thing. He's going to want to believe I made him first."

"I'm lonely," Adam told God in the Garden of Eden. "I need to have someone around for company."

"Okay," replied God. "I'll give you the perfect companion. She is beautiful, intelligent, and gracious—she'll cook and clean for you and never say a cross word."

"Sounds great," Adam said. "But what's she going to cost?"

"An arm and a leg," answered God.

"That's pretty steep," replied Adam. "What can I get for a rib?"

A guy goes into confession and says to the priest, "Father, I'm eighty years old, married, have four kids and eleven grandchildren, and last night I had an affair and I made love to two eighteen-year-old girls. Both of them. Twice."

And the priest says, "Well, my son, when was the last time you were at confession?"

"Never, Father, I'm Jewish."

"So then, why are you telling me?"

"I'm tellin' everybody!"

One morning the devil decided to go to church. He appeared suddenly, just before the offering, in a shower of flame and sparks and smoke. He ran up and down the aisle screaming, and all of the congregation ran out except for an old man sitting in back. The devil leaned over him, shook his spear, let out a ferocious roar, and cried, "I am Satan, Beelzebub, the Prince of Darkness. I am evil incarnate. Do you not fear me?"

The old man said, "Why should I? Been married to your sister for forty-eight years."

What were the last words spoken at the Last Supper?
"Everyone who wants to be in the picture, get on this side of the table."

Jesus was walking through the streets, and he noticed a group of people throwing stones at an adulteress. He stopped and said to the crowd, "Let the one who is without sin cast the first stone." All of a sudden, a big stone came out of the crowd and hit the woman right on the head. Jesus stopped, taken aback, then looked up and said, "Mom!"

Every year, St. Peter conducted a tour down on earth. "This year," he told the Virgin Mary, "I'm going to survey all your shrines and compare them to the shrines I've seen in previous years." He took his tour and visited shrines around the world before he came back to heaven and reported to Mary, "I've got great news! There are more people at your shrines than anyone else's. But I noticed one thing—every single statue portrayed you with a sad expression on your face. Why is that?" And Mary said, "You might not understand my feelings." And St. Peter said, "Now, Mary, I've had many people tell me their innermost feelings—can't you open up to me?" And Mary said, "Well, you see, Peter...I really wanted a girl."

This guy goes into his barber, and he's all excited. He says, "I'm going to go to Rome. I'm flying on Alitalia and staying at the Rome Hilton, and I'm going to see the Pope." The barber says, "Ha! Alitalia is a terrible airline, the Rome Hilton is a dump, and when you see the Pope, you'll probably be standing in back of about 10,000 people."

So the guy goes to Rome and comes back. His barber asks, "How was it?"

"Great," he says. "Alitalia was a wonderful airline. The hotel was great. And I got to meet the Pope."

"You met the Pope?" said the barber.

"I bent down to kiss the Pope's ring."

"And what did he say?"

"He said, 'Where did you get that crummy haircut?'"

Why was Isaac twelve years old when God called Abraham to sacrifice his son?

Because if he had been a teenager, it wouldn't have been a sacrifice.

A guy enters the monastery. He has to take a vow of silence, but once a year he can write a word on the chalkboard in front of the head monk. The first year it's tough not to talk, but Word Day comes around and the monk writes "The" on the chalkboard. The second year is painful—it's very difficult not to talk—but finally Word Day rolls around. The monk scratches "food" on the chalkboard and enters his third year, which is excruciating. But the monk struggles through it, and when Word Day rolls around again, he writes "stinks." And the head monk says, "What's with you? You've been here for three years and all you've done is complain."

Abraham decided to upgrade his PC to Windows 10 and Isaac couldn't believe it. He said, "Dad, your old PC doesn't have enough memory." And Abraham said, "My son, God will provide the RAM."

This man went to his rabbi and said, "I'm very troubled by my son. He went away and he came back a Christian."

The rabbi said, "You know, it's funny you say that. My son, too, left home and came back a Christian."

They decided to pray about it, and God said, "You know, it's funny you say that…"

Do you think that Moses led the Israelites through the desert for forty years because God was testing him, or because he wanted them to really appreciate the promised land when they finally got there, or was it because Moses refused to ask anybody for directions?

A man was praying to God. He said, "God?"

God responded, "Yes?"

And the guy said, "Can I ask a question?"

"Go right ahead," God said.

"God, what is a million years to you?"

God said, "A million years to me is only a second."

"Hmm," the man wondered. Then he asked, "God, what is a million dollars worth to you?"

God said, "A million dollars to me is as a penny."

So the man said, "God, can I have a penny?"

And God said, "Sure! Just a second."

Three older Jewish mothers were sitting on a park bench in Miami Beach talking about how much their sons love them.

Sadie said, "You know the Manet painting hanging in my living room? My son, Irving, bought that for me for my seventy-fifth birthday. What a good boy he is, and how much he loves his mother."

Gertie said, "You call that love? You know that new Cadillac I just got for Mother's Day? That's from my son Bernie. What a doll."

Golda, in turn, replied, "That's nothing. You know my son Stanley? He's in analysis with a psychotherapist on Park Avenue. Five sessions a week—and what does he talk about? Me."

The Lutheran minister is driving down to New York, and he's stopped in Connecticut for speeding. The state trooper smells alcohol on his breath and sees an empty wine bottle on the floor. He asks, "Sir, have you been drinking?"

And the minister says, "Just water."

The sheriff says, "Then why do I smell wine?"

The minister looks down at the bottle and says, "Good Lord, he's done it again!"

So Tommy goes into a confessional and says, "Bless me, Father, for I have sinned. I have been with a loose woman."

The priest says, "Is that you, Tommy?"

"Yes, Father, it is I."

"Who was the woman you were with?"

"I cannot tell you, Father, for I do not wish to ruin her reputation."

"Was it Brenda?"

"No, Father."

"Was it Fiona?"

"No, Father."

"Was it Ann?"

"No, Father."

147

"Very well, Tommy. Go say five Our Fathers and four Hail Marys."

Tommy goes back to his pew, and his buddy Sean slides over and asks, "What happened?"

And Tommy says, "I got five Our Fathers, four Hail Marys, and three good leads."

The Jewish mother's telegram: "Begin worrying. Details follow."

A nun comes into the office of the mother superior and whispers, "Mother Superior, we…uh…we have discovered a case of syphilis."

"Wonderful. I was getting tired of the Chablis."

A maitre d' goes over to a middle-aged Jewish couple eating in his restaurant. He asks them, "Is anything all right?"

Why did the Amish couple get divorced?
He was driving her buggy.

What goes CLOP CLOP CLOP, BANG BANG, CLOP CLOP CLOP?
An Amish drive-by shooting.

Why don't Amish people water-ski?
The horses would drown.

A pastor skips services one Sunday to go bear hunting in the mountains. As he turns the corner along the path, he and a bear collide. The pastor stumbles backwards, slips off the trail, and begins tumbling down the mountain with the bear in hot pursuit. Finally, the pastor crashes into a boulder, sending his rifle flying in one direction and breaking both of his legs. The pastor is lying there; he's lost his gun, and the bear is coming closer. So he cries out in desperation, "Lord, I repent for all I've done. Please make this bear a Christian." The bear skids to a halt at the pastor's feet, falls to its knees, clasps its paws together, and says, "Lord, I do thank you for the food I am about to receive."

Three couples—an elderly couple, a middle-aged couple, and a young newlywed couple—wanted to join a Baptist church. The pastor says, "We have special requirements for new parishioners. You must abstain from having sex for two weeks."

The couples agreed and came back at the end of two weeks.

The pastor goes up to the elderly couple and asks, "Were you able to abstain from sex for the two weeks?"

The old man replies, "No problem at all, Pastor."

"Congratulations! Welcome to the church!" says the pastor.

The pastor goes to the middle-aged couple and asks, "Well, were you able to abstain from sex for the two weeks?"

The man replies, "The first week was not too bad. The second week I had to sleep on the couch for a couple of nights, but, yes, we made it."

"Congratulations! Welcome to the church," says the pastor.

The pastor then goes to the newlyweds and asks, "Well, were you able to abstain from sex for two weeks?"

"Well, Pastor, we were not able to go without sex for the two weeks," the young man replies.

"What happened?" inquires the pastor.

"My wife was reaching for a lightbulb on the top shelf and dropped it. When she bent over to pick it up, I couldn't help myself, and we had sex right there on the floor."

The pastor says, "Well, then, you're not welcome in the Baptist church."

"That's okay," says the young man. "We're not welcome at the grocery store anymore either."

The preacher was dissatisfied with how little his congregation put in the collection plates on Sundays, so he learned hypnosis. He began preaching his sermons in a monotone. He swung a watch slowly in front of the lectern, and at the end of the sermon he said, "Give!" and the collection plate was full of twenty-dollar bills. It worked for weeks. The congregation sat mesmerized during the sermon, staring at the watch swinging, and when he said, "Give!" they gave everything they had. Then one Sunday, at the end of the sermon, the chain on the watch broke, and the preacher said, "Oh, crap!"

This woman is visiting in Israel and notices that her little travel alarm needs a battery. She looks for a watch repair shop but she doesn't read Hebrew. Finally she sees a shop with clocks and watches in the window and goes in and hands the man her clock.

He says, "Madam, I don't repair clocks. I am a rabbi. I do circumcisions."

She says, "Why all the clocks in the window?"

And he says, "And what should I have in my window?"

A bum walked up to the Jewish mother on the street and said, "Lady, I haven't eaten in three days."

And the lady replied, "Try, honey. Force yourself."

The drag queen walks into a Catholic church as the priest is coming down the aisle swinging the incense pot. And he says to the priest, "Oh, honey, I love your dress, but did you know your handbag's on fire?"

This old guy was dying, and he said to his wife, "Honey, call for a priest." And she said, "But Sam, we're Jewish." And he said, "What? I should make the rabbi sick?"

A little boy and his grandmother were walking along the seashore when a huge wave appeared out of nowhere and swept the child out to sea. The grandmother, horrified, falls to her knees and says, "God, please return my beloved grandson. Please, I beg of you. Send him back safely." And, lo, another huge wave washed in and deposited the little boy on the sand at her feet. She picked him up, looked him over, and, looking up at the sky, said, "He had a hat!"

What's the difference between Jews and Christians?

Jews get really angry, but Christians just get a little cross.

What is 666?

That's the number of the beast.

And 668?

The next-door neighbor of the beast.

What's 666-point-00000?

That's the high-precision beast.

And zero-point-666 is the Millibeast.

And 1-900-666-6666 is where you can call and talk to a beast, live, one-on-one.

And $665.95 is the retail price of the beast. $699.25 with 5 percent sales tax. $769.95 with all accessories.

Why was Jesus born in a manger?
Because Mary belonged to an HMO.

Son: Mom, hi. How are you? How's everything in Florida?
Mom: Not too good. I've been very weak.
Son: Why are you weak?
Mom: Never mind.
Son: What's wrong?
Mom: Never mind. It's okay.
Son: Why are you weak, Mom?
Mom: I haven't eaten in thirty-eight days.
Son: That's terrible. Why haven't you eaten in thirty-eight days?
Mom: Because I didn't want my mouth to be filled with food if you should call.

A man was so proud of his fancy new Cadillac that he invited a priest, a minister, and a rabbi to come and bless it. The priest approached the auto, sprinkled holy water over it, and chanted in Latin. The minister invoked the name of the almighty and led them all in silent prayer. The rabbi sang a psalm and cut off the end of the tailpipe.

A man went to church, and afterward he stopped to shake the preacher's hand and say, "Preacher, I'll tell you, that was a damned fine sermon. Damned good."

The preacher said, "Thank you, sir, but I'd rather you didn't use that sort of language in the house of the Lord."

The man said, "I was so damn impressed with that sermon I put $5,000 in the collection plate."

The preacher said, "No shit?"

A new pastor was out visiting his parishioners one Saturday afternoon. All went well until he came to one house. Although it was obvious someone was home, no one came to the door, even after he had knocked several times. Finally, he pulled out his card, wrote "Revelation 3:20" on the back, and stuck it in the door.

The next day as he was counting the offering he found his card in the collection plate. Below his message was the notation "Genesis 3:10."

Revelation 3:20 reads: "Behold I stand at the door, and knock: if any man hear my voice, and open the door, I will come in to him, and will dine with him, and he with me."

Genesis 3:10 reads: "And he said, I heard thy voice in the garden, and I was afraid, because I was naked."

A priest and a rabbi had been friends for many years. One evening over a cup of coffee the priest turned to the rabbi and said, "My friend, we've known each other for a long time, and there's something I've always wondered. Have you ever tasted ham?"

"Well," said the rabbi, looking a little sheepish, "I must admit, when I was a very young man and curious, I tasted some ham. Now tell me, my old friend," the rabbi said, "there's something I've always wondered. Have you ever been with a woman?"

"My friend," answered the priest, "I must confess, when I was a young man, before I entered the priesthood, yes, I was with a woman."

The rabbi smiled at the priest and said, "It's better than ham, isn't it?"

Hyman Goldfarb went to Buckingham Palace to be knighted by the queen. When he knelt for her to put the sword on his shoulder, he was supposed to say something in Latin, but he forgot it.

So instead he said something in Hebrew, a question from the Passover seder, "Ma nishtana ha leila hazeh."

And the queen turned to her grand chamberlain and said, "Why is this knight different from all other knights?"

Our church is so liberal it's only open on Tuesdays.

Two bees ran into each other. One asked the other how things were going.

The second bee said, "Really bad. Too much rain. No flowers or pollen."

The first bee said, "Here's what you do. Just fly down five blocks and turn left and keep going until you see all the cars. There's a bar mitzvah going on, and there are all kinds of fresh flowers and fresh fruit. Just wear a yarmulke so they don't think you're a WASP."

A cruise ship sinks and three men make it to a desert island. The first man, a Catholic, kneels down and prays to the Lord to be saved from the island. The second man, a Lutheran, kneels down and prays to the Lord to be saved from the island. The third man, a Jew, says, "Hey. Two years ago I gave a million dollars to the Jewish Federation. Last year I gave two million. This year I pledged three million. Don't worry, they'll find me."

So the voter says to the politician, "I wouldn't vote for you if you were St. Peter himself."

"If I were St. Peter himself, you wouldn't be in my district."

After church on Sunday morning, a young boy suddenly announced to his mother, "Mom, I've decided I'm going to be a minister when I grow up."

"That's okay with us," the mother said, "but what made you decide to be a minister?"

"Well," the boy replied, "I'll have to go to church on Sunday anyway, and I figure it will be more fun to stand up and yell."

My son recently took up meditation. At least it's better than sitting doing nothing.

The Christian family wanted to buy a Christian dog, so they found one that would fetch the Bible. And then when you told the dog to look up First Corinthians, it did it right away. And if you didn't feel well, the dog would leap up on your lap and put a paw on your forehead and say, "Heel."

Why do Baptists object to fornication?
They're afraid it might lead to dancing.

What's the difference between Baptists and Methodists?
Baptists won't wave to each other in the liquor store.

You should always invite two Baptists to go fishing with you
because if you invite one, he'll drink all your beer.

Two Baptist ministers are talking about the immorality of
the country today, and one of them says, "I didn't sleep with
my wife before I was married. How 'bout you?"
And the other says, "I don't know. What was her maiden
name?"

One of the angels asked God where he was going on
vacation. He said, "Not Earth again. That's for sure. I
went there about two thousand years ago, got a Jewish girl
pregnant, and they haven't stopped talking about it since."

Adam and Eve had the perfect marriage. He didn't have to
listen to her talk about men she knew before him, and she
didn't have to put up with his mother.

Adam was the perfect figure of a man, and Eve was
indescribably beautiful. So where do all the ugly people come
from?

God created Adam before he created Eve because he didn't
want someone telling him how to create Adam.

How long did Cain hate his brother? As long as he was Abel.

If there had been three wise women who went to Bethlehem, they would have asked for directions, arrived on time, helped deliver the baby, cleaned the stable, made a meal, and brought some practical gifts.

The priest's bicycle was stolen and he thought somebody in his congregation might have done it, so the next Sunday he preached on the commandment "Thou shalt not steal," and then he noticed the commandment "Thou shalt not commit adultery," and then he remembered where he had left his bicycle.

A salesman from Budweiser went to the Vatican to get an audience with the Pope, and he said, "Holy Father, I'm prepared to give you ten million dollars to change the words of the Lord's Prayer to 'give us this day our daily beer.'" The Pope refused. "Okay, fifty million." The Pope refused again, and the salesman said, "Okay, here's my card, call me if you change your mind." When the salesman left, the Pope got on the phone and said, "Monsignor—it's me. Tell me, when does our contract with General Mills expire?"

The priest was caught fooling around with his housekeeper. Apparently they found his vest in her pantry and her pants in his vestry.

Do you think it's okay to have sex before you're married, Father?
Not if it delays the ceremony.

A scientist wanted to find out once and for all if there was a God, so he built the most powerful computer ever and he accessed all imaginable data banks, all the libraries of the world, science institutes, universities, and scanned in every published book since the invention of the printing press. Finally, he sat down at his keyboard and typed in the question, "Is there a God?" And the computer said, "There is now."

A Jewish man was seeing a psychiatrist for an eating and sleeping disorder. He said, "I am so obsessed with my mother. As soon as I go to sleep, I start dreaming, and everyone in my dream turns into my mother. I wake up in such a state, all I can do is go downstairs and eat a piece of toast."

The psychiatrist replies: "What, just one piece of toast, for a big boy like you?"

A man goes to confession in Amsterdam:
"Forgive me, Father, for I have sinned."
"What is it, my son?"
"During World War II, I hid a Jew in my attic."
"Well, that's not a sin. That's a good deed."
"But I made him promise to pay me 20 guilders for every week he stayed."
"Well, that's not good, but you did it for a good cause."
"Okay, but I have one other question."
"What is that, my son?"
"Do I have to tell him the war is over?"

Why do Jews always answer a question with another question?
Well, and why shouldn't we?

As the prisoner was strapped to the electric chair, the priest said, "Son, is there anything I can do for you?"
The prisoner said, "Yeah, when they pull the switch, I'd like you to hold my hand."

A man went to the doctor with two black eyes. The doctor said, "These are really bad. Were you in a fight or in an accident?"
The man replied, "I got these in church."
"In church!" the doctor replied. "How could that happen?"
"Well," the man explained, "we were kneeling at prayer. When we stood up, I noticed the woman in front of me had her skirt caught in between her butt cheeks. I thought it looked uncomfortable, so I reached over and tugged it out. She turned around and socked me."
"That explains one black eye," said the doctor. "How did you get the other one?"
"After she turned back around, I thought about it. I figured she didn't like what I had done, so I put it back."

BAR JOKES

A bird in a tuxedo walked into a bar. The bartender said: "Nice tuxedo." The bird said: "How do you know I am not a penguin?"

A North Korean, a Chinese, a Japanese, a Vietnamese, a South Korean, a Burmese, a Mongolian, a Cambodian, a Lao, a Filipino, a Malaysian, and a Singaporean walk into a bar. The bartender says, "I'm sorry, but I can't let you come in here without a Thai."

A German walks into a bar and orders a martini. The bartender asks, "Dry?" The German says, "Nein, just one for now."

The barman says, "We don't serve time travelers in here."
   A time traveler walks into a bar.

The past, the present, and the future walked into a bar. It was tense.

A mathematician walked into a bar and ordered root beer in a square glass.

A germ walked into a bar, and the bartender said, "We don't serve bacteria in this place." The germ said, "But I work here. I'm staph."

A guy walked into a bar. The bartender said, "You've got a steering wheel down your pants."

The guy said, "I know. It's driving me nuts."

A drunk walked into a bar and saw a woman sitting there and he walked over to her and kissed her. She jumped up and slapped him. He said, "I'm sorry. I thought you were my wife. You look exactly like her." She said, "You worthless idiot, you no good drunk!" He said, "And you sound like her, too."

A guy walks into a bar and says to the bartender, "Make you a bet. If I win, I get a free drink. Can you spell a word with ten letters that starts with GAS?" The bartender thinks about it, and says no. The guy says, "AUTOMOBILE!"

A guys walks into a bar, and there's a seal sitting at the far end of the room. The seal says to the man, "I like the way you smell. You've got a great haircut. Your jacket looks great on you. Nice tan." The man says to the bartender, "Who is he?" The bartender says, "That's the Seal of Approval."

A young man from Texas walks into a bar and asks the bartender for a drink. The bartender replies, "Ya got any ID?" The Texan says, "An idee about what?"

A B-flat, a D-flat, and an F walk into a bar. The bartender says to them, "I'm sorry, we don't serve minors here." So the D-flat leaves and the B-flat and the F have an open fifth between them.

Why do elephants drink so much?
To try to forget.

Eight Canada Geese walk into a bar. What do they order?
V-8.

Van Gogh is sitting at the bar. The bartender asks, "Would you like a whiskey?"
Van Gogh replies, "I got one 'ere."

Why did the mouse run under the beer truck?
Because he wanted to get smashed.

An Irishman walks into a bar in Cork and asks the barman:
"What's the quickest way to get to Dublin?"
"Are you walking or driving?" asks the barman.
"Driving," says the man.
"That's the quickest way," says the barman.

A vacationer from New York found his way into a bar in Billings, Montana, and began some serious drinking. After he was well past the legal limit, he stood up and shouted, "Every last Democrat is a horse's ass!" The crowd jumped on him and beat him up.

After a week he returned to the same bar, had some drinks, and stood up and shouted, "Every last Republican is a horse's ass!" The crowd descended upon him and beat him into Silly Putty again. He asked the bartender, "Who are these people anyway?"

"You don't understand," the bartender replied. "This is horse country."

So these two Irishmen walked out of a bar.

A dog went into a bar and ordered a drink. He said to the bartender, "What are you staring at?"
 The bartender replied, "Just surprised to see a dog in here drinking a martini. Don't see that very often."
 The dog said, "At these prices, I'm not surprised."

A man walks into a bar with his dog and says, "This is a talking dog. I'll bet you a drink." The bartender takes the bet and the man says to the dog, "What's up overhead?" Dog says, "Roof!" The bartender says, "Awwww, make him say more than that." The man says to the dog, "Describe sandpaper." The dog replies, "Rough!" The bartender is still not satisfied. The guy asks the dog, "Who is the best baseball player who ever lived?" The dog replies, "Ruth!" The bartender says, "Get that dog out of here." As they walk out the door, the dog asks the man, "What should I have said? Mickey Mantle?"

So a dog walks into a bar and asks the bartender, "Do you have any jobs?" And the bartender says, "Why don't you try the circus?" And the dog says, "Why would the circus need a typist?"

A guy stumbles out of a bar and vomits all over a rat and thinks to himself, "Whoa, I don't remember eating that!"

A man walked into a bar looking sad, and the bartender asked him, "What's the matter?" The man said, "My wife and I had a fight, and she told me she wasn't going to speak to me for a month. And the month is up today."

A pile of vomit walked into a bar and sat down and started to cry.

The bartender said, "What's wrong?"

And the vomit said, "I'm just sentimental. This is where I was brought up!"

A man walks into a bar with a chunk of asphalt under his arm and says, "Beer please, and one for the road."

So a five-dollar bill walks into a bar. The bartender says, "Get out-a here! We don't serve your type. This is a singles' bar."

A termite went into a bar and asked, "Is the bar tender here?"

This skeleton walks into a bar and says, "Give me a beer and give me a mop."

This fly walks into a bar, walks up to a woman sitting at the bar, and says, "I like that stool you're sitting on."

A Frenchman walks into a bar. He has a parrot on his shoulder, and the parrot is wearing a baseball cap. The bartender says, "Hey, that's neat—where did you get that?" And the parrot says, "France—they've got millions of them there."

"Hey, bartender. Pour me a cold one."

"Hey, go on, kid, you wanna get me in trouble?"

"Maybe later. Right now I just wanna beer."

An anteater walks into a bar and says that he'd like a drink. "Okay," says the bartender. "How about a beer?"
"No-o-o-o-o-o-o-o-o-o," replies the anteater.
"Then how about a gin and tonic?"
"No-o-o-o-o-o-o-o-o-o."
"A martini?"
"No-o-o-o-o-o-o-o-o-o."
Finally, the bartender gets fed up and says, "Hey, buddy, if you don't mind me asking—why the long no's?"

A pair of jumper cables walked into a bar and asked for a drink. The bartender said, "Okay, but I don't want you starting anything in here."

So there was this dyslexic guy who walked into a bra.

Charles Dickens walks into a bar and orders a martini. The bartender asks, "Olive or Twist?"

A blind man walks into a bar, grabs his dog by its hind legs, and swings him around in a circle. The bartender says, "Hey buddy, what are you doing?" And the blind man says, "Don't mind me, I'm just looking around."

Into the bar comes a grasshopper. And the bartender says, "Hey, we've got a drink named after you!" And the grasshopper says, "Is that right? Why would anyone name a drink Bob?"

A horse walks into a bar. And the bartender says, "Why the long face?"

165

Two ropes go into a bar. The bartender says, "Get out of here. We don't serve ropes in here."

The ropes go outside and one says to the other, "I have an idea." He ties himself up, messes up his hair, and goes back in. The bartender says, "Hey. No ropes." The rope says, "I'm not a rope."

The bartender says, "You're not a rope?"

"Nope. I'm a frayed knot."

Two guys were walking their dogs—one had a German shepherd and the other had a Chihuahua. The man with the shepherd suggested going into a bar for a drink. The other man says, "They're not going to let dogs into the bar." And the first guy says, "No? Watch this." He puts on some dark glasses, acts like the German shepherd is a Seeing Eye dog, walks into the bar, and orders a drink. And no one says anything.

So the second guy takes out some dark glasses, slips them on, and walks his Chihuahua into the bar. The bartender says, "Sorry—we don't allow dogs in here." And the man says, "It's okay—it's my Seeing Eye dog." The bartender laughs and says, "This Chihuahua is your Seeing Eye dog?" And the guy says, "They gave me a Chihuahua?"

A pork chop goes into a bar and orders a drink. The bartender says, "Sorry, we don't serve food here."

A cowboy walks into the bar and asks for a whiskey. Suddenly another cowboy rushes in and yells, "Joe, Joe, hurry up, your house is on fire!" The cowboy runs to the door and then stops and thinks, "Hey! I ain't got no house!"

The cowboy sits back down and drinks his whiskey. Suddenly another cowboy runs into the bar shouting, "Joe, Joe, hurry up, your father is dying!" The cowboy jumps up, runs out, jumps on his horse, and then remembers, "I ain't got no father!"

He walks back to the bar, sits down, and finishes his drink. And another cowboy bursts in and yells, "Joe, Joe, hurry up, you won the lottery and there's a million bucks for you at the post office!" The cowboy jumps to his feet, runs out of the bar, jumps on his horse, gallops to the post office, dashes in, and then he says, "Hey! My name ain't Joe!"

A guy comes in with a frog on his head, and the bartender says, "Where did you get that?" And the frog says, "It started out as a little bump on my butt."

This guy walks into a pub, sits down, and says, "Give me two beers. Rough day at work." And the bartender says, "Oh? What do you do?" The guy says, "I take care of the corgis— you know, the dogs the royal family owns."

The bartender says, "Tough job, huh?"

The guy says, "Well, all that inbreeding has led to low intelligence and bad temperament. And the dogs aren't that smart either."

A brain goes into a bar and says to the bartender, "I'll have a pint, please." The bartender says, "Sorry, I can't serve you. You're out of your head."

This guy walks into a bar and has a drink. And he looks in his pocket and orders another drink, looks in his pocket and orders another drink, looks in his pocket and orders another drink, looks in his pocket, and so on. And the bartender says, "What are you doing? What's in your pocket?" And the guy says, "It's a picture of my wife. When she starts looking good to me, I know it's time to go home."

A man goes into a bar and says, "Give me a drink before the trouble starts." And the bartender gives him a drink.

He drinks it and says, "Give me another drink before the trouble starts."

He downs that one and says, "Give me another drink before the trouble starts."

He drinks that and says, "Give me another drink before the trouble starts."

And the bartender says, "When's this trouble going to start?"

The man says, "The trouble starts as soon as you realize that I don't have any money."

The tourist goes into a bar, and there's a dog sitting in a chair, playing poker.

He says, "Is that dog really playing poker?" And the bartender says, "Yeah, but he's not too good. Whenever he has a good hand, he starts wagging his tail."

This cowboy walks into a bar and orders a beer. His hat is made of brown wrapping paper, his shirt and vest are made of waxed paper, and his chaps, pants, and boots are made of paper. His spurs are made of tissue paper. Pretty soon they arrest him for rustling.

René Descartes is in a bar. At last call, the bartender asks him if he'd like another drink. Descartes says, "I think not." And he disappears.

A man walks into a bar. There's a beautiful woman sitting at the bar, and they sit and have a drink together. She leans over and says, "I want you to make me feel like a real woman." So he takes off his jacket and says, "I need this ironed."

A northerner walks into a bar down South around Christmastime, and there's a little nativity scene on the bar. And the guy says, "That's a nice nativity scene. But how come the three wise men are wearing firemen's hats?" And the bartender says, "Well, it says right there in the Bible—the three wise men came from afar."

A pig walked into a bar, ordered fifteen beers, and drank them. The bartender asked, "Would you like to know where the bathroom is?"

"No," said the pig. "I'm the little pig that goes wee-wee-wee all the way home."

This duck walks into a bar, and the bartender looks at him and says, "Hey, buddy, your pants are down around your ankles!"

A bear walks into a bar and says, "I'd like a beer and......a packet of peanuts." The barman says, "Why the big pause?"

A panda walks into a bar, sits down, and orders a sandwich. He eats the sandwich, pulls out a gun, and shoots the waiter dead. As the panda stands up to go, the bartender shouts, "Hey! Where are you going? You just shot my waiter, and you didn't pay for your sandwich." The panda yells back at the bartender, "Hey man, I'm a panda. Look it up!"

The bartender opens his dictionary to "panda" and reads: "A tree-dwelling marsupial of Asian origin, characterized by distinct black and white coloring. Eats shoots and leaves."

A guy goes into a bar, orders four shots of the most expensive thirty-year-old single-malt Scotch, and downs them one after the other.

The barkeep says, "You look like you're in a hurry."

"You would be too if you had what I have," says the guy.

"What have you got?" asks the bartender.

"Fifty cents."

A drunk guy walks into a bar and looks up to see a lady with a French poodle. The drunk slurs, "Where did you get that pig?"

The lady, with a look of surprise, snaps back, "I'll have you know that it is a Frrrench poodle."

The drunk looks at her and says, "I was talking to the French poodle."

This duck waddles into a bar, and the bartender says, "What can I get for you?" The duck says, "Got any grapes?" The bartender says, "No, we serve beer and whiskey and stuff like that." The duck says, "Okay," and he leaves.

The next day, the same duck comes in, hops up on the stool, and says, "Got any grapes?" The bartender say, "No—I've told you two days in a row that we don't have any grapes.

You come in here again and I'm going to nail your beak to the bar!" So the duck leaves.

The very next day, the same duck comes back into the bar and says, "Got any nails?" The bartender says, "No, why?" And the duck says, "Got any grapes?"

A man walks out of a bar and sees a bum panhandling on the corner. And the bum says, "Mister, do you have a dollar you could spare me?"

The man thinks about the question for a bit and asks the bum, "If I give you a dollar, are you going to use it to buy liquor?"

"No," says the bum.

The man then asks the bum, "If I give you a dollar, are you going to use it for gambling?"

Again the bum says, "No."

So the man says to the bum, "Do you mind coming home with me so I can show my wife what happens to someone who doesn't drink or gamble?"

Waiter: And how did you find your steak, sir?

Diner: Well, I just pushed aside a pea and there it was…

A salesman walks into the bar and asks, "You know where Bubba lives?"

"Sure," says the bartender, and he gives him directions. "But you gotta be careful. Don't honk your horn when you pull up in front of Bubba's house."

"Why not?" asks the salesman.

"Well, you see, about three months ago, Bubba's wife ran off with a banjo player named Junior. And every time Bubba hears somebody honk, he's afraid the banjo player is bringing her back."

A drunk staggers out of a bar and into a nearby cathedral. He eventually stumbles his way down the aisle and into a confessional. After a lengthy silence, the priest asks, "May I help you, my son?"

"I dunno," comes the drunk's voice from behind the partition. "You got any toilet paper on your side?"

A thief breaks into a bar and is heading right for the cash register when he hears a voice behind him say, "God is watching." He turns around, but he doesn't see anything, so he goes back to the cash register. Again he hears, "God is watching." So he turns around and sees a parrot over in the corner. He goes over to it and says, "What's your name?"

"John the Baptist," replies the bird.

"That's a funny name for a parrot," says the thief. "Who named you that?"

The parrot says, "My owner. The same guy who named the Rottweiler 'God.'"

A man walked into a bar, sat down, and ordered a beer. As he sipped the beer he heard a soothing voice say, "Nice tie." Looking around he noticed that the bar was empty except for himself and the bartender at the end of the bar. A few sips later the voice said, "Beautiful shirt." At this, the man called the bartender over. "Hey, I must be losing my mind," he told him. "I keep hearing these voices saying nice things, and there's not a soul in here but us."

"It's the peanuts," answered the bartender.

"Say what?"

"You heard me. It's the peanuts...they're complimentary."

This guy goes into a bar and orders three separate shot glasses of Irish whiskey.

He drinks all three. He does this day after day after day, and the bartender finally says, "You know, I can put all three of those shots into one glass for you."

The guy says, "No, I prefer it this way. See, I have two brothers—they're over in Ireland, and I love them. This glass right here is for Finnian and this one here is for Fergus, and this one is for me. This way I can feel like we're all here together having a drink."

And the guy continues to come in day after day after day, and the bartender continues to set up three glasses. Then one day, the guy says, "Give me two shots today."

"What happened? Did something happen to one of your brothers?" the bartender asks.

"No, no, no," the guy says. "They're okay. It's just that I decided to quit drinking."

Three mice walked into a bar. The first mouse had a shot of whiskey and said, "When I see a mousetrap, I lie on my back and set it off with my foot. When the bar comes down, I catch it in my teeth, bench-press it twenty times to work up an appetite, and then make off with the cheese."

The second mouse drank two shots of whiskey and said, "Yeah, well, when I see rat poison, I collect as much as I can, take it home, grind it up into a powder, and add it to my coffee each morning so I can get a good buzz going for the rest of the day."

The third mouse said, "I can't stay long. I've got a date with the cat."

This old couple walk into the bar, and the husband goes over and starts flirting with some young women. And the bartender says to the wife, "Doesn't it bother you that your husband is always making passes at the younger women around here?"

"No, no, no, not really," the wife says. "I mean, dogs chase cars, but that doesn't mean they know how to drive."

A man walks into a bar and orders a beer. He sips it and sets it down. A monkey swings across the bar and pisses in the pint. The man asks the barman, "Who owns the monkey?" The barman indicates the piano player. The man walks over to the piano player and says, "Do you know your monkey pissed in my beer?" The pianist replies, "No, but if you hum it I'll play it."

A man walked into a bar carrying an ape in his arms. "I just bought this fella as a pet," he explained. "We have no children, so he's going to live with us, just like one of the family. He'll eat at our table, even sleep in the bed with me and the wife." "But what about the smell?" someone asked. "Oh, he'll just have to get used to it, the same way I did."

A cowboy walks out of a bar and a second later comes back in, mighty mad. "Okay," he growls. "Now which one of you sidewindin' hombres went outside an' painted mah horse bright red while I was a-drinkin'?"

Nobody answers, and the cowpoke draws his six-shooter and yells, "I said which one of you mangy polecats painted mah horse red?!"

Slowly one of the cowboys at the bar stands up. He is six feet, nine inches tall, and he pulls a small cannon from his holster. "I done it," he growls.

The first cowboy puts his gun back in the holster and says, "Just wanted to let you know the first coat's dry."

A redneck swaggers into a bar. "Hey barkeep, set me up with a cold one," he says. Then he looks to the end of the bar and asks the bartender, "Hey, is that Jesus down there?" The barkeep nods. "Well, set him up with a cold one, too."

As Jesus gets up to leave, he walks over to the redneck, touches him, and says, "For your kindness, you are healed!"

The redneck jumps back and exclaims, "Don't touch me! I'm drawing disability!"

A man walks into the bar with a giraffe. He says, "A beer for me, and one for my giraffe." And they stand around drinking for hours, until the giraffe passes out on the floor. The man pays his tab and gets up to leave, and the bartender says, "Hey! You're not going to leave that lyin' on the floor, are you?"

The man says, "That's not a lion, it's a giraffe."

A Texan walks into a pub in Ireland and clears his voice to the crowd of drinkers. He says, "I hear you Irish are a bunch of drinkers. I'll give five hundred American dollars to anybody in here who can drink ten pints of Guinness back-to-back." The room is quiet, and no one takes the

Texan's offer. One man even leaves. Thirty minutes later the same gentleman who left shows up and taps the Texan on the shoulder. "Is your bet still good?" asks the Irishman. The Texan says yes and asks the bartender to line up ten pints of Guinness. Immediately the Irishman tears into all ten of the pint glasses, drinking them all back-to-back. The other pub patrons cheer as the Texan sits in amazement. The Texan gives the Irishman the $500 and says, "If ya don't mind me askin', where did you go for that thirty minutes you were gone?" The Irishman replies, "Oh, I went to the pub down the street to see if I could really do it."

A man walked into a bar and sat down next to a man with a dog at his feet. "Does your dog bite?" he asked. "No," was the reply. So he reached down to pet the dog, and the dog bit him. "I thought you said your dog doesn't bite!" he said. "That's not my dog!"

Four brewery presidents walk into a bar. The guy from Corona sits down and says, "Hey, Señor, I would like the world's best beer, a Corona." The bartender gives it to him.

The guy from Budweiser says, "I'd like the best beer in the world. Give me 'The King of Beers,' a Budweiser." The bartender gives him one.

The guy from Coors says, "I'd like the only beer made with Rocky Mountain spring water. Give me a Coors." He gets it.

The guy from Guinness sits down and says, "Give me a Coke." The bartender is a little taken aback, but gives him what he ordered.

The other brewery presidents look over at him and ask, "Why aren't you drinking a Guinness?"

The Guinness president replies, "Well, I figured if you guys aren't drinking beer, neither would I."

A dog walks into a bar and says, "Hey, guess what? I'm a talking dog. Ever seen a talking dog before? How about a drink for the talking dog?"

The bartender answers, "Okay. The toilet's right back there."

A pickle walks into a bar and the bartender says, "Hey, you're a pickle! What are you doing here?"

The pickle says, "Well, for starters, I'm celebrating the fact that I can walk."

A priest, a rabbi, a lawyer, a redneck, a blonde, and a dog walk into a bar. The bartender looks up and says, "Is this some kind of joke?"

A mangy-looking guy goes into a bar and orders a drink. The bartender says, "No way. I don't think you can pay for it." The guy says, "You're right. I don't have any money, but if I show you something you haven't seen before, will you give me a drink?" The bartender says, "Only if what you show me ain't risqué." "Deal!" says the guy, and reaches into his coat pocket and pulls out a hamster. He puts the hamster on the bar, and it runs to the end of the bar, down off the bar, across the room, up the piano, jumps on the keyboard, and starts playing Gershwin songs. And the hamster is really good. The bartender says, "You're right. I've never seen anything like that before. That hamster is truly good on the piano."

The guy downs the drink and asks the bartender for another. "Money or another miracle, else no drink," says the bartender.

The guy reaches into his coat again and pulls out a frog. He puts the frog on the bar, and the frog starts to sing. He has a marvelous voice and great pitch. A fine singer. A stranger from the other end of the bar runs over to the guy and offers him $300 for the frog. The guy says, "It's a deal." He takes the $300 and gives the stranger the frog. The stranger runs out of the bar.

The bartender says to the guy, "Are you some kind of nut? You sold a singing frog for $300? It must have been worth millions." "The frog ain't singing," says the guy. "The hamster is also a ventriloquist."

A woman walked into a bar and asked for a double entendre. So the barman gave her one.

A well-dressed young businessman walks into a bar. The bartender asks, "What can I get you?" The well-dressed man replies, "I'll have a glass of twelve-year-old Scotch." The bartender returns with the drink. The man takes a sip, winces, and spits it out, exclaiming, "That's ten-year-old Scotch! How dare you insult a man of my stature with inferior Scotch!" The bartender explains that the bar doesn't carry twelve-year-old Scotch, and he had thought the man wouldn't notice the two-year difference.

The well-dressed man next asks for fifteen-year-old bourbon. The bartender returns with the drink. The man takes a sip, winces, and spits it out, exclaiming, "That's twelve-year-old bourbon! How dare you insult a man of my stature with inferior bourbon." The bartender apologizes, citing his earlier explanation. The situation repeats itself regarding the well-dressed man's next request, this time for a glass of thirty-year-old port wine.

Meanwhile, an old drunk at the end of the bar calls the bartender down and produces a glass. Handing the glass to the bartender, he says, "Give this to that well-dressed man, and tell him it's on me."

The bartender gives the drink to the well-dressed man, indicating the old drunk at the end of the bar. The man takes a sip, winces, and spits it out. "My Lord!" he cries. "That tastes like urine!"

"It is," replies the old drunk. "Now tell me how old I am."

A man walks into a bar with a newt on his shoulder. He tells the bartender that the newt's name is Tiny.

"Why?" asks the bartender.

"Because he's my newt!"

This baby seal walks into a bar and the bartender says, "What'll ya have?"

The seal says, "Anything but a Canadian Club…"

A man walks into a bar and asks the bartender, "Do you have any Campari?"

The bartender says, "Do I have Campari! Look down here!" And he takes him to the basement and there's a hundred cases of Campari.

"Boy, you must sell a lot of Campari."

"No, but the man who sells me Campari—he sells a lot of Campari."

A penguin walked into a bar and said, "Has my father been in here today?"

The bartender said, "I don't know. What does he look like?"

A man walks into a bar and says, "I know the sign says 'No Smoking' but would you mind if I smoke in here?"

"It's okay with me. Just make sure you put the lit end into your mouth."

A man walked out of the bar and got in his car and a policeman came over.

"Sir, your eyes seem to be bloodshot. Have you been drinking?"

"Officer, your eyes seem to be glazed. Have you been eating doughnuts?"

A cowboy was sitting at a bar. A guy came and sat next to him and looked at the cowboy hat and asked, "Are you a real cowboy?"

The cowboy replied, "Yes, I believe I am a real cowboy. I spend my day riding around on a horse, looking after cattle and sleeping under the stars."

Later, a woman came and sat next to him and asked, "Are you a real cowboy?"

"Yes, I spend my entire day riding around on the range looking after horses and cattle, I suppose I am a cowboy. What about you? What are you?"

"I'm a lesbian. I spend my whole day thinking about women. I get up in the morning, I have a shower and I think about women. I have breakfast and I think about women. I go to work and I think about women."

Ten minutes later, another guy came and sat next to the cowboy and asked, "Are you a real cowboy?"

"Well, ten minutes ago I thought I was."

A man walked into the bar and ordered a drink, and the bartender said, "I thought you quit drinking."

"No, I just wanted to cut my drinking in half, so I joined A."

An Irishman walks into a bar, and there is a little brass lamp at the end of the bar. He touches it, and a genie comes out and gives him three wishes. He says, "Ah, faith! I wish for a bottle of Guinness that will never run dry." Poof! A bottle appears, and he drinks it, and holds it up and it magically fills itself up again. He drinks it down, it refills again, then the genie asks, "And what are your other two wishes?"

"Just give me two more like this one."

ADULTS-ONLY JOKES

"Is that pornography you're carrying?"
"I don't even have a pornograph!"

Miss Beatrice, the church organist, was in her nineties
and had never been married. She was a sweet old lady, so
the pastor was surprised to see, sitting on the keyboard, a
condom. He said, "Miss Beatrice, tell me about this." She
said, "I found it on the ground when I was walking through
the park and it says it prevents the spread of disease, and do
you know I haven't had the flu all winter?"

What did the bra say to the top hat?
You go on a head. I'll give these two a lift.

"Henry," the old woman says, "Your fires don't burn as hot
as they used to!" "Martha," he says, "your flue don't draw the
way it used to!"

Bumper sticker seen on the tailgate of a rusted pick-up truck:
If Dolly Parton was a farmer, she'd be flat busted, too.

"Mrs. Peterson, are you sexually active?"
"No, Doctor, mostly I just lie there."

My husband took a Viagra and it got stuck in his throat and
now he has a stiff neck.

How do they circumcise a whale?
They send down four skin divers.

After checking out all the well-dressed guests at the party, a man spotted an attractive woman standing alone across the room. When he approached and asked her name, she coyly replied, "Carmen." Trying to maintain some sort of conversation with her, he responded with "That's beautiful. Is 'Carmen' a family name?" "No," she said. "I gave it to myself, because it reflects the things I like most in the world —cars and men." Then she asked, "What's your name?" "Golf-tits," he replied.

"Do you smoke after sex?"
  "I don't know. I never looked."

Sex is not the answer. Sex is the question. The answer is yes!

It's only premarital sex if you're intending to get married.

Do you go for casual sex, or should I dress up?

Why don't women blink during foreplay?
  They don't want to miss it.

The Lord created alcohol so that ugly people can have sex, too.

Sex on television can't hurt you unless you fall off.

According to Sigmund Freud, what comes between fear and sex?
  Fünf.

What's the difference between beer nuts and deer nuts?
Beer nuts are $1.69 and deer nuts are under a buck.

What did the doe say when she came out of the woods?
Boy, I'll never do that again for two bucks.

Did you hear about the thieves who stole an entire shipment
of Viagra?
Police are looking for a gang of hardened criminals.

An old lady who never married specified in her will that her
tombstone say, "Born a virgin, lived a virgin, died a virgin."
That was too many words to put on the stone so they just
wrote, "Returned unopened."

A psychologist did a study of 300 people and their sex lives.
Some of them said they had sex almost every night, others
said they had sex once a week, and others said they had sex
once or twice a month. One man said he had sex only once a
year. The psychologist felt bad for him and went over, patted
him on the back, and said, "That's too bad. I'm really sorry
for you." The man grinned up at him and said, "Yes, but
tonight's the night."

"Hi. Couldn't help but notice the book you're reading."
"Yes, it's about finding sexual satisfaction. It's interesting.
Did you know that, statistically, American Indian and Polish
men are the best lovers? By the way, my name is Jill. What's
yours?"
"Flying Cloud Kowalski. Nice to meet you."

Three women were returning to their Hungarian village when they spotted a man, obviously very inebriated, walking ahead of them. As they watched, he stumbled and fell face down into a mud puddle. When they walked up to him, one woman turned him over to see if she recognized him. However, his face was so covered with mud she couldn't tell, so she bent over and unzipped his pants. She remarked, "Well, he's not my husband."

The second woman, peering over the first woman's shoulder, agreed, "You're right, he's not your husband."

The third woman, somewhat older than the other two, bent over to look and said, "He's not even from our village."

Three women go out to a nightclub to see male dancers. One of the women wants to impress the others, so she pulls out a $10 bill and waves the dancer over. She licks the $10 bill and sticks it to his left buttock. Not to be outdone, the second woman pulls out a $20 bill, licks it, and slaps it on the other cheek. The dancer looks down at the third woman and raises his eyebrows. Thinking for a minute, she reaches into her purse. She pulls out her ATM card, swipes it down the crack, grabs the $30, and goes home.

A man goes into a restaurant. A beautiful waitress comes over to serve him and asks what he would like. He says, "I want a quickie."

She slaps him and says, "Just give me your order, mister!"

Another customer leans over and says, "I believe that's pronounced 'quiche'."

A dedicated shop steward is at a convention in Las Vegas and decides to go into a brothel. He asks the madam, "Is this a union house?"

"No, it's not," she replies.

"So, how much do the girls earn?" the union man asks.

"Well, if you pay me $100, the house gets $80 and I pay the girl $20."

The man says, "That's terrible!" He stomps out. Finally he finds a brothel where the madam says, "Yes, this is a union house."

"And if I pay you $100, what cut does the girl get?"

"She gets $80."

"That's great!" the man says. "I'd like Tiffany."

"I'm sure you would," says the madam, "but Ethel here has seniority."

Did you hear about the guy who had sex with his canary?

Came down with a bad case of chirpies. And the worst thing about it is it's untweetable.

An old woman is sitting in a rocking chair on her porch, petting her cat, Puff. A fairy appears and says, "I'm here to give you three wishes."

The old woman says, "I wish I were twenty-one years old and beautiful again." Poof! She is.

"Now I wish I had a million dollars and this old house were a mansion." Poof! Done.

"And now, I wish that Puff were the handsomest man in the world and deeply in love with me."

Poof! Suddenly she's in the arms of the handsomest man in the world. He kisses her and says, "Darling, aren't you sorry you had me fixed?"

What is the similarity between Viagra and Disney World?
You have to wait an hour for a three-minute ride.

A teenage couple had been dating for a couple of weeks, and the relationship seemed to be going rather well. The young girl told the boy that if he were to come over for dinner, meet the parents, and make a good impression, she would reward him by making love to him.

Well, he was pretty excited, as it would be their first time, and he immediately went down to the local pharmacy to buy some condoms. But, it being his first time, he didn't know what kind to buy, so he asked the pharmacist for help. The pharmacist spent a good hour discussing the different kinds of condoms, what they do, how to pick a size, etc. He then asked the boy which he would like. To which the boy responded, "Well, being as it is going to be the first time, why don't I get the family pack." The pharmacist rang it up and sent him on his way.

Finally the night arrived. Of course the boy was very nervous but was determined to make a good lasting impression on the girl's parents. Everyone sat down to dinner, and the mother said, "Let us bow our heads and pray." Everyone bowed their heads and said grace. When they were finished, everyone looked up...except the boy. He continued to bow his head and mumble in prayer. After about twenty minutes, he is still praying and the girl taps him on the leg and whispers, "I never knew you were so religious." And the boy says, "I never knew your dad was a pharmacist!"

A traveling salesman stops at the nearest farmhouse and asks if he can spend the night. The farmer says okay and tells him he can go upstairs and sleep in the same room as his daughter. The salesman goes upstairs and, as he enters the daughter's room, notices another salesman in bed with her. "Oh, my God!" he proclaims. "I must be in the wrong joke!"

Mama Stork, Papa Stork, and Baby Stork sat down to dinner and Mama said, "What did you do today, Papa?"
    And Papa said, "I was out making someone very happy."
    And Mama said, "I was out making someone very happy, too. What were you doing, Baby?"
    And Baby Stork said, "I was out scaring the crap out of college students."

A lady who lived in a small Minnesota town had two pet monkeys she was very fond of. One of them took sick and died. A couple of days later the other one died of a broken heart. Wishing to keep them, the kindly lady took them to the taxidermist. The man asked her if she would like them mounted. "Oh, no," she replied, "just have them holding hands."

What do you get when you take Viagra with beans?
    A stiff wind.

There were a lot of Viagra jokes a few years ago, but they seem to have petered out.

Three engineers are arguing about which is better, mechanical, electrical, or civil engineering. The mechanical engineer says, "God must've been a mechanical engineer: look at the joints in the human body." The second says, "No, God must've been an electrical engineer: look at the nervous system." And the third says, "God had to be a civil engineer: who else would've run a waste disposal pipeline right through a great recreational area?"

"Mrs. Johnson had quintuplets. Isn't that something? Did you know that happens only once in four million times?"
"My gosh, when did they ever have time to go to work?"

A woman approaches a man in a bar and says, "Hi. You look lonely. I'll do anything you want for two hundred dollars." The guy says, "Okay, how about you paint my house?"

I had an uncle who was so dumb, the closest he ever got to a 4.0 was his blood alcohol content.

My uncle peed in a wheat field once and was arrested for going against the grain.

"Excuse me, would you mind giving up your seat? I'm pregnant."
"Certainly. But I must say, you don't look pregnant."
"Well, it's only been about half an hour."

"Son, I think it's time we talked about sex."
"Sure, Dad. What do you want to know?"

"Daddy, Megan and I want to get married."

"I see, Danny. Well, how will you support her?"

"I get two dollars allowance each week, and she gets an allowance too."

"But what if there's a baby?"

"So far, we've been lucky."

On the chest of a barmaid at Yale
Were tattooed the prices of ale
And on her behind
For the sake of the blind
Was the same information in Braille

Smokey the Bear's wife wants to have kids, but every time she gets hot, he hits her with a shovel.

What is the fastest way to determine the sex of a chromosome? Pull down its genes.

TOTALLY TASTELESS JOKES

The suicide bombing instructor stood up in front of his class and said, "Pay attention, I'm only going to show you this once."

Have you heard the one about the deaf man? Neither has he.

There's a huge party at the orphanage tonight. Their parents are gone.

What's the difference between a bad golfer and a bad sky diver? The bad golfer goes, Twhack! "Damn it!" The bad sky diver...

There was a Bible salesman who sold a hundred Bibles a day though he had a terrible stutter. He'd walk up and knock on a door and say, "I'm suh, suh, suh, suh, suh, suh, suh, selling buh, buh, buh, buh, buh, buh, buh, buh Bibles. Wuh, wuh, wuh, wuh, wuh, wuh, wuh, would you like to buh, buh, buh, buh, buh, buh, buh, buy one or should I reh, reh, reh, reh, reh, reh, reh read it to you a la la la la la la la la la la la la loud?"

What's the difference between an oral and a rectal thermometer? The taste.

Did you hear the one about the kid who lost his chewing gum in the chicken coop and found it twice?

An old cowboy walks into the barbershop for a shave and a haircut and tells the barber he can't get all his whiskers off because his cheeks are wrinkled from age. The barber gets a little wooden ball from a cup on the shelf and tells the old cowboy to put it inside his cheek to spread out the skin. When he's finished, the old cowboy tells the barber that was the cleanest shave he's had in years. But he wants to know what would have happened if he had swallowed the little ball. The barber says, "Just bring it back in a couple of days like everyone else."

Did you hear about the construction worker who got the whole left side of his body cut off? He's all right.

Did you hear about the constipated mathematician? He worked it out with a pencil.

How do you make a cat sound like a dog?
    You pour gasoline on it and light it with a match and it goes, "WHOOOF!"

How do you make a dog sound like a cat?
    Put it in the deep freeze for a week, then cut it in half with a circular saw—it goes,
"MMEEEEEEOOOOOOOOOWWWWWWWWW!"

Raggedy Ann was dating the Pillsbury Dough Boy, but then she got a yeast infection.

What's brown and sits on a piano?
    Beethoven's last movement.

Did you hear about the new movie called "Constipated"?
   It hasn't come out yet.

What's the most fattening drink?
   A martini has about 700 calories, but if you drink enough of them, you don't keep any of the calories.

The snake pit in the Los Angeles zoo was accidentally filled in. Now the snakes don't have a pit to hiss in.

Did you hear about the cow who had an abortion?
   She was decaffeinated.

A little boy came home crying: "A car hit Jimmy's dog. Hit him right in the ass."
   His mom said, "No, honey, you mean rectum."
   "Rectum? Almost killed him!"

How does the blind parachutist know when he's getting close to the ground?
   The leash goes slack.

What's green and red and goes fifty miles per hour?
   A frog in a blender.

Why do farts smell?
   So that deaf people can enjoy them, too!

The cannibals ate the missionary to get a taste of religion but they felt sick afterwards because it's hard to keep a good man down.

Where do cannibals get their vegetables from? The coma ward.

What did the cannibal give his wife for Valentine's Day? A box of farmers' fannies.

So these two cannibals are eating a clown and one says, "Does this taste funny to you?"

Did you hear about the cannibal who passed his brother in the woods one day?

Two cannibals were sitting by a fire and one says, "Gee, I hate my mother-in-law."
   And the other says, "So, try the potatoes."

Why did the cannibal eat the tightrope walker?
   He wanted a balanced meal.

Did you hear about the cannibal who was expelled from school?
   He was buttering up his teacher.

Two guys are captured by cannibals. They're stuck naked in a big pot of water over a fire, and the water gets hotter and hotter. All of a sudden, one guy starts laughing, and the other guy says, "What's so funny?"
   "I just peed in their soup!"

Two cannibals meet one day. The first cannibal says, "You know, I just can't seem to get a tender missionary. I've baked them, I've roasted them, I've stewed them, I've barbecued them, I've tried every sort of marinade. I just can't seem to get them tender."

The second cannibal asks, "What kind of missionary do you use?"

The other replies, "You know, the ones that hang out at that place at the bend of the river. They have those brown cloaks with a rope around the waist, and they're sort of bald on top with a funny ring of hair on their heads."

"Aha!" the second cannibal replies. "No wonder—those are friars!"

Have you noticed how bad Stan's breath is?

Are you kidding? It's so bad, people look forward to his farts!

They announced today that the Green Bay Packers and the Tampa Bay Buccaneers are going to merge and form one team called the Tampacks. It may be a mediocre team, though. It'll only be good for one period and there'll be no second string.

What do you get when you mix holy water with castor oil?

A religious movement!

What happened to the fly on the toilet seat?

He got pissed off!

A guy walks into a cafe and asks for a bowl of chili. The waitress says, "The guy next to you got the last bowl." He looks over and sees that the guy's bowl of chili is full. He says, "If you're not going to eat that, mind if I take it?" The other guy says, "No, help yourself." He starts to eat it and about halfway down, his fork hits something. It's a dead mouse, and he vomits the chili back into the bowl. The other guy says, "That's about as far as I got, too."

A woman goes to the store to buy some fishing gear for the weekend. She asks an employee for any suggestions. A blind man who works at the store suggests a rod and reel costing $20. She agrees and moves to the counter to pay for her purchase.

The blind man walks behind the counter to the register. In the meantime the woman breaks wind. At first she is embarrassed, but then she realizes there is no way he could tell it was her. Being blind, he wouldn't know she was the only person around. He rings up the sale and says, "That will be $25.50."

She says, "But didn't you say it was $20?"

He says, "Yes, ma'am. The rod and reel is $20, the duck call is $3, and the catfish stink bait is $2.50."

Why does Piglet smell so bad?
He always plays with Pooh.

Did you know diarrhea is hereditary?
It runs in your genes.

What's invisible and smells like carrots?
Rabbit farts.

The Queen was showing the Archbishop of Canterbury around the royal stables when one of the stallions farted so loudly it couldn't be ignored. "Oh dear," said the Queen. "How embarrassing. I'm frightfully sorry about that."

"It's quite understandable," said the Archbishop, adding after a moment, "As a matter of fact, I thought it was the horse."

Two airline mechanics get off work at LaGuardia, and one says, "Let's go have a beer." The other says, "Why don't we try drinking jet fuel? I hear it tastes like whiskey, and you don't have any hangover in the morning." So they drink about a quart of it apiece. It tastes great and they have a good time. The next morning, one of them calls up the other and says, "Hey, how do you feel?"

"I feel great."

"Me, too. No hangover."

"Just one thing. Have you farted yet?"

"No…"

"Well, don't. I'm calling from Phoenix!"

A man walks into his house with a handful of dog turds, and he says to his wife, "Look what I almost stepped in!"

Did you hear about the blind skunk who fell in love with a fart?

What's the difference between boogers and broccoli?

Kids won't eat broccoli.

There was this woman who had a problem with silent gas. She went to the doctor and she said, "This is so embarrassing. I have this problem of farting silently. You probably haven't noticed, but I've let three of them since

I've been in this office with you. Is there anything you can do?"

He said, "Yes, but the first thing is to get you fitted for a hearing aid."

What is the difference between a saloon and an elephant's fart?

One is a barroom and the other is a BARRRROOOOOOOM!

So, Professor, you're back from the Rawalpindi archipelago, huh? Discover anything interesting out there?

Yes. The tribe has discovered a kind of palm frond that can be made into suppositories to cure constipation.

Do they really work?

Hey, with fronds like those, who needs enemas?

What did the elephant say to the naked man?

"It's cute, but can you really breathe through that thing?"

There once was a blind man who decided to visit Texas. When he got on the plane, he felt the seats and said, "Wow, these seats are big!" The person next to him answered, "Everything is big in Texas." When he finally arrived in Texas, he decided to visit a restaurant. Upon arriving he ordered a drink and got a mug placed between his hands.

He exclaimed, "Wow, these mugs are big!" The bartender replied, "Everything is big in Texas."

After a couple of drinks, the blind man asked the bartender where the bathroom was located. The bartender replied, "Second door to the right." The blind man headed for the bathroom but accidentally tripped and passed by the second door. Instead, he entered the third door, which led to the swimming pool, and he fell into the pool.

Scared to death, the blind man started shouting, "Don't flush, don't flush!"

"Gladys, it's like a miracle. Every night when I get up and go to the bathroom, God turns the light on for me, and when I'm finished, he turns the light off."

"Harry—you're doing it in the refrigerator again!"

What was Helen Keller's favorite color?
Corduroy.

Did you know Helen Keller had a dollhouse in her back yard?
No, and neither did she.

How did Helen Keller drive?
One hand on the wheel and one hand on the road.

Why were Helen Keller's hands purple?
She heard it through the grapevine.

Why did Helen Keller play the piano with one hand?
Because she sang with the other.

How did Helen Keller burn her ear?
She answered the iron.
How did she burn her other ear?
They called back.

How did Helen Keller burn her fingers?
She tried to read the waffle iron.

Why are Helen Keller's stockings yellow?
Because her Seeing Eye dog can't see either.

Why can't Helen Keller drive?
Because she's a woman.

Why do you feel so sophisticated when you're in the bathroom?
European.

Did you hear about the Easter egg hunt for the Alzheimer's patients?
They hid their own eggs.

My company put me up in a pretty low-class hotel. I called the front desk and said, "I've got a leak in my sink."
They said, "Go ahead."

This sailor met a pirate in a bar, and the sailor couldn't help but notice that the pirate was the worse for wear. He had a peg leg, and a hook, and an eyepatch.
So the sailor asked the pirate how he got the peg leg, and the pirate answered, "Well, matey, I got washed overboard one night while we was in a fierce storm. An' dern me if a shark didn't go and bite off me leg."
Then the sailor asked, "So how'd you get the hook?"
And the pirate answered, "Well, we was in a fierce fight while boarding a ship one time, and that's when I got me hand cut off."

Finally, the sailor asked, "So how'd you get the eyepatch?" And the pirate responded, "A seagull pooped in me eye."

And the sailor said, "You mean to tell me you lost an eye just because a seagull pooped in it?"

The pirate said, "Well, it was the first day I had me hook."

What drove the thirty-nine members of Heaven's Gate to suicide?

You put that many people together, force them to work in Windows 95, and it's bound to happen.

(I heard some of them were UNIX programmers.)

As the drunk said as he leaned over the toilet, "Two beers, coming up!"

This lieutenant was leading his troops into battle, and his sergeant said, "Sir, there's a whole platoon of enemy coming toward us."

And the lieutenant said, "All right, sergeant, bring my red shirt. If I should be wounded, I don't want my men to see the blood and be demoralized."

The sergeant said, "I forgot to say they have tanks and heavy artillery and…"

The lieutenant said, "Sergeant, bring me my brown pants!"

Four big executives are playing golf together. On the second tee they hear a phone ring, and Michael Eisner reaches into his golf bag, pulls out a cellular phone, and talks to his office awhile.

They play the second hole. On the third tee there's a little buzz. Warren Buffett puts one finger in his ear and one finger to his mouth and talks. Afterward he explains that he has a tiny microphone installed in one fingernail and a tiny speaker in another, so he can keep in touch with the office. Everyone is impressed.

They play the third hole. On the fourth tee, Ted Turner starts talking—no phone or anything. Afterward he explains that he has a microphone in a filling in his tooth and a speaker in his ear, so he can always talk to the office. They are even more impressed and move on.

Suddenly they see Bill Gates pull his pants down, squat, and reach into his golf bag for a roll of toilet paper. He looks up and says, "It's okay. I'm expecting a fax."

Why do airlines say that in case of an emergency water landing, the seat cushions can be used as a floatation device? If we're going down, my seat cushion's going to be used as a toilet.

Did you know that in 1553, the Norwegians invented the toilet seat?

Really?

Yeah. Later, the Italians invented the hole in the middle of it.

A county extension agent is visiting a farm and needs to use the toilet, but he remembers that there is no running water. So he runs around back to the outhouse, opens the door, and the hired man is sitting there. But the hired man says, "It's okay. Come on in, it's a two-holer." So the agent goes in and sits down. Soon, the hired man stands up, and as he pulls up his pants, some change tumbles out of his pocket and goes down the hole. The hired man shakes his head, pulls out his wallet, and drops a ten-dollar bill down the hole. The extension agent says, "What did you do that for?" And the hired man says, "Well, I ain't goin' down there for just thirty-five cents."

Do you prefer port or sherry, sir?
    Port, by all means. To me, port is the apotheosis of wine. A glass of vintage port is almost orchestral in its complexity, and between the bouquet and the finish, there is such a panoply of colors, of tonal textures. And sherry makes me fart.

The man went to his proctologist and there on the examining table was a tube of K-Y jelly, a pair of rubber gloves, and a bottle of beer.
    What's the beer for?
    It's a butt light.

I was at this banquet and my false teeth were hurting me, so the guy sitting next to me reaches into his pocket and pulls out some dentures, and says, "Try these." So I do. But they're too tight. He gives me another set and says, "Try these." I try them and they're fine. I wear them for the rest of the banquet, then I give them back. I say, "Thanks. Lucky for me I was sitting next to a dentist." He says, "No, I'm an undertaker."

"I went out with twins last night."
    "Really? Did you have a good time?"
    "Well—yes and no."

What do you call a man with a seagull on his head?
Cliff.

What do you call a man with a spade in his head?
Doug.

What do you call a woman with no arms or legs on
a bar-b-que grill?
Patty.

What do you call a man with no arms or legs on a bar-b-que
grill?
Frank.

What do you call two guys on your wall with no arms and no
legs?
Kurt and Rod.

What do you call a man with no arms or legs who lives
in a bush?
Russell.
…hanging on the wall?
Art.
…in a swimming pool?
Bob.
…in a ditch?
Phil.

What do you call a guy with no feet?
Neil.

What do you call a woman with one leg shorter than the other?

Eileen.

What if she's Asian?

Irene.

What's different about a bulimic's birthday party?

The cake jumps out of the girl.

How can you tell if a woman is wearing panty hose?

If she farts, her ankles swell.

What did the maxi-pad say to the fart?

"You are the wind beneath my wings."

How do you make a dog drink?

Put it in a blender.

What goes "Marc! Marc!"?

A dog with a harelip.

LAWYER/JUDGE JOKES

"I have good news and bad news," the defense lawyer says to his client. "What's the bad news?" The lawyer says, "Your blood matches the DNA found at the murder scene." "Dammit!" cries the client. "What's the good news?" "Well," the lawyer says, "your cholesterol is down to 140."

A man calls a law office and hears "Weinstein, Weinstein, Weinstein, Weinstein attorneys. May I help you?" He says, "Yes, may I speak to Mr. Weinstein?" He is told, "I'm sorry, Mr. Weinstein passed away two years ago." He says, "Well, then can I speak to Mr. Weinstein?" The voice on the phone replies, "I am so sorry, Mr. Weinstein retired last year." Frustrated he asks, "Then, can I speak to Mr. Weinstein?!" He hears the reply, "I am sorry, Mr. Weinstein is in court today." Finally, in total frustration he asks, "May I speak to Mr. Weinstein". The voice on the other end of the phone replies, "Speaking."

What do you call a lawyer who's gone bad?
  Senator.

What is the difference between a wood tick and a lawyer?
  A wood tick falls off you when you die.

The airliner was having engine trouble, so the cabin crew told the passengers to take their seats and prepare for an emergency landing, which they all did, except for a lawyer who went around passing out business cards.

A lawyer was playing golf when he got hit by a ball. When the player came over looking for the ball, the lawyer said "I'm a lawyer, and this will cost you $5,000."

"I'm sorry," said the golfer, "but I did say 'fore'."

"I'll take it," said the lawyer.

A priest and a lawyer died and went to heaven on the same day, and St. Peter showed them both to their rooms. The lawyer's room was extremely large and lavish, but the priest's room was a little ten-by-ten cell with one window and a cot. The priest said, "St. Peter, I have spent my entire life serving God, why do I get a crummy room and the lawyer gets the best room?"

St. Peter replied, "Well, we get thousands of priests up here, but this is the first lawyer we've ever had."

What do you have when you've got six lawyers buried up to their necks in sand?

Not enough sand.

A surgeon, an engineer, and a lawyer were arguing about which profession was the oldest, and the doctor said, "Well, on the sixth day of Creation, God took a rib from Adam, so surgery is the oldest profession." The engineer said, "But, before that, God created the heavens and earth from chaos, so engineering is the oldest profession." And the lawyer said, "Yes, but who do you think created the chaos?"

A lawyer sent a note to a client:

"Dear Jim: Thought I saw you on the street the other day. Crossed over to say hello, but it wasn't you, so I went back. One-tenth of an hour: $25."

Why won't sharks eat lawyers?
Professional courtesy.

The teacher was asking her students what their parents did for a living, and Timmy stood up and said, "My daddy's a doctor and my mommy's a doctor too." And little Sarah stood up and said, "My mommy's an engineer and my daddy's an accountant." And then little Billy stands up and says, "My mommy's a writer and my daddy plays the piano in a whorehouse."

The teacher was horrified and later she called Billy's father, and said, "Why would you ever tell your child a thing like that?" And the father said, "Well, actually I'm a defense lawyer. But how do you explain a thing like that to a seven-year-old?"

Why does New Jersey have so many toxic waste dumps and Washington, D.C., has so many lawyers?
New Jersey got first choice.

The judge said to his dentist: Pull my tooth, the whole tooth, and nothing but the tooth.

A lawyer had just undergone surgery. As he came out of the anesthesia, he said, "Why are all the blinds drawn, Doctor?"
"There's a big fire across the street, and we didn't want you to wake up and think the operation was a failure."

A young lawyer meets the devil at a bar association convention and the devil says, "Listen, if you give me your soul and the souls of everyone in your family, I'll make you a full partner in your firm."

And the young lawyer says, "So…what's the catch?"

The lawyer is cross-examining the doctor about whether he checked the pulse of the deceased before he signed the death certificate.

"No," he said, "I didn't check his pulse."

"And did you listen for a heartbeat?" said the lawyer.

"No, I did not," said the doctor.

"So," said the lawyer, "when you signed the death certificate, you had not taken steps to make sure he was dead."

And the doctor said, "Well, let me put it this way. The man's brain was in a jar on my desk, but for all I know he could be out practicing law somewhere."

How many lawyers does it take to roof a house?

Depends on how thin you slice them.

Prosecutor: Did you kill the victim?

Defendant: No, I did not.

Prosecutor: Do you know what the penalties are for perjury?

Defendant: Yes, I do. And they're a hell of a lot better than the penalty for murder!

Taking his seat in his chambers, the judge faced the opposing lawyers. "So," he said, "I have been presented by both of you with a bribe." Both lawyers squirmed. "You, attorney Leon, gave me $15,000. And you, attorney Campos, gave me $10,000."

The judge reached into his pocket and pulled out a check. He handed it to Leon. "Now then, I'm returning $5,000, and we're going to decide this case solely on its merits."

Two lawyers went into the restaurant and ordered two drinks. Then they got sandwiches out of their briefcases and started to eat. The waiter said, "Hey, you can't eat your own sandwiches in here!" So the lawyers traded sandwiches.

How was copper wire invented?
Two lawyers were arguing over a penny.

A New York man was forced to take a day off work to appear for a minor traffic summons. He grew increasingly restless as he waited hour after endless hour for his case to be heard. When his name was called late in the afternoon, he stood before the judge only to hear that court would be adjourned, and he would have to return the next day.

"What for?" he snapped at the judge.

His honor, equally irked by a tedious day and the sharp query, roared, "Twenty dollars for contempt of court. That's why!"

Then, noticing the man checking his wallet, the judge relented. "That's all right. You don't have to pay now."

The man replied, "I'm just seeing if I have enough for two more words."

What did the lawyer name his daughter?
Sue.

"Are you a lawyer?"

"Yes."

"How much do you charge?"

"A hundred dollars for four questions."

"Isn't that awfully expensive?"

"Yes. What's your fourth question?"

Why is it unethical for lawyers to have sex with their clients?
Because it'd mean being billed twice for essentially the
same service.

The defendant knew he didn't have a prayer of beating the
murder rap, so he bribed one of the jurors to find him guilty
of manslaughter. The jury was out for days before they finally
returned a verdict of manslaughter. Afterward the defendant
asked, "How come it took you so long?"
The juror said, "All the others wanted to acquit."

A lawyer comes to visit his client on death row, and he says,
"I have some good news for you."
And the client says, "What good news are you talking
about? You lost my case, I was convicted of a murder I did not
commit, and I've been sentenced to die in the electric chair!"
The lawyer says, "Yes, but I got the voltage lowered."

I dated a lawyer for a while, until one time she told me,
"Stop and/or I'll slap your face."

The lawyer is painting his house, and a hobo comes around
and asks if he can do something to earn a few dollars. The

lawyer says, "Sure, take a can of this paint and go around to the back of the house and paint my porch."

The hobo does this and fifteen minutes later comes back and says he's finished. The lawyer says, "Already?"

And the hobo says, "Yeah, but it isn't a Porsche. It's a Mercedes!"

ENGINEER JOKES

An engineer gets home from work and sees a note on the fridge from his wife. "This just isn't working, I'm at my mother's." He opens the fridge, the light goes on, and he finds it's working fine.

Two engineers were standing at the base of a flagpole, trying to figure out how to determine the height of it. A woman walked up, took a wrench from her purse, loosened a few bolts, laid the pole down, took a tape measure, and said, "Eighteen feet, six inches." The engineers said, "We need the height, and you measured the length!"

The difference between mechanical engineers and civil engineers is that mechanical engineers build weapons and civil engineers build targets.

How do you torture an engineer?
     Tie him to a chair, stand in front of him, and fold up a road map the wrong way.

Two engineering students met on campus one day, and one said, "Hey—nice bike! Where did you get it?" The other said, "Well, I was walking to class the other day when this beautiful woman rides up on this bike. She jumps off, takes off all of her clothes, and says, 'I'll give you anything you want!' So I took the bike." The other said, "Good choice. Her clothes wouldn't have fit you anyway."

The mathematician, the physicist, and the engineer were given a red rubber ball and told to find the volume. So the mathematician measured the diameter and evaluated a triple integral. The physicist filled a beaker with water, put the ball in the water, and measured the total displacement. And the engineer looked up the model and serial number in his red-rubber-ball table.

What did the arts graduate say to the engineering graduate?
Would you like fries with your order, sir?

The optimist sees a glass that's half full. The pessimist sees a glass that's half empty. An engineer sees a glass that's twice as big as it needs to be.

Three people were going to the guillotine. The first was a lawyer, who was led to the platform, blindfolded, and had his head put on the block. The executioner pulled the lanyard, but nothing happened. To avoid a messy lawsuit, the authorities allowed the lawyer to go free.
The next man to the guillotine was a priest. They put his head on the block and pulled the lanyard, but nothing happened. The blade didn't come down. They thought it must have been divine intervention, so they let the priest go.
The third man to the guillotine was an engineer. He waived his right to a blindfold, so they led him to the guillotine and put his head on the block. As he lay there, he said, "Hey, wait. I think I see your problem."

Engineers say, "If it ain't broke, it doesn't have enough features."

An engineer walks into his boss' office and his boss is holding a tiny object up to the light. The engineer asks, "What is that you have?"

The boss says, "It looks like plastic but feels like rubber."

The engineer says, "Well, let me have a look at it." So the boss hands it over and the engineer rolls it around between his thumb and his fingers.

"Yes," says the engineer, "it's interesting. It's kind of viscous but also kind of solid. Where'd you get it?"

The boss says, "Out of my nose."

STRICTLY BUSINESS JOKES

There are two rules for succeeding in business. The first one is "Never tell them everything you know."

A large company, feeling it was time for a shakeup, hired a new CEO. This new boss was determined to rid the company of all slackers. On a tour of the facilities, the CEO noticed a guy leaning on a wall. The room was full of workers and he wanted to let them know that he meant business!

The new CEO walked up to the guy leaning against the wall and asked, "How much money do you make a week?" A little surprised, the young fellow looked at him and replied, "I make $300 a week. Why?"

The CEO then handed the guy $1,200 in cash and screamed, "Here's four weeks' pay. Now GET OUT and don't come back."

Feeling pretty good about himself, the CEO looked around the room and asked, "Does anyone want to tell me what that goof-off did here?" From across the room came a voice, "He's the pizza delivery guy."

I needed some time off from work so I decided to act crazy. I hung upside down from the ceiling and when the boss asked me what I was doing, I said, "I'm a lightbulb." "You're going crazy," he said. "Take a few days off." I left and my officemate followed me. The boss asked where she was going. She said, "I can't work in the dark."

A local United Way office realized that it had never received a donation from the town's richest man, a leading CEO. The contributions manager cornered him after a Sunday service. "Our research shows that out of a yearly income of at least $50,000,000, you give not a penny to charity. Wouldn't you like to give back to the community in some way?"

The CEO mulled this over for a moment, then replied, "First, did your research also show that my mom is dying after a long illness, and had medical bills that are several times her annual income?" Embarrassed, the United Way rep mumbled "Um...no." "Or that my brother, a disabled veteran, is blind and confined to a wheelchair? Or that my sister's husband died in a traffic accident, leaving her penniless with three kids?' The humiliated United Way rep, completely beaten, said simply, "I had no idea—" On a roll, the CEO cut him off, "So if I don't give any money to them, why should I give any to you?"

A boss gave his new secretary a miniskirt for her first salary. The next month he raised it.

Two men took the test to qualify for a job and both men answered nine out of ten questions correctly, but they gave the job to the first man: he answered Question No. 10 "I don't know" and the other man answered it, "Neither do I."

A computer is perfectly reliable until the moment you switch it on.

The function of a computer expert is not to be right about more things; it is to be wrong for more sophisticated reasons.

The secretary was leaving the office when she saw the CEO standing by a shredder with a piece of paper in his hand. "Listen," said the CEO, "this is a very important document. Can you make this thing work?" The secretary turned the machine on, inserted the paper, and pressed the start button. "Great," said the CEO as his paper disappeared inside the machine. "I just need one copy."

Computers can never completely replace humans. They may become capable of artificial intelligence, but they will never master real stupidity.

Why is Christmas just like a day at the office?
    You do all the work and the fat guy in the suit gets all the credit.

A programmer is someone who solves a problem you didn't know you had in a way you don't understand.

This customer comes into the computer store. "I'm looking for a mystery adventure game with lots of graphics. You know, something really challenging."
    "Well," replied the clerk, "have you tried Windows 98?"

The crusty old managing partner finally passed away, but his firm kept receiving calls asking to speak with him. "I'm sorry, he's dead," was the standard answer. Finally, the receptionist who fielded the calls began to realize it was always the same voice, so she asked who it was and why he kept calling. The reply was, "I used to be one of his junior associates, and I just like to hear you say it."

A man is flying in a hot-air balloon and realizes he is lost. He reduces height and spots a man down below. He lowers the balloon more and shouts, "Excuse me, can you tell me where I am?"

The man below says, "Yes, you're in a hot-air balloon, hovering thirty feet above this field."

"You must work in information technology," says the balloonist.

"I do," replies the man. "How did you know?"

"Well," says the balloonist, "everything you have told me is technically correct, but it's of no practical use to anyone."

The man below says, "You must be a corporate manager."

"I am," replies the balloonist. "How did you know?"

"Well," says the man, "you don't know where you are or where you're going, but you expect me to be able to help. You have the same problem you had before we met, but now it's my fault."

God decides it's time to have the world end. He calls in Barack Obama, Vladimir Putin, and Bill Gates. He tells them that the world is going to end in seven days. So Obama goes to the American people, and Putin goes to the Russian people, and they say, "We have some good news and some bad news. The good news is, there is a God. The bad news is, the end of the world is coming."

And Bill Gates goes back to Microsoft and says, "I have some good news and some even better news. The good news is, I'm one of the three most important people on Earth, and the even better news is we don't have to fix Windows 10!"

IRS/ACCOUNTANT JOKES

An accountant is someone who solves a problem you didn't know you had in a way you don't understand.

What's an accountant's idea of trashing his hotel room? Refusing to fill out the guest comment card.

An accountant was passing a beggar in the street, and the man said, "I have not eaten for three days." The accountant replied, "How does that compare with the same period last year?"

The accountant couldn't get to sleep so he tried counting sheep. But then he made a mistake and it took him all night to find it.

The old accountant retired after fifty years, and in the top drawer of his desk they found a note that said: "Debits in the column toward the file cabinet. Credits in the column toward the window."

A man wrote a letter to the IRS: "I have been unable to sleep knowing that I have cheated on my income tax. I understated my taxable income and have enclosed a check for $150. If I still can't sleep, I will send the rest."

A kid swallowed a coin and it got stuck in his throat. His mother yelled for help. A man passing by hit him in the small of the back, and the coin came out.

"I don't know how to thank you, Doctor—," his mother started.

"I'm not a doctor," the man replied. "I'm from the IRS."

Two accountants are in a bank when armed robbers burst in. While several of the robbers take the money from the tellers, others line up the customers, including the accountants, and proceed to take their wallets, watches, etc. While this is going on, the first accountant jams something into the second accountant's hand. Without looking down, the second accountant whispers, "What is this?" To which the first accountant replies, "It's that $50 I owe you."

ECONOMIST JOKES

A conservative economist was lecturing to his class and he saw that one student had fallen asleep and he pounded on the table and the student woke up and said, "Cut taxes and reduce government spending."

An economist is an expert who will know tomorrow why the things he predicted yesterday did not happen today.

A woman hears from her doctor that she has only half a year to live. The doctor advises her to marry an economist and to live in South Dakota. The woman asks, "Will this cure my illness?"

The doctor answers, "No, but the half year will seem pretty long."

A party of economists was climbing in the Alps. After several hours they became hopelessly lost. One of them studied the map for some time, turning it up and down, sighting on distant landmarks, consulting his compass and the sun. Finally he said, "Okay, see that big mountain over there?"

The others agreed. "Well, according to the map, we're standing on top of it."

What's the difference between an economist and a confused old man with Alzheimer's?

The economist is the one with the calculator.

A mathematician, an accountant, and an economist apply for the same job. The interviewer calls in the mathematician and asks, "What does two plus two equal?" The mathematician replies, "Four." The interviewer asks, "Four exactly?" The mathematician looks at the interviewer incredulously and says, "Yes, four exactly."

Then the interviewer calls in the accountant and asks the same question: "What does two plus two equal?" The accountant says, "On average, four—give or take 10 percent—but on average, four."

Then the interviewer calls in the economist and poses the same question: "What does two plus two equal?" The economist gets up, locks the door, closes the shade, sits down next to the interviewer, and says, "What do you want it to equal?"

Why was astrology invented?
To make economics seem scientific.

Three econometricians went out hunting and came across a large deer. The first econometrician fired but missed by a meter to the left. The second econometrician fired but missed by a meter to the right. The third econometrician didn't fire but shouted in triumph, "We got it! We got it!"

An economist is someone who didn't have enough personality to become an accountant.

Economists have forecast nine out of the last five recessions.

DOCTOR/PSYCHIATRIST JOKES

"Mr. Phelps, Dr. Wynsczkrepskyvich will see you now."
"Which doctor?"
"No, he's an M.D. like all the others."

Client: "Doctor, people always ignore me."
Psychiatrist: "Next!"

The good thing about a doctor with Alzheimer's is he can give you his own second opinions.

A man went to a hospital to visit a friend and got lost and walked into a ward where old men sat and drank whisky. He asked a man where he was and the man cried out, "Some hae meat, and canna eat, And some wad eat that want it; But we hae meat and we can eat, And sae the Lord be thankit." And he asked the next man who cried: "So fair art thou my bonnie lass, so deep in love am I, that I would love thee still my love til all the seas gang dry." So he asked the nurse and she said, "This is the Burns unit."

So who is this Rorschach guy, and why did he draw so many pictures of my parents arguing?

Santa Claus went to a psychiatrist because he was afraid of going down chimneys. He was diagnosed with santaclaustrophobia.

A psychiatrist said to his patient, "Don't worry, you're not delusional. You only think you are."

Doctor, I can't stop eating. I am such a pig!
  How long has this been going on?
  Oh, about a weeeeeeeeeeek!

How about a local anesthetic?
  I'd prefer an import.

Old doctors never die. They just lose their patience.

A man went to the doctor with a leaf of lettuce sticking out of his ear. The doctor examined him and said, "I'm sorry to tell you, but this is just the tip of the iceberg."

A woman goes to the dentist. As he leans over to begin working on her, she grabs his crotch and says, "You and I are going to be very careful not to hurt each other, aren't we."

Doctors tell us there are over seven million people who are overweight. These, of course, are only round figures.

"Doctor," said the patient. "I can't stop singing 'The Green, Green Grass of Home.'" "Sounds like Tom Jones Syndrome to me," the doctor replied. "Is that common?" "It's not unusual."

What do you call a doctor who graduated at the bottom of his class?
  Doctor.

Why did the urologist lose his license?
  He got in trouble with his peers.

Did you hear about the veterinarian who is also a taxidermist?

The sign outside his office reads, "Either way, you get your dog back."

A Texan oil baron went to the dentist for a checkup. "I'm pleased to say your teeth are just fine," said the dentist. "I know," replied the oilman, "but drill anyway. I feel lucky."

A man goes to the doctor. The man has a strawberry growing out of his head. The doctor says, "Let me give you some cream to put on that."

Doctor: What seems to be the matter?
Patient: I have a sore throat, Doctor. I ache. I have a fever.
Doctor: Sounds like some kind of virus.
Patient: Everyone in the office has it.
Doctor: Well then, maybe it's a staff infection.

The doctor was showing the visitor around the insane asylum, and showing him a test to decide whether people should be admitted as patients. "We fill a bathtub with water, and we hand the person a teaspoon, a cup, and a pail." "Oh," said the visitor, "So the normal person will use the pail to empty the tub." The doctor replied, "No, actually, a normal person would pull the plug. So, would you like a private room?"

A guy goes to the doctor's office and the doctor says, "I haven't seen you for a while."

The guy says, "I know, I've been sick."

Doctor, you've got to help me. I can't stop thinking I'm a goat.
I see. And how long have you had this problem?
Ever since I was a kid.

A woman goes into a dentist's office and says, "I think I'd just as soon have a baby as get a tooth pulled."
The dentist says, "Make up your mind. I have to adjust the chair."

"I'm a little nervous, Doctor. This is my first operation."
"Mine too."

"I think I'm a moth."
"I think you need a psychiatrist."
"I know."
"So, why did you come in here to the gas station?"
"The light was on."

What's the difference between a nurse and a nun?
A nun only serves one God.

"Sir, I'd give you maybe three minutes to live."
"Isn't there anything you can do for me, Doctor?"
"Well, would you like me to boil you an egg?"

"I have terrible news, Mr. Larson. You have cancer and you have Alzheimer's."
"Well, Doctor, at least I don't have cancer."

"Doctor, I feel like a pair of curtains."
"Come now, pull yourself together."

227

"Doctor, there is an invisible man in your waiting room."
"Tell him I can't see him now."

"Doctor, you told me I have a month to live and then you sent me a bill for $1,000! I can't pay that before the end of the month!"
"Okay, you have six months to live."

"Doctor, am I going to die?"
"That's the last thing you're going to do."

"Doctor, my fingers hurt. Do you think I should file my nails?"
"No, just throw them away."

Patient: How much to have this tooth pulled?
Dentist: Ninety dollars.
Patient: Ninety dollars for just a few minutes' work?
Dentist: I can do it slower if you like.

A man consults a therapist and states, "Doc, I'm suicidal. What should I do?"
The doctor replies, "Pay in advance."

"Mrs. Larson, you're not going deaf in your left ear. You seem to have a suppository stuck in there!"
"Well, now I know what happened to my hearing aid."

"Doctor, I don't know what's wrong with me, but I hurt all over. If I touch my shoulder here, it hurts, and if I touch my leg here, it hurts, and if I touch my head here, it hurts, and if I touch my foot here, it hurts."

"I believe you've broken your finger."

Pharmacist: Sir, pardon me for asking, but every week you come in here to my drugstore and buy two dozen condoms.

Customer: Yes?

Pharmacist: It's none of my business, but how on earth do you use that many condoms a week?

Customer: I feed them to my poodle and now when she poops, she poops in little plastic bags.

"What's wrong, Doctor? You look puzzled."

"I can't figure out exactly what's wrong with you. I think it's the result of heavy drinking."

"Well then, I'll just come back when you're sober."

The doctor calls up the patient and says, "I have some bad news and some worse news. The bad news is that you have only twenty-four hours left to live." And the patient says, "That is very bad news. What could be worse than that?"

And the doctor says, "I've been trying to reach you since yesterday."

Patient: Doctor, every time I sneeze, I have an orgasm.

Doctor: Are you taking anything for it?

Patient: Ground pepper!

A ninety-year-old man went to his doctor and said, "Doctor, my wife, who is eighteen, is expecting a baby."

The doctor said, "Let me tell you a story. A man went hunting, but instead of his gun, he picked up an umbrella by mistake. And when a bear suddenly charged at him, he pointed his umbrella at the bear, shot at it, and killed it on the spot."

"Impossible. Somebody else must have shot that bear."

"Exactly my point."

A man accidentally cut off all his fingers with a power saw. When he got to the hospital, the doctor said, "Thank goodness for microsurgery. Give me the fingers and I'll sew them back on."

The man said, "I wasn't able to pick them up."

Woman: So give it to me straight, Doctor. I want to know the truth.

Doctor: Very well. Your husband is in terrible shape, and if you want him to live, you're going to have to make sure he's well fed and comfortable and happy at all times, and you're going to have to make love to him three times a day.

Woman: Three times a day?

Doctor: Three times a day.

Husband: So what'd the doctor say?

Woman: He says you're going to die.

Did you hear the one about the two carrots who are riding in a car? They get into a terrible accident, and they're rushed to the hospital. One of the carrots just has some scrapes and bruises, but the other is rushed to the operating room.

Hours later, the doctor comes out and says, "I have some good news and some bad news. The good news is that your friend is going to live. The bad news is that he's going to be a vegetable for the rest of his life."

"What happened to you, Mr. Peebles? You look awful."
"Well, Doctor, you told me to take this medicine for three days and then skip a day, and all that skipping wore me out."

Patient: Say, Doctor? What was wrong with that nun who just came running out of your office? She looked terribly pale.
Doctor: Well, I examined her and told her she was pregnant.
Patient: Is she?
Doctor: No, but it sure cured her hiccups!

A woman goes to the doctor and says, "Doctor, Doctor, you have to help me. Every time I go to the bathroom, dimes come out!"
The doctor tells her to relax, go home, rest with her feet up, and come back in a week.
A week later the woman returns and says, "Doctor, Doctor, it's gotten worse! Every time I go to the bathroom, quarters come out! What's wrong with me?" Again the doctor tells her to relax, go home, rest with her feet up, and come back in a week.
Another week passes. The woman returns and yells, "Doctor, Doctor, I'm still not getting better! Every time I go to the bathroom, half-dollars come out! What the heck is wrong with me?"
The doctor says, "Relax, relax, you're just going through your change."

The old family physician took his son into partnership after the son got his M.D. The old doctor then went off on a two-week vacation, his first in years. When he got home, he asked his son if there'd been any problems at the clinic. The son said no, everything went well. "In fact," he said, "you know that rich old widow, Mrs. Ferguson? I cured her of her chronic indigestion."

"Well, that's fine," said the old doctor. "But Mrs. Ferguson's indigestion is what put you through medical school."

Patient: Nurse, I keep seeing spots in front of my eyes.
     Nurse: Have you ever seen a doctor?
     Patient: No, just spots.

So, this man walks into the pharmacy and says, "Have you got cotton balls?"

The pharmacist says, "What is this, a joke?"

The man came to see the doctor about his constant fatigue and the doctor said, "I'm afraid you're going to have to give up sex."

The man said, "But I'm a young guy. I'm in the prime of my life. How can I just give up sex?"

"Well," the doctor said, "you do what everyone does. You get married and you taper off gradually."

"Doctor! Something's wrong! I'm shrinking!"

"Take it easy, sir. You'll just have to be a little patient."

The doctor calls up the patient and says, "I've got some good news and some bad news for you." And the patient says, "What's the good news, Doctor?" And the doctor says, "They're going to name a disease after you."

Woman: Doctor, for the last eight months, my husband has thought that he's a lawn mower.
  Doctor: That's terrible. Why didn't you bring him in sooner?
  Woman: Because the neighbor just returned him this morning.

A man walks into the psychiatrist's office with a cucumber up his nose, a carrot in his left ear, and a banana in his right ear. He says, "What's the matter with me?"
  The psychiatrist says, "You're not eating properly."

Pharmacist: May I help you, sir?
  Customer: Yes, I, uh, well, this is sort of embarrassing, but I'm going out on a date tonight, and you know, I need some...
  Pharmacist: You need some protection.
  Customer: Right.
  Pharmacist: Small, medium, or large?
  Customer: Uhhhh. Medium, I guess.
  Pharmacist: Okay, that'll be $2.35 including tax.
  Customer: Tacks! I thought they stayed on by themselves!

A man was very unhappy that he had no romance in his life whatsoever. So, he went to a Chinese sex therapist, Dr. Chang, who looked at him and said, "Okay, take off all your crose." Which the man did.

"Now, get down and crawl reery fass to the other side of room." Which the man did. "Okay, now crawl reery fass to me." Which the man did. Dr. Chang said, "Your probrem velly bad. You haf Ed Zachary Disease." The man said, "What is Ed Zachary Disease?"

"It when your face rook Ed Zachary rike your ass."

Doctor: What's wrong with your brother?
Boy: He thinks he's a chicken.
Doctor: Really? How long has he thought this?
Boy: Three years.
Doctor: Three years!
Boy: We would've brought him in sooner, but we needed the eggs.

A woman went to a dentist to have a tooth pulled and there was instant electricity between the two. They made love right there in his office. She came back week after week after week and they made love over and over and over again. Until one day he told her they'd have to end the affair, as beautiful as it was, because she only had one tooth left.

When the X-ray specialist married one of his patients, everybody wondered what he saw in her.

"Hello? Is this the state mental hospital?"
"Yes, it is."
"Can I speak to Mr. Russell in room twenty-seven?"
"One moment and I'll connect you… (pause) I'm sorry, Mr. Russell is not answering."
"Good. That means I must have really escaped."

A man is feeling poorly, so he goes to his doctor. After numerous tests the doc says, "I'm sorry, but you have an incurable condition and there is nothing more I can do for you." The man pleads with the doctor to suggest anything he might do to improve his condition, and the doctor then suggests that he go to the spa and take a daily mud bath. "Is there any hope of a cure?" the man asks. "No," says the doctor, "but it will help you get used to dirt."

Patient: Doctor, you've got to help me. Some mornings I wake up and think I'm Donald Duck, other mornings I think I'm Mickey Mouse.

Doctor: Hmm, and how long have you been having these Disney spells?

Patient: I'm feeling terrible. Am I dying?

Doctor: I'll have to examine you. Hmmmmm…I'm afraid I have some bad news. You're dying and you don't have much time.

Patient: Oh no! How long have I got?
Doctor: Ten…
Patient: Ten? Ten what?
Doctor: Nine…
Patient: Nine? Nine what—months? weeks? what?!
Doctor: Eight…seven…six…

A painter got a call from the gallery that was showing his work. The gallery owner said, "I have good news and bad news. A fellow came in this morning and asked if your work is the kind that would increase in value after the artist's death. I said yes, and he bought all fifteen paintings. The bad news is that he's your doctor."

A guy goes to the doctor, and the doctor tells him he only has a day to live. He goes home to tell his wife, who asks him what he wants to do with his final hours. Of course he wants to spend them having sex. They have great sex all night long. Finally, about two a.m., the wife says she's tired and wants to go to sleep. He says, "Oh, come on, can't we do it just one more time?"

And she says, "Look, I've got to get up in the morning—you don't!"

There's so much more that medical science knows now than it ever used to. When my wife went in for her sonogram, she found out that the baby is a lesbian.

Never go to a doctor whose office plants have died.

How did it go at the doctor's today, honey?

The doctor told me I have to take medication every day for the rest of my life.

What's so terrible about that?

He only gave me four pills.

Doctor: Sir, how did you happen to break your leg?

Patient: Well, Doctor, it was like this. Twenty-five years ago, I was on the road and it got dark and…

Doctor: Never mind that. Tell me how you broke your leg this morning.

Patient: Well, twenty-five years ago, I was on the road and it got dark, and I needed a place to stay. There was only this one farmhouse near, so I knocked on the door and the farmer answered. I told him my situation, and he said, "Well, you can stay here, but you'll have to share a room with my beautiful daughter." I said that would be okay, and I went up and crawled into bed. She was already asleep, and that night, right after I'd gone to sleep, she woke me up and asked me if there was anything I wanted. I said no, everything was fine. She said, "Are you sure?" I said, "I'm sure." She said, "Isn't there anything I can do for you?" I said, "I reckon not."

Doctor: What does this have to do with your broken leg?

Patient: Well, this morning, it dawned on me what she meant by that, and I fell off the roof!

"Doctor, I think I'm suffering from memory loss."
"Have you ever had it before?"

Why do surgeons wear masks during operations?
So they can't be identified.

One reason surgeons are paid more than auto mechanics is that auto mechanics don't have to repair the engine while it's running.

My doctor tried kidnapping for a while, but nobody could read the ransom notes.

Doctor: Nurse, how is that little girl doing who swallowed ten quarters last night?
Nurse: No change yet.

"I was depressed, Doctor, so I tried to kill myself by taking a thousand aspirins."

"What happened?"

"Well, after the first two I felt better."

"Am I going to be okay, Doctor?"

"Sir, there's nothing to worry about, the operation is quite routine and not at all complicated."

"Good. I hope you remember that when you're writing up the bill."

Psychiatrist: Mr. Phelps, I can say with confidence that after fifteen years of psychotherapy you are cured.

Patient: Well, that's good, I guess. But on the other hand, fifteen years ago I was God. Now I'm nobody.

I asked my doctor if I should have a vasectomy. He said to let a sleeping dog lie.

Patient: Doctor, I have this terrible problem. I think I'm a dog. I walk around on all fours, I keep barking in the middle of the night and I eat dog food.

Doctor: Very interesting. Lie down on the couch, please.

Patient: I'm not allowed on the couch.

Visitor: I'm here to see a friend who was admitted to the hospital this morning. He was run over by a steamroller.

Nurse: He's in Room 105, 106, 107, 108, and 109.

Psychoanalysis is easier for a man, because when it's time to go back to childhood, he is already there.

Father: I'm dying.
Son: Yes, Dad.
Father: Somehow I never expected this to happen to me.
Son: I know, Dad.
Father: I'm not ready to go.
Son: Where do you want to be buried, Dad?
Father: Surprise me.

A man is walking by an insane asylum and hears all the residents chanting, "Thirteen! Thirteen! Thirteen!" He's very curious about all this, so he finds a hole in the fence, looks in and someone pokes him in the eye with a sharp stick. Everyone in the asylum starts chanting "Fourteen! Fourteen! Fourteen!"

A guy goes into a doctor's office wearing nothing but a piece of Saran Wrap around his waist. The doctor says, "I can clearly see you're nuts."

Doctor: You are in perfect health. You'll live to be at least 65.
Patient: But Doctor, I am 65!
Doctor: See? What did I tell you?

After twelve years of analysis, I finally was able to get in touch with my emotions and break down and cry.
What happened?
One day, my analyst looked at me and said, "No hablo inglés."

Patient: Doctor! I can't feel my legs!
Doctor: That's because we had to amputate your arms.

"Hello, doctor?"

"Yes?"

"My wife is pregnant, and her contractions are only two minutes apart!"

"Is this her first child?"

"No, this is her husband!"

We've got bad news and we have good news, Mrs. Olson. The bad news is that we've amputated the wrong leg. The good news is that your bad leg is getting better.

We've got bad news and we have good news, Mrs. Olson. The bad news is that we've had to amputate the other leg, too. The good news is that the lady in the next room made a very good offer on your shoes.

COP JOKES

A man called the police and said, "I found a suitcase in the forest with a cat and four kittens in it." The police dispatcher said, "That's terrible. Are any of them moving?" The man said, "I didn't ask, but that would explain the suitcase."

A man driving down the road gets pulled over by a policeman. The policeman says, "You're drunk." And the driver says, "Well thank God for that, I thought the steering had gone!"

A juggler, driving to his next performance, is stopped by the police.
"What are those knives doing in your car?" asks the officer.
"I juggle them in my act," says the juggler.
"Oh yeah?" says the cop. "Let's see you do it." So the juggler starts tossing and juggling the knives.
A guy driving by sees this and says, "Wow, am I glad I quit drinking. Look at the test they're making you do now!"

The town cop is parked outside a bar at midnight, watching for drunk drivers, when he sees a man stumble out the door, trip over the curb, try thirty cars before opening the door to his own, and fall asleep on the front seat. One by one the drivers of the other cars drive off, and finally the guy wakes up, starts his car, and pulls out of the parking lot. The cop pulls him over and gives him a Breathalyzer test. The results shows a 0.0 blood-alcohol level, and the cop is puzzled. He asks, "How can that be?"
The guy says, "Well, tonight was my turn to be the decoy."

The state trooper is driving down the highway when he sees a truck driver pull over, walk to the side of his truck with a tire jack, bang on the side of the truck several times, and then drive away. Two miles down the road he does the same thing. Another two miles, same thing. The trooper pulls the truck over and asks the truck driver to explain. And the driver says, "The load limit is ten tons, and I'm carrying fifteen tons of parakeets, so I've got to keep some of them flying around."

A cop pulls a woman over and says, "Let me see your driver's license, lady."

The woman replies, "I wish you people would get it together. One day you take away my license and the next day you ask me to show it."

This cop pulled a guy over and said, "Sir, I need you to breathe into this Breathalyzer for me."

"I can't do that. I'm an asthmatic. If I do that, I'll have a really big asthma attack."

"Okay. Then I need you to come down to the station with me and we'll have to do some blood work."

"I can't do that, either. I'm a hemophiliac. If I do that, I'll bleed to death."

"Okay. Then I need a urine sample from you."

"I can't do that, either. I'm a diabetic. If I do that, my sugar will get really low."

"Okay. Then I need you to step out of the car and walk this white line."

"I can't do that, either."

The cop said, "Why not?"

The guy said, "Because I'm drunk."

All the toilet seats were stolen from police headquarters. The police have nothing to go on.

This old rancher in Montana hates wearing a seat belt. One day he's driving on the highway with his wife and sees a state patrol car behind him. He says to his wife, "Quick, take the wheel! I gotta put my seat belt on!" So she does, and right then the patrolman pulls them over.

He walks up to the car and says to the rancher, "Say, I noticed you weren't wearing your seat belt."

The rancher says, "I was too, but you don't have to take my word for it. My wife here is a good Christian woman, ask her. She'll tell you the truth. She doesn't lie about anything."

The cop says to the wife, "So? How about it, ma'am?"

And the wife says, "I've been married to Buck for twenty years, officer, and one thing I've learned in all that time is this: You never argue with him when he's drunk."

The police officer sees a car weaving back and forth down the highway, and he takes off after it. He pulls up alongside and sees the driver is a little old lady, and she's knitting as she drives. He can't believe it, and he yells at her, "Pull over! Pull over!"

And she yells, "No, it's a scarf!"

MUSICIAN JOKES

"Will the band play anything you ask them to?"
"Yes, of course."
"Okay, ask them to play pinochle."

A man went to sing for the patients at the hospital. He sang some opera, some Broadway, some pop songs, and at the end, he said, "Thank you so much, and I hope you all get better." They said, "We hope you get better too."

With your mandolin, you spend half of your time tuning it, and the other half playing out of tune.

Three trombone players are in a car. Who's driving?
The police.

What do you call a beautiful girl on a trombonist's arm?
A tattoo.

What's the difference between a pop musician and a jazz musician?
The pop musician plays three chords for a thousand people, and the jazz musician plays a thousand chords for three people.

What happens if you play blues music backwards?
Your wife comes back and treats you okay and you don't wake up in the morning.

What do you call a building full of guitarists?
Jail.

Have you heard of the new diet for guitar players?
It's called the Chet Atkins diet. All you do is pick at your food.

Did you hear Willie Nelson got hit by a car?
He was playing on the road again.

Why was the piano invented?
So the band would have a place to set their beer.

Why is the trumpet an instrument of worship?
Because a man blows in it, but God only knows what comes out of it.

What do you get when you cross a tuba player and a goalpost?
A goalpost that can't march.

How long does it take to tune a viola?
Nobody's bothered to find out.

What's the longest viola joke in the world?
The Walton Viola Concerto.

A conductor is a person who is able to follow many people at the same time.

No wonder we have so much air pollution when so much of it has passed through saxophones.

What's the difference between a baritone saxophone and a chain saw?

The exhaust.

How do you know when a trombone player is at your door?

The doorbell drags.

Once there was a tenor with such a big ego, when he was invited to sing *La Forza del Destino* he thought he was going to sing the title role.

A bunch of bass players walk into a bar. The orchestra is playing Beethoven's Ninth Symphony, and there's a long section near the end where the basses don't play, so the bass players decide to go out and have a few beers. They tie a string to the conductor's score, so that when he turns the page, it will tug on the string, and the bass players will know to come back for the end of the symphony.

So the performance goes on, and eventually, the conductor looks up and realizes he's in big trouble: It's the bottom of the Ninth, the score is tied, and the basses are loaded!

The singer says to her piano player, "I'd like to do 'My Funny Valentine' tonight, but how about we arrange it a little?"

The piano player says, "Okay, how about this: we do the first chorus in G minor, then modulate to G# minor for the second chorus in 5/4 time, then modulate to A minor in 3/4 time for the bridge, then cut off the last three bars!"

She says, "That sounds complicated."

And the piano player says, "Well, that's how you did it last night!"

A banjo is like an artillery shell—by the time you hear it, it's too late.

What's the difference between a banjo and a lawnmower?
You can tune a lawnmower.

What's the difference between a banjo and a vacuum cleaner?
You have to plug in a vacuum cleaner before it sucks.

Do you know the definition for perfect pitch?
When you throw the banjo into the Dumpster and it lands right on the accordion.

What's the difference between an accordion and an onion?
No one cries when you cut up an accordion.

Definition of an optimist:
• An accordion player with a pager.
• A choir director with a mortgage.

Hey, buddy. How late does the band play?
Oh, about half a beat behind the drummer.

What do you call a guy who hangs out with musicians?
A drummer.

How do you get a drummer out of your house?
Pay him for the pizza.

How can you tell that there's a drummer at your front door?
Gradually, the knocking gets faster and faster.

Why do drummers leave their sticks on the dashboard when they park?
So they can use the handicapped zones.

Why are orchestra intermissions limited to 20 minutes?
So you don't have to retrain the drummers.

What's the difference between a drummer and a drum machine?
With a drum machine you only have to punch the information in once.

What's the difference between drummers and government bonds?
Government bonds eventually mature and earn money.

How can you tell when the drum riser is level?
Drool comes out of both sides of the drummer's mouth.

What's the last thing a drummer says before he's out of a band?
"Hey guys, why don't we try one of my songs?"

Why do bands have bass players?
To translate for the drummer.

One day the bass player hid one of the drummer's sticks. The drummer said, "Finally! After all these years, I'm a conductor!"

A policeman went up to a street musician and asked, "Excuse me, sir, do you have a license to play that violin in the street?"

And the violinist answered, "Well, actually, no."

"In that case I'm going to have to ask you to accompany me."

"Of course, officer. What would you like to sing?"

The gig's going really well. I mean really well. The crowd is going wild—people are dancing, yelling, and applauding loudly after every song, and the house is packed. There's someone who looks to be a talent agent in the back. The whole band is having a great night, hitting every groove, pulling off every little detail to make it right.

The guitarist thinks, "We're going to be famous. I'm going to be famous! Everyone's going to know my name. I'm going to have a lot of sex."

The drummer thinks, "We're going to be rich. So rich. I'm going to buy a ton of gear."

The singer/rhythm guitarist thinks, "This is wonderful. I can finally support my designer drug habit."

The bassist thinks, "G - D - C - D - G."

Did you hear about the bassist who was so out of tune his section noticed?

Why does a violinist have a handkerchief under his chin when he plays?

Because there's no spit valve.

I recommend that you don't buy a Stradivarius. He stopped making parts for them.

A double bass player arrived a few minutes late for the first rehearsal of the local choral society's annual performance of Handel's *Messiah*.

He picked up his instrument and bow, and turned his attention to the conductor. The conductor asked, "Would you like a moment to tune?"

The bass player replied with some surprise, "Why? Isn't it the same as last year?"

Why are violins smaller than violas?
They're really the same size, but violinists have bigger heads.

Why are viola jokes so short?
So violinists can understand them.

How do you tell the difference between a violinist and a dog?
The dog knows when to stop scratching.

What do a viola and a lawsuit have in common?
Everyone's happy when the case is closed.

How do you get two viola players to play in perfect unison?
Shoot one of them.

Why do so many people take an instant dislike to the viola?
It saves time.

What's the difference between the first and last desk of a viola section?
Half a measure and a semi-tone.

Did you hear about the violist who bragged that he could play 16th notes?

The rest of the orchestra didn't believe him, so he proved it by playing one.

How can you tell if a viola is out of tune?

The bow is moving.

What's the difference between a cello and a viola?

A cello burns longer.

Did you hear about the violist who dreamed she was playing in the pit for *The Nutcracker*, and she woke up and found out that she was?

A viola player came home late at night to find police cars and fire trucks outside his house. The chief of police intercepted him.

"I'm afraid I have terrible news for you. While you were out, the conductor came to your house, killed your family and burned your house down."

The viola player was stunned. "You're kidding! The conductor came to my house?"

What's the difference between a viola and a coffin?

The coffin has the dead person on the inside.

During a concert, a fight broke out between the oboe player and the viola player. At the intermission, the orchestra leader went to investigate.

"He broke my reed," said the oboe player.

"He undid two of my strings," countered the viola player, "and he won't tell me which ones."

What's the definition of a quarter tone?
Two oboes playing in unison.

What's the difference between a saxophone and a lawn mower?
• Lawn mowers sound better in small ensembles.
• The neighbors are upset if you borrow a lawnmower and don't return it.
• The grip.

What's the difference between a baritone sax and a chain saw?
Vibrato.

How can you tell which kid on a playground is the child of a trombonist?
He doesn't know how to use the slide, and he can't swing.

A girl went out on a date with a trumpet player, and when she came back her roommate asked, "Well, how was it? Did his embouchure make him a great kisser?"
"Nah," the first girl replied. "That dry, tight, tiny pinched-up mouth; it was no fun at all."
The next night she went out with a tuba player, and when she came back her roommate asked, "Well, was he a good kisser?"
"Ugh!" the first girl exclaimed. "Those huge, rubbery, blubbery, slobbering lips! Oh, it was just gross!"

The next night she went out with a French horn player, and when she came back her roommate asked, "Well, how was his kissing?"

"Well," the first girl replied, "his kissing was just so-so, but I loved the way he held me!"

Why can't a gorilla play trumpet?
He's too sensitive.

What's a tuba for?
1½" by 3½" unless you request "full cut."

What is the difference between a dead trombone player lying in the road and a dead squirrel lying in the road?
The squirrel might have been on his way to a job.

What is the dynamic range of the bass trombone?
On or off.

What do you get when you drop a piano down a mine shaft?
A-flat minor.

Pianist to singer: "You keep your hands off my piano and I'll keep my hands off your throat."

The doorbell rang, and the lady of the house discovered a workman, complete with tool chest, on the front porch.
"Madam," he announced, "I'm the piano tuner."
The lady exclaimed, "Why, I didn't send for a piano tuner."
The man replied, "I know, but your neighbors did."

A pianist gave a solo recital. When it was over, he got a big ovation, and a woman in the front row stood up and shouted, "Play it again! Play it again!" He stepped forward and bowed. She yelled, "Play it again until you get it right!"

I play piano just like Frederic Chopin—with both hands.

Why couldn't Mozart find his teacher?
Because he was Haydn.

Why did Beethoven kill his chicken?
It kept saying "Bach, Bach, Bach…"

They laughed when I sat down at the piano. I forgot to bring a stool.

How do you get to the Catskills?
Stop practicing.

Two musicians are walking down the street, and one says to the other, "Who was that piccolo I saw you with last night?"
The other replies, "That was no piccolo. That was my fife."

I'm in a three-piece band. We only know three pieces.

I play in a small quartet. There's only three of us.

How do you make a bandstand?
Take away their chairs.

So a seven-year-old kid says to his dad, "When I grow up, I want to be a musician."

And the dad says, "Make up your mind."

The organ is the instrument of worship, for in its sounding we sense the majesty of God and in its ending we know the grace of God.

What do you call a guitarist without a girlfriend?

Homeless.

Two out-of-work Jewish musicians are sitting on a park bench in Brooklyn.

The first one says, "Oy!"

The other one says, "I'm hip."

St. Peter's checking IDs. He asks a man, "What did you do on Earth?"

The man says, "I was a doctor."

St. Peter says, "Okay, go right through those pearly gates. Next! What did you do on Earth?"

"I was a school teacher."

"Go right through those pearly gates. Next! And what did you do on Earth?"

"I was a musician."

"Go around the side, up the freight elevator, through the kitchen…"

What's the difference between a musician and a fourteen-inch pizza?

The pizza can feed a family of four.

How do you get a guitar player to stop playing?
Put sheet music in front of him.

How does a guitar player make a million dollars?
He starts out with seven million.

Either heaven or hell will have continuous background
music. Which one you think it will be tells a lot about you.

The other day I saw one of those pop singers with an
exposed belly but no navel. It's either a show-biz gimmick or
the ultimate rejection of mother.

I was a musical prodigy. At three I composed an opera. At
four I wrote a minuet. At five I wrote a complete symphony.
And at five thirty, as usual, I went down and had a cup of tea.

My friend was trying to write a drinking song but he couldn't
get past the first few bars.

To be a real folk-singer you have to collect the songs straight
from the horse's mouth. The way to do this is to go to a
village and find the oldest inhabitant and ask him to sing you
the songs his mother taught him. You'll probably find out
that he's deaf, and if he isn't deaf he can't sing, and if he can
sing he doesn't want to, and by the time you've persuaded
him and he does sing, you won't understand a word of what
he's singing about. This is how folk songs have been passed
down from generation to generation.

A jazz musician dies and goes to heaven. He is told, "Hey man, welcome! You have been elected to the Jazz All-Stars of Heaven—right up there with Satchmo, Miles, Django, all the greats. We have a gig tonight. Only one problem—God's got this girlfriend who's a singer…"

Why do bagpipers always walk when they play?
     To get away from the noise.

There was a young Scottish boy called Angus who decided to try life in Australia. He found an apartment in a small block and settled in.
     After a week or two, his mother called from Aberdeen to see how her son was doing in his new life. "I'm fine," Angus said. "But there are some really strange people living in these apartments. The woman next door cries all night long, and the guy upstairs bangs his foot on the floor all the time."
     "Well, ma laddie," says his mother, "I suggest you don't associate with people like that."
     "Oh," says Angus, "I don't, Ma'am. I stay inside my apartment all day and night, playing my bagpipes."

Why do high school choruses travel so often?
     To keep would-be assassins guessing.

How do you know you have a singer at your front door?
     Can't find the key; doesn't know when to come in.

Twelve tenors and a baritone were climbing Mount Everest and they fell down into the crevasse. All of them managed to hang on to the rope, but it was clear that the rope couldn't hold them all. They decided one man would have to let go.

The baritone said, "Okay, I'm only a baritone. There are so many baritones and so few tenors. The music world cannot bear to lose you, so I'll sacrifice myself to save your lives." And the tenors all applauded and fell to their deaths.

What's the difference between a soprano and the PLO?
You can negotiate with the PLO.

What's the difference between a soprano and a Rottweiler?
Jewelry.

What's the difference between a Wagnerian soprano and a Wagnerian tenor?
About 10 pounds.

How do you tell if a Wagnerian soprano is dead?
The horses seem very relieved.

What's the difference between an alto and a tenor?
Tenors don't have hair on their backs.

First woman: What did you hear at the opera yesterday?
Second woman: Oh, lots of things. The Williamses are going to Hawaii this winter. Elsa is pregnant again…

A new conductor was at his first rehearsal. It was not going well. He was as wary of the musicians as they were of him. As he left the rehearsal room, the timpanist sounded a rude little "bong." The angry conductor turned and said, "All right! Who did that?"

What do you get when you play country music backwards?
　You get your wife back, your dog back, your car back…

What do you get when you play New Age music backwards?
　New Age music.

What does it say on a blues singer's tombstone?
　"I didn't wake up this morning…"

What's the difference between a puppy and a singer-songwriter?
　Eventually the puppy stops whining.

How many musician jokes are there?
　Just one—all the rest are true.

AND A FEW MORE JOB JOKES

There is a Hollywood agent who has lost all of his clients and he is just about to close his doors when the Devil appears. And the Devil says, "Here's the deal. You get Leo DiCaprio, Robert Redford, and Sean Penn and in return I get your soul." So the agent says, "What's in it for you?"

A salesman knocks on a door and a little kid answers. The kid's got a cigar in one hand and a beer in the other. The salesman says, "Are your parents home?" The kid says, "What do you think?"

A scientist doing an experiment with liquid chemicals was trying to solve a problem when he fell in and became part of the solution.

Did you hear about the scientist whose wife had twins? He baptized one and kept the other as a control.

You can spot a chemist in the restroom because they wash their hands before they go.

Why are there no English majors on the Starship *Enterprise*? Because they don't have jobs in the future, either.

The computer programmer gave his son a basketball for his birthday and the boy said, "Thank you, but where's the user's manual?"

The computer programmer's wife had a baby and the doctor handed the baby to the father. His wife said: "So, is it a boy or a girl?" The programmer said, "Yes."

Famed anthropologist Mary Leakey died at the age of eighty-three, and she was buried near her home, where she will rest in peace until some nosy anthropologist digs her up.

I didn't want to believe that my dad was stealing from his job at the transportation department, but when I got home all the signs were there.

There was a computer and printer repair shop that found that they made more money on repairs if they encouraged their customers to try reading the manual and fixing the problems themselves first.

There was once a young man who wanted to become a great writer and to write stuff that millions of people would read and react to on an emotional level, cry, howl in pain and anger, so now he works for Microsoft, writing error messages.

Why did the auto mechanic go to art school?
    So he could learn to make a van go.

Did you hear about the mechanic who was addicted to brake fluid?
    He said it was no problem—he could stop any time.

A statistician is someone who is good with numbers but lacks the personality to be an accountant.

A professor is someone who talks in someone else's sleep.

An elementary schoolteacher is a woman who used to think she liked small children.

A consultant is someone who takes the watch off your wrist and tells you the time.

A guy stuck his head into a barber shop and asked, "How long before I can get a haircut?" The barber looked around the shop full of customers and said, "About two hours." The guy left.

A few days later the same guy stuck his head in the door and asked, "How long before I can get a haircut?" The barber looked around at the shop and said, "About three hours." The guy left.

A week later the same guy stuck his head in the shop and asked, "How long before I can get a haircut?" The barber looked around the shop and said, "About an hour and a half." The guy left. The barber turned to a friend and said, "Hey, Bill, do me a favor. Follow that guy and see where he goes. He keeps asking how long he has to wait for a haircut, but then he doesn't ever come back." A little while later, Bill returned to the shop, laughing hysterically. The barber asked, "So where does that guy go when he leaves?" Bill looked up, tears in his eyes, and said, "Your house."

The newspaper photographer was assigned to get aerial photos of a forest fire. The editor told him to rush to the airport and the plane would be waiting to take him up. So he raced to the little country airport, and the plane was warming up, so he jumped in with his equipment and yelled, "Let's go!" The pilot swung the plane into the wind and took off. The photographer told him to fly over the fire, and the pilot said, "Why?" The photographer said, "I'm a photographer. I have to take pictures." The pilot said, "You mean you're not the instructor?"

Did you hear about the flasher who was thinking of retiring? He decided to stick it out for one more year.

A teacher was telling her third-grade class that they needed to bring in a couple dollars to get a copy of the class picture. "This is going to mean so much to you in thirty years," she said. "You'll look at it and you'll say, there's my friend Julie, she's a lawyer now, and there's my friend Jim…"

A voice from the back of the room interrupted, "And there's my teacher. She's dead."

Two cowboys are riding across the prairie and they come across an Indian lying down with his ear on the ground. They get off their horses and ask him what he's doing. He says, "Two wagons, four horses, two men, two women, one small child, one cow, two goats, and one large brown dog."

They say, "Wow, you can tell all of that by listening to the ground?!" He says, "No, they ran over me half an hour ago."

Why was the archeologist depressed? His career was in ruins.

A drill sergeant ran his platoon of recruits all over the camp in the hot sun with heavy packs on. As they stood there, exhausted, he put his face right up to one recruit's face and said, "I'll bet you're wishing I would die so you could come and urinate on my grave, aren't you?"

And the recruit says, "No, sir! When I get out of the army I'm never gonna stand in another line again."

Did you hear that archeologists just recently identified the cause of the Dark Ages?

It was most definitely the Y1K problem.

Four people were riding in a train coach. A woman and her beautiful nineteen-year-old daughter were on one side, and facing them were the army general and his escort, an army private. The train enters a tunnel, and the cabin becomes dark. A kiss is heard, followed by a slap. The mother thinks, "That young man stole a kiss from my daughter, and she rightfully slapped him."

The daughter thinks, "That young man tried to kiss me and kissed my mother by mistake and got slapped."

The general thinks, "That young man stole a kiss, and I got slapped by mistake."

The private thinks, "I'm pretty smart. I kiss the back of my hand and get to hit the general."

The old retired general goes into the base hospital for his annual physical. "Any complaints about your physical condition?" the doctor asks.

"My sex life isn't as good as it used to be," complains the general.

"Really, General, when was the last time you had sexual relations?" asks the doctor.

"1958!" says the general.

"Well, no wonder," says the doctor, "that's an awfully long time ago and you're an old man!"

The general, angry, replies, "Whaddya mean, it's only a little after 2100 right now!"

A biologist, an engineer, and a mathematician were sitting outside an empty house. They saw two people go in, and a while later, three people came out. The engineer said, "Our initial count must have been wrong." The biologist said, "They must have reproduced." The mathematician said, "Now, if one person goes back into the house, it will be completely empty!"

The human cannonball decided to retire. The circus owner cried, "But you can't! Where am I going to find a man of your caliber?"

This man got a job with the county highway department painting lines down the center of the highway. The supervisor told him he was expected to paint two miles of highway a day, and the man started work the next day. The first day the man painted four miles. The supervisor thought, "Great." The next day the man only painted two miles but the supervisor thought, "Well, it's good enough." But the third day the man only painted one mile and the boss said, "Is there a problem?"

The man said, "Well, I'm getting farther and farther away from the bucket."

Teacher: Class, it's an interesting linguistic fact that, in English, a double negative forms a positive. In some languages, though, such as Russian, a double negative is still a negative. However, there is no language in which a double positive can form a negative.

Student: Yeah, right.

The CIA, the FBI, and the NYPD are competing to see which organization is the greatest apprehender of criminals. A rabbit is released into a forest and each organization tries to bring the rabbit in.

The CIA places animal informants throughout the forest and hidden microphones on the trees. And after three months, they conclude that rabbits do not exist.

The FBI goes in. After two weeks with no leads, they burn the forest, killing everything in it.

The NYPD goes in. Two hours later they come out leading a badly beaten bear by the ear. The bear is yelling: "Okay, okay, I'm a rabbit, I'm a rabbit."

A manager is a person who thinks that nine women ought to be able to produce a child in one month.

A consultant is a man who knows 147 ways to make love, but doesn't know any women.

An actuary is someone who brings a fake bomb on a plane, because that decreases the chances that there will be another one.

An auditor is someone who arrives after the battle and bayonets all the wounded.

A banker is a fellow who lends you his umbrella when the sun is shining and wants it back the minute it begins to rain.

A philosopher is a person who doesn't have a job but at least understands why.

A newspaper editor is a person whose business it is to separate the wheat from the chaff, and to see that the chaff is printed.

A psychologist is a man whom you pay a lot of money to ask you questions that your wife asks free of charge.

A sociologist is someone who, when a beautiful woman enters the room and everybody looks at her, looks at everybody.

My boss is so mean, if you get in two minutes late he fines you and if you get in two minutes early he charges you rent.

My only regret was that I had but one life to give for my country. If I'd had two, I would have felt a lot safer.

I earned my sergeant's stripes the hard way. I started out as a lieutenant.

Copy-editing is a very stressful line of work for women. Every time one of us misses a period, we get really nervous.

Useful Phrases for the Workplace:
- Thank you. We're all refreshed and challenged by your unique point of view.
- The fact that no one understands you doesn't mean you're an artist.
- You are validating my inherent mistrust of strangers.
- I will always cherish the initial misconceptions I had about you.
- What am I? Flypaper for freaks!?
- I'm not being rude. You're just insignificant.
- I'll try being nicer if you'll try being smarter.

Sergeant: Private!
    Private: Yes, sir.
Sergeant: You failed to show up for camouflage class yesterday.
    Private: How do you know that, sir?

What to say if you get caught sleeping in your work cubicle:
- It's okay: I'm still billing the client.
- Do you discriminate against people who practice yoga?
- I wasn't sleeping. I was trying to pick up a contact lens without using my hands.

For every philosopher, there exists an equal and opposite philosopher.

I got an A in philosophy last semester by proving that my professor doesn't exist.

The philosopher went out on his first date with a woman and took her to a restaurant. They sat quietly for a while and he finally says, "Do you like philosophy?"

She says, "No."

He says. "Do you have a sister?"

"No."

He says, "If you had a sister, do you think she'd like philosophy?"

A terrible actor was doing *Hamlet* and was so bad that during the "To be or not to be" soliloquy the audience threw their shoes at him. The actor stepped downstage and said, "Look—folks—I didn't write this crap."

OLE AND LENA JOKES

Ole and Lena were sitting in the living room watching TV when Lena said, "Ole, did you hear that Sven got a brand new bicycle for Hilda?" "Uff da," said Ole. "That's a really good deal."

Ole's best friend Sven snuck over to Ole's house when he was gone and started fooling around with his wife, Lena. The phone rang, and Lena answered it. She said, "Hi, Ole. Oh, okay," and hung up. Sven says, "Holy cow, I s'pose I better get dressed and high tail it outta here." Lena says, "Take your time. Ole said he'll be late 'cause he's playing cards with you."

Ole came home carrying a rock, a chicken, and a pail, and he asked Lena to open the door for him. She said, "No, I'm afraid you might suddenly want to make love to me." He said, "How could I make love to you with a rock, a chicken and a pail in my arms?" "Well," she said, "you could set the chicken down, put the pail over it, and then set the rock on top of the pail."

So Lena had an affair with a man across the river named Clarence. Ole went to beat the man up, but he saw a sign on the bridge that read Clarence is 13 feet 6 inches, so he changed his mind.

Ole and Lena were at the bank. A robber ran into the bank waving a gun, but his mask fell off, and the teller saw him, so the robber shot the teller. Another man looked straight at him, and the robber shot him too. The robber yelled, "Anybody else here see my face?" Ole looked down at the floor and said, "Well, I think my wife Lena got a pretty good look at you."

Ole was marooned on a desert island for thirty years. When a rescue boat finally arrived, he was showing the crew all the things he had built such as living quarters, barns, and stables. When he came to a small structure with a steeple, he said, "This is my church." They asked, "If this is your church, then what's that building with the steeple over there?" He said, "Oh, that's the church I used to go to."

Ole comes home with Sven and as they walk through the house they notice Lena is in the living room making love to another man. They continue on into the kitchen, and Ole pulls out two beers from the fridge and says, "Here's one for you and one for me." Sven asks, "But what about the guy in the living room?" Ole says, "He can get his own beer."

Ole had a cow that when he reached down to milk her, she let out a fart. He told Sven and Sven sat down to milk the cow and the moment he pulled on the cow's teat, she let out a big fart. He said, "Your cow come from North Dakota?" "What makes you say that" said Ole. "Because my wife does the same thing."

Why did Ole sell his water skis?
    He couldn't find a lake with a hill in it.

Ole and Lena were at the drive-in movie. Ole says, "Say Lena, you wanna get in the back seat?"
    Lena says, "Naw, Ole, I'd just as soon stay up here with you."

Ole and Lena walked into a fancy grocery store. "Will you look at that Ole—they got these green fuzzy potatoes."

"Those aren't potatoes, Lena. Those are kiwis—what they use to make the shoe polish."

Sven and Ole were out hunting when there was a terrible accident. Sven accidentally shot Ole. Sven was horrified. He ran to his friend crying, "Ole, Ole, I'll save you. Hang on until I can get you to the hospital."

In the emergency room Sven said, "Doctor, Doctor, is Ole going to live?"

The doctor said, "To tell you the truth, he'd have a better chance if you hadn't gutted him."

Ole got a job as a diesel fitter.

Is that right?

Ja, every day he went to the ladies' lingerie department and looked over the underwear until he found something nice and he said, "Yeah, diesel fitter."

Nurse: Do you want the urinal, Ole?

Ole: No, I yust finished reading da *Tribune*.

Three dead bodies turn up at the mortuary, all with smiles on their faces. The coroner calls the police to tell them what happened.

"First body: Frenchman, 80, died making love to his mistress. Second body: Scotsman, 25, won a thousand pounds in the lottery, spent it all on whiskey, died of alcohol poisoning. Third body: Sven, Norwegian from Minnesota, struck by lightning."

"So why the smile?" the inspector asked.

"He thought he was having his picture taken."

Ole was the only Lutheran in his little town of all Catholics. That was okay, but the neighbors had a problem with his barbecuing venison every Friday. Since they couldn't eat meat on Friday, the tempting aroma was getting the best of them. So the neighbors got together and went over and persuaded Ole to join their church. The big day came and the priest had Ole kneel. He put his hand on Ole's head and said, "Ole, you were born a Lutheran, you were raised a Lutheran, and now," he said as he sprinkled some incense over Ole's head, "now you are a Catholic!"

Ole was happy and the neighbors were happy. But the following Friday evening at suppertime, there was again that aroma coming from Ole's yard. The neighbors went to talk to him and as they approached the fence, they heard Ole saying: "You were born a whitetail deer, you were raised a whitetail, and now," he said with a sprinkle of seasoning, "now you are a walleye!"

Ole took a flight from Minneapolis to Seattle, and when the plane landed, he said, "Vell, dere goes five dollars down da drain for dat flight insurance!"

Ole was stopped by a game warden in northern Minnesota leaving a lake well known for its walleye. He had two buckets of fish. Since it was during the spawning season, the game warden asked, "Do you have a license to catch those fish?"

Ole replied, "No, sir! Dese here are my pet fish. Every night I take dese fish here down to da lake and let dem svim around for a while. Den I vhistle and dey yump back into dere buckets and I take dem home."

"That's a bunch of hooey," said the game warden. "Fish can't do that."

Ole said, "Vell, den, I'll just show you." Ole poured the fish into the lake and stood waiting.

After several minutes, the game warden turned to Ole and said, "Well?"

"Vell vhat?" responded Ole.

"When are you going to call them back?"

"Call who back?" asked Ole.

"The fish!"

"What fish?"

Ole was upstairs dying and he felt terrible and then he smelled the lefse baking in the kitchen and he thought, Oh that sweet Lena, she's fixing me lefse, and he went downstairs and took a piece of lefse and Lena reached over and slapped his hand and said, "You leave that alone. I'm baking that for the funeral!"

Lena went to the local newspaper. "I want to put a notice in the paper: 'Ole died.'"

"That's terrible," said the editor. "But don't you want the full obituary, Lena?"

"No, no," said Lena, "just a notice: two words: 'Ole died.'"

"Fine," said the editor, "but there is a five-word minimum, so you can say three more words. Is there anything else you might want to say?"

Lena said, "Okay. Make it: 'Ole died, Boat for sale.'"

Ole was first dating Lena, and he took her to New Ulm. In the restaurant Ole said, "Hey, Lena, would you like a cocktail before dinner?"

"Oh, no, Ole," said Lena. "What would I tell my Sunday School class?"

After dinner, he said, "Hey, would you like a cigarette?"
"Oh, no, Ole," said Lena. "What would I tell my Sunday School class?"

Ole was driving Lena home when they passed the Romeo Motel. He said, "Hey, Lena, how would you like to stop at that motel with me?"

"Yah, Ole, dot would be nice," said Lena.

Ole asked, "But vat are you going to tell your Sunday School class?"

"The same ting I always tell them. You don't have to smoke and drink to have a good time!"

Ole: I need to buy some boards there, Sven.
    Sven: How long you want 'em, Ole?
    Ole: Long time. I'm building a house, ya know.

Sven asked Ole if he and Lena used anything when they had sex. Ole said, "Ya, for sure, we use Vaseline."

"Vaseline?" said Sven.

"Yeah," Ole said, "Vaseline. We put it on the doorknob to keep the kids out."

Ole and Lena and their little boy Sven go to New York City, and they see amazing things they've never seen before, like elevators. Lena takes Sven into a building and there is an elevator. Lena stood and watched—an old man in a wheelchair rolled up to the elevator and pressed a button. The doors opened, the man rolled in, the doors closed, the lights flashed. Then the doors opened again, and a handsome young man walked out. And Lena turned to Sven and said, "Go get your Pa."

Ole and Sven go on a fishing trip to Canada and come back with only three fish. Sven says, "The way I figger it, Ole, each of them fish cost us $400."

Ole says, "Well, at dat price it's a good ting we didn't catch any more of 'em than we did."

Ole came home from work one day and found Lena sitting on the edge of the bed, naked. He asked her, "Lena, why are you sitting there without any clothes on?"

And Lena said, "I don't have no clothes to wear."

Ole said, "Don't be silly—you got lots of clothes." And he went over to the closet, flung open the door, and said, "Lena, look—here's a blue dress, here's a yellow dress, here's Sven, here's a flowered dress…"

Lena was competing in the Sons of Norway swim meet. She came in last in the hundred-yard breast stroke, and she said to the judges, "Oh say, I don't vant to complain, but I tink those other two girls ver using dere arms!"

Sven and Ole went out duck hunting. They worked at it for a couple hours and finally Sven says, "I wonder why aren't we getting any ducks, Ole?"

"I don't know," says Ole. "I wonder if we're throwing the dog high enough."

Ole was fishing with Sven in a rented boat. They could not catch a thing. Ole said, "Let's go a bit furder downstream." So they did, and they caught many monstrous fish. They had their limit, so they went home. On the way home, Sven said, "I marked da spot right in da middle of da boat, Ole."

"You stupid," said Ole. "How do you know ve vill get da same boat next time!"

Did you hear about Ole's nephew Torvald who won the gold medal at the Olympics?

He had it bronzed.

Ole got a car phone and on his way home on the freeway, he calls up Lena and says, "Oh, Lena, I'm calling you from the freeway on my new car phone."

And Lena says, "Be careful, Ole, because on the radio they say that some nut is driving the wrong way on the freeway."

And Ole says, "One nut—heck, there are hundreds of them!"

Ole is hiking in the mountains of Norway, and he slips on a wet rock and falls over the edge of a 500-foot cliff. He falls twenty feet and grabs hold of a bush that's growing out of a rock. There he is, hanging, looking into this deep fjord down below him—certain death—and his hands start to perspire. He starts to lose his grip on the bush, and he yells out, "Is anybody up there?"

And he hears a deep voice ring out in the fjord, "I'm here, Ole. It's the Lord. Have faith. Let go of that bush and I will save you."

Ole looks down, looks up, and says, "Is anyone else up there?"

Ole: Hello? Funeral home?

Funeral home: Yes?

Ole: My wife, Lena, died.

Funeral home: Oh, I'm sorry to hear that. We'll send someone right away to pick up the body. Where do you live?

Ole: At the end of Eucalyptus Drive.

Funeral home: Can you spell that for me?

Ole: How 'bout if I drag her over to Oak Street and you pick her up dere?

So there was a big snowstorm and a snow emergency was declared. Ole had to park his car on the odd-numbered side of the street. Two days later, more snow, and he had to park it on the even-numbered side of the street. The next day, another snowstorm, another snow emergency, odd-numbered side of the street, and Ole said, "Heck, Lena, I'm tired of this. I'm gonna leave the dang car in the garage and if they want to tow it, let 'em tow it."

Sven and Ole are walking home from the tavern late at night, and they head down the railroad tracks. Sven says, "This is the longest flight of stairs I ever climbed in my life." And Ole says, "Yeah, it's not the stairs that bother me, it's these low railings."

Ole: Sven, how many Swedes does it take to grease a combine?

Sven: I don't know, Ole.

Ole: Only two if you run them through real slow.

Sven and Ole go to the beach. After a couple hours, Sven says, "This ain't no fun. How come the girls ain't friendly to me?"

Ole says, "Well, I tell you, Sven, maybe if you put a potato in your swim trunks that would help."

So Sven does, but he comes back to Ole later, and he says, "I tried what you told me with da potato, but it didn't help."

Ole says, "No, Sven—you're supposed to put da potato in da front."

Sven: So, Ole—I see you got a sign up that says "Boat for Sale." But you don't own a boat. All you got is your old John Deere tractor and your combine.

Ole: Yup, and they're boat for sale.

Ole: Say, I went and bought Lena a piano for her birthday and then about a week later I traded it in for a clarinet, because you know, with a clarinet, you can't sing.

Lena: I'd better warn you, my husband will be home in an hour.

Henrik: But I haven't done anything I shouldn't do.

Lena: I know, but if you're going to, you'd better hurry up.

"Sven, you should be more careful about pulling down your window shades. I saw you and your wife making love last night."

"Ha, the joke's on you, Ole! I wasn't home last night!"

Ole goes to the doctor and says, "Doc, I got two problems. First, I seen on da TV dat guy talkin' about how Vigoro can help your sex life dere. So I been dissolvin' a tablespoon of

Vigoro in half a glass of water an' drinkin' it before bed every night, but so far it ain't done me a bit of good."

And the doctor says, "Ole, that's supposed to be Viagra. Vigoro ain't no medicine. It's just a fertilizer."

And Ole says, "Oh, vell, dat explains da berries, den."

Ole: Well, guess what, Lena. I just bought a condominium.

Lena: Well, that's good, Ole. Now I can throw away my diagram.

The county game warden dies, and Sven and Ole devise a plan that will hopefully land one of them in the position. They flip a coin, and Ole calls it. "You'd be callin' the mayor, Sven," he says.

So Sven calls up the mayor and says, "Mayor, I hear the game warden died last night. If it's all right with you, I'd like to take his place."

The mayor replies, "It's all right with me if it's all right with the undertaker."

Sven and Ole went fishing and the fish were biting pretty good, and while they were reeling in the fish, Sven he fell out of the boat. And Ole he got his fish in the boat and got the hook out and then he dove in for Sven, and he brought him up and laid him in the boat and he give him mouth to mouth. And Ole he thinks, "Pew, that sure was bad coffee Sven drank this morning." And then he looks and he says, "Hey, Sven didn't have a snowmobile suit on when he fell out of the boat. I wonder who this is?"

Lena: Oh, Ole. I'm glad you got home. A burglar broke into the house last night while I was sleeping.
Ole: Did he get anything, Lena?
Lena: He sure did. But only because I thought it was you.

Lena: My two specialties are meatballs and peach pie.
Ole: I see. And which one is this?

Ole: When I die, I want to be buried at sea. Just because Lena keeps saying she's going to dance on my grave.

Sven: Well, that's a lovely family, Ole. Five boys. Looks like you got a boy every single time.
Ole: Oh, no, sometimes we didn't get anything.

Sven: Lena, I hear that Ole's father and mother were first cousins.
Lena: Ya. That's why he looks so much alike.

Sven: Working hard, Ole?
Ole: Nope. I'm fooling the boss. I'm carrying the same load of cement up and down the steps all day.

Ole was visiting the Vatican and went to see the Sistine Chapel. The tour guide told him that it took four years to paint the ceiling. Ole said, "Yeah, I used to have a landlord like that myself."

Ole: Hey, Sven! Lookit here. I just bought a rare antique coin. More than two thousand years old. Look, it says 93 B.C. right on the front of it.

Lena: I'm so proud of my two boys. They became pilots. The other guys haul the cow manure out of the barn, and my boys pile it.

Did you hear about the skeleton they found in Willmar last week?
Yeah, it was the winner of the 1965 Sons of Norway hide-and-seek contest.

One day, Sven and Ole were hunting and suddenly a man came running out of the bushes, yelling, "Don't shoot! Don't shoot! I'm not a deer!" Ole raised his gun and shot him dead.
Sven said, "Ole, why did you shoot that man? He said he wasn't a deer!"
Ole answered, "Oh! I thought he said he was a deer!"

So Ole and Lena were going to take a cruise to celebrate their 50th anniversary, and Lena said, "On the boat, I just want to make love like we did when we were young!"
So Ole went to the drugstore and bought a bottle of pills for seasickness and a box of condoms. And the druggist said, "You know, if it makes you that sick, why do it?"

Sven: So, Ole, I hear that Ole Jr.'s gone to college.
Ole: Yeah, that's right, Sven.
Sven: So what do you think he'll be when he graduates?
Ole: Probably about 35 or 40.

Ole was sitting in a coffeeshop in Hinckley when a man he recognized walked in, so he said, "Hey, Larson! Boy, look at you. When I knew you, you had a headful of hair, and now you're bald and you shaved off your moustache and you're wearing glasses."

The guy replies, "I'm Benny Carlson—"

Ole says, "And you changed your name, too!"

Lena: Ole, how come you're sitting in the living room with no clothes on?

Ole: Well, nobody's going to come visit me so what does it matter?

Lena: But you got your hat on.

Ole: Well, you never know…

Ole is dying. On his deathbed, he looks up and says, "Is my wife here?"

Lena replies, "Yes, Ole, I'm here, next to you."

So Ole asks, "Are my children here?"

"Yes, Daddy, we're all here," say the children.

"Are my other relatives also here?"

And they say, "Yes, we are all here."

Ole says, "Then why is the light on in the kitchen?"

Sven: So, Ole, I see you burnt your ears pretty bad. What happened then?

Ole: Well, I was ironing a shirt, you know, and the telephone rang, and I put the iron to my ear.

Sven: Oh, for dumb. And what about the other?

Ole: Well, then I went to call the doctor…

Ole and Lena were celebrating their twenty-fifth anniversary. After the guests left, Lena looked at Ole and punched him real hard in the shoulder. "That's for twenty-five years of bad sex."

Ole thinks about it and then reaches over and punches Lena hard in the shoulder, "That's for knowing the difference!"

IOWA JOKES

Did you hear about the Iowans who went to the drive-in movie and got rowdy and ripped up the seats?

Did you hear about the Iowa coyote?
He chewed off three legs and was still caught in the trap.

Did you hear what happened to the Iowa ice hockey team?
They drowned during spring training.

The Iowan walks into the hardware store to buy a chainsaw. He says, "I want one that will cut down about ten trees in an hour." So the clerk sells him one.
The next day, the Iowan comes in all upset and says, "Hey, this chainsaw only cut down one little tree in one hour!"
The clerk says, "Gee, let me take a look at it."
He pulls on the starter rope, the saw starts up, and the Iowan says, "What's that noise?"

Why don't they take coffee breaks in Iowa?
It takes too long to retrain them.

What do they call 100 John Deeres circling a McDonald's in Iowa?
Prom night.

The Iowan was asked to use the word "fascinate" in a sentence.
He said, "My sister has a sweater with ten buttons, but her chest is so big she can only fascinate."

How do you know when an Iowan has been using your computer?

There are eraser marks on the screen.

How do you make an Iowan's eyes light up?

Stick a flashlight in his ear.

Did you hear about the Iowan who stayed up all night to see where the sun went?

It finally dawned on him.

The Iowan checks into a hotel for the first time in his life and goes up to his room. Soon he calls the desk and says, "You've given me a room with no exit. How do I leave?"

The desk clerk says, "Sir, that's absurd. Have you looked for the door?"

The Iowan says, "Well, there's one door that leads to the bathroom. There's a second door that goes into the closet. And there's a door I haven't tried, but it has a 'Do Not Disturb' sign on it."

The Minnesota man and the Iowa man have just finished using the men's room and the Iowan stops to wash his hands. He says, "In Iowa, we're brought up to wash our hands after we pee."

The Minnesotan says, "In Minnesota, we're brought up not to pee on our hands."

Did you hear about the Iowa woman who went to the department store to return a scarf?

She claimed that it was too tight.

Why don't Iowans eat pickles?
They can't get their heads in the jar.

The Iowan came to Minneapolis to see the sights and asked the hotel clerk about the time of meals. "Breakfast is served from seven to eleven, dinner from twelve to three, and supper from six to eight," explained the clerk.

"Look here," inquired the Iowan in surprise, "when am I going to get time to see the city?"

Two Iowans were sitting in the doctor's waiting room. One of them was crying. The other Iowan asked, "Why are you crying?"

The first Iowan replied, "I came here for a blood test, and they had to cut my finger."

Upon hearing this, the second one started crying. The first one was astonished and asked the other, "Why are you crying?"

The second Iowan says, "I'm here for a urine test."

Why do Iowans use birth-control pills?
So they'll know what day of the week it is.
And why do they stop using birth-control pills?
Because the pills keep falling out.

Why don't Iowans make Jell-O?
They can't figure out how to get two cups of water into those little bags.

Why can't an Iowan dial 911?
He can't find the eleven.

What about the Iowan who went to the library and checked out a book called *How to Hug*?

He got home and found out it was volume seven of the encyclopedia.

So this Iowan died and went to heaven. St. Peter said, "Before I let you in, you have to pass a test."

"Oh, no!" said the Iowan.

St. Peter said, "Don't worry. This is easy. Just answer this question: Who was God's son?"

The Iowan thought. Finally, she said, "Andy!"

St. Peter said, "Andy?"

The Iowan said, "We sang it in church: 'Andy walks with me, Andy talks with me, Andy tells me I am his own.'"

Why do Iowans hate to make chocolate chip cookies?

It takes too long to peel the M&M's.

On his first day at work, a recent University of Iowa graduate was handed a broom by his new boss and told to sweep the floor. He looked at the boss with disgust and said, "Hey! I'm a graduate of the University of Iowa, you know!"

The manager took the broom back and said, "Really? Sorry about that. Here, let me show you how it's done."

The Iowan walks down the road wearing one shoe. He meets a man from Minnesota who says, "How did you lose your shoe?"

"Didn't lose a shoe. I found one."

MINNESOTA JOKES

Why are most Iowa jokes so short?
So Minnesotans can remember them.

Four retired guys, two from California and two from Arizona, are walking down a street in Phoenix. Then they turn a corner and see a sign that says, "Old Timer's Bar—ALL DRINKS 10 CENTS!" They go in. The old bartender says in a voice that carries across the room, "Come on in and let me pour one for you. What'll it be, Gentlemen?" There seems to be a fully stocked bar, so the four men each asked for a martini. In short order, the bartender serves up four iced martinis and says, "That'll be 10 cents each, please." They can't believe their good luck. They pay the 40 cents, finish their martinis, and order another round. Again, four excellent martinis are produced with the bartender again saying, "That's 40 cents, please." They pay the 40 cents, but their curiosity is more than they can stand. They've each had two martinis and so far they've spent less than a dollar. Finally one of the men couldn't stand it any longer and asks the bartender, "How can you afford to serve martinis as good as these for a dime a piece?" "Here's my story. I'm a retired tailor from Brooklyn, and I always wanted to own a bar. Last year I hit the lottery for $25 million and decided to open this place. Every drink costs a dime—wine, liquor, beer, all the same." "Wow! That's quite a story," says one of the men. The four of them sipped at their martinis and couldn't help but notice three other guys at the end of the bar who didn't have a drink in front of them, and hadn't ordered anything the whole time they were there. One man gestures at the three at the end of the bar without drinks and asks the bartender, "What's with them?" The bartender says, "They're seniors from Minnesota. They're waiting for happy hour."

One day a man finds a magic lamp. He rubs the lamp and the genie pops out. The genie says she can grant the man one wish. The man says he'd like to live forever. The genie says she's sorry she's not authorized to grant that type of wish. The man thinks for a moment and then he says, "Okay, I'd like to live until the Vikings win the Super Bowl."

So the Minnesotans were sent to hell and they really enjoyed it, the warmth and all, so Satan turned the temperature down to forty below, and they were even happier because, if hell froze over, that meant the Vikings won the Super Bowl.

What do you call forty guys watching the Super Bowl on television?
    The Minnesota Vikings.

The Vikings' placekicker tried to commit suicide after they lost to Atlanta.
    He got the rope around his neck, but he couldn't kick the bucket out from under him.

Did you hear that their coach wouldn't let the Vikings eat cereal?
    When they get close to a bowl, they choke.

If a Palestinian and a Minnesotan get married, what do they call their child?
    Yasir Yabetcha.

Guy #1: You know, once it got so cold in Minnesota…
Guy #2: How cold did it get?
Guy #1: So cold, I woke up in the morning and found these little chunks of ice in my bed, and when I warmed them up they went, "ppppppppppppppp!"

What did the Minnesotan say to the Pillsbury Doughboy?
"Hey, man—nice tan."

Where do you find the trees in Minnesota?
Between da twos and da fours.

A boy worked in the produce section of the supermarket. A man came in and asked to buy half a head of lettuce. The boy told him they only sold whole heads of lettuce, but the man was persistent. The boy said he'd go ask his manager what to do.

The boy walked into the back room and said, "There's some jerk out there who wants to buy only half a head of lettuce."

As he finished saying this he turned around to find the man standing right behind him, so he added, "And this gentleman wants to buy the other half."

The manager okayed the deal. Later the manager said to the boy, "You almost got yourself in a lot of trouble earlier, but I must say I was impressed with the way you got yourself out of it. You think on your feet, and we like that around here. Where are you from, son?"

The boy replied, "Minnesota, sir."

"Oh really? Why did you leave Minnesota?" asked the manager.

The boy replied, "They're all just whores and hockey players up there."

"My wife is from Minnesota," the manager said.

The boy replied, "Really!? What team did she play for?"

NORTH DAKOTA JOKES

The Lewis family owned a small farm in Canada, a stone's throw from the North Dakota border. Their land had been the subject of a minor dispute between the United States and Canada for generations. One day, Mrs. Lewis's son came into the kitchen, holding a letter. "I just got some news, Mom," he said. "The government has come to an agreement with the people in Washington. They've decided that our land is really part of the United States. We have the right to approve or disapprove of the agreement. What do you think?" "Hmmmm," his mother said. "Tell them we accept! I don't think I could stand another one of those Canadian winters!"

Two North Dakotans are skydiving. One jumps out of the plane and pulls the cord—nothing happens. So he pulls the emergency cord—still nothing. The other one jumps out of the plane and yells, "Oh! So you wanna race, huh?"

Two North Dakotans go into a bar, and they buy drinks for everybody in the place. They're celebrating and whooping it up, slapping everybody on the back. So the bartender says, "What are you whooping it up for? What's the occasion?"

They say, "We just finished a jigsaw puzzle, and it only took us two months!"

The bartender says, "Two months! What's the big deal? It shouldn't take that long to do a jigsaw puzzle!"

"Oh yeah?" says one of the North Dakotans. "On the box it said two to four years!"

How is a divorce in North Dakota like a hurricane in Florida?

Either way, you lose the trailer.

The train for Chicago leaves at 1:15, the train for Duluth leaves at 1:30, and the train for Fargo leaves when the big hand is on the 9 and the little hand is on the 1.

What is a seven-course meal in North Dakota?

A hamburger and a six-pack.

AND A FEW JOKES BEYOND US

"Are you a pole vaulter?"
"No, I'm Norwegian, and my name isn't Valter."

An Arab prince needed a blood transfusion. He had a very rare blood type, but they found a donor in Glasgow with the same rare type. The prince was so grateful he gave him a BMW and a sack of diamonds. A year later, the prince needed another transfusion. The Scotsman donated his blood, and the prince gave him a pint of whisky and a thank-you note, because now he had Scottish blood in his veins.

"So, how's life in North Korea?"
"Well, I can't complain."

Why do French people eat snails?
    Because they don't like fast food.

Wherever there are four Irishmen, you'll find a fifth.

A couple of Irish guys tried to write a song, but they couldn't get past the first two bars.

What is Irish Alzheimer's?
    You forget everything but the grudges.

What does the show *60 Minutes* and an Irish mother have in common?
    They both begin with tsk-tsk-tsk-tsk.

A Swiss man, looking for directions, pulls up at a bus stop where two Americans are waiting. "Entschuldigung, koennen Sie Deutsch sprechen?" he asks. The two Americans just stare at him. "Excusez-moi, parlez vous Francais?" he tries. The two continue to stare. "Parlare Italiano?" No response. "Hablan ustedes Espanol?" Still nothing. The Swiss guy drives off, extremely disgusted.

The first American turns to the second and says, "Y'know, maybe we should learn a foreign language."

"Why? That guy knew four languages, and it didn't do him any good."

How do you know you're at a redneck wedding?
Everybody is sitting on the same side of the church.

What do you call a Northern Iraqi farmer?
A cheese Kurd.

Paddy was driving down the street in a sweat because he had an important meeting and couldn't find a parking place. Looking up to heaven he said, "Lord, take pity on me. If you find me a parking place I will go to Mass every Sunday for the rest of me life and give up me Irish whiskey." Miraculously, a parking place appeared. Paddy looked up again and said, "Never mind, I found one."

John and Jane, two American tourists, went to Germany for a vacation. As they were walking through a park they noticed a man urinating in public. The woman, disgusted, said, "Gross!" The German man turned to her and replied, "Danke!"

Chinese civilization goes back 4,000 years and Jewish civilization goes back 5,000 years. So what did those people eat for a thousand years?

Why do Irishmen like deep sea diving?
Because deep down, they are quite intelligent.

A wagon train got lost crossing the Plains and they're low on food and they see an old Norwegian sitting under a tree. They stop and ask him, "Is there food around here?" He says, "Well, I don't know, but I tell you, I wouldn't go that way— there's a big bacon tree over that hill." "A bacon tree?" "Yeah, so I wouldn't go that way."

The wagon train talked about it and a bacon tree sounded good to them so they went over the hill and over the next hill and a thousand Indians were waiting for them and attacked them from all sides and took them prisoner except for the leader who went crawling back to the old Norwegian and said, "There was no bacon tree there, just a mob of Indians who took everybody captive."

The Norwegian said, "Vait a minute." He picked up his Norwegian-English dictionary and looked through it, and then said, "Oh, it wasn't a bacon tree. It was a ham bush."

Why do Norwegians wear suspenders?
To keep their shoulders down.

Did you know that in a bowl of Irish bean soup there are exactly 239 beans?
If there were one more bean, it would be too farty.

The Greek and the Italian were arguing about the superiority of their respective cultures. The Greek said, "We built the Acropolis." "Well," the Italian said, "We came up with the Coliseum." The Greek said, "But we invented advanced mathematics." The Italian said, "Yes, but we had the Holy Roman Empire." The Greek then said, "We invented sex," and the Italian said, "Yes, but it was the Italians who introduced it to women."

Where are the Virgin Islands?
Far from the Isle of Man.

The teacher asked the little Mexican kid to make up a sentence with the colors green, yellow, and pink in it. He said "The telephone went green, green. I pinked it up and said, 'yellow.'"

Son: Mama, I have da biggest feet in da third grade. Is dat becoss I'm Norvegian?
Mom: No, it's because you're nineteen.

A Frenchman, a German, and a Jew are lost in the desert, wandering for hours. The Frenchman says, "I'm tired. I'm thirsty. I must have wine."
The German says, "I'm tired. I'm thirsty. I must have beer."
The Jew says, "I'm tired. I'm thirsty. I must have diabetes."

A mine owner advertised for new workers and three guys turned up—an Irishman, an Italian, and a Japanese. The owner tells the Irishman, "You'll be in charge of the mining."

He tells the Italian, "You'll be in charge of the lift." He tells the Japanese, "You'll be in charge of making sure we have supplies." The next day the three men went into the mine, and at the end of the day one man was missing, the Japanese. They searched for him for hours. Just as they were about to give up, he jumped out from behind a rock yelling, "Supplies! Supplies!"

What do you call a Norwegian under a wheelbarrow?
A mechanic.

What's the difference between a Norwegian and a canoe?
A canoe will sometimes tip.

What do you call a Norwegian car?
A Fjord.

Did you hear about the Norwegian who lost fifty dollars on the football game?
Twenty-five on the game, and twenty-five on the instant replay.

Did you hear about the Miss Norway Contest where the winner came in third?

I went into this Cajun/Norwegian restaurant. They served blackened toast.

Did you hear about the Finnish husband who loved his wife so much he almost told her?

A Texan was trying to impress a guy from Boston with an account of the heroism at the Alamo. He says, "I guess you don't have many heroes where you're from?"

The Bostonian replies, "Well, have you ever heard of Paul Revere?"

And the Texan says, "Paul Revere? Isn't he the guy who ran for help?"

How can you tell when you're talking to a Finnish extrovert?
He looks at your shoes.

A Texan, a Russian, and a New Yorker went to a restaurant in London, and the waiter said, "Excuse me, but if you order the steak you might not get one, as there is a shortage." The Texan said, "What's a shortage?" The Russian said, "What's a steak?" The New Yorker said, "What's excuse me?"

A tourist is heading for his car when he sees a guy breaking into his trunk. He yells, "Hey, this is my car!"

The guy says, "Okay, you take the radio and I'll take the tires."

How did the Irish Jig get started?
Too much to drink and not enough restrooms.

The reason New Yorkers are depressed is because the light at the end of the tunnel is New Jersey.

Did you hear about the hurricane that hit New Jersey and inflicted $11 million worth of improvements?

A Norwegian guy likes to go to bed with two women, so
when he falls asleep they can talk to each other. He would
marry a pregnant woman just to save himself the trouble.
He is so repressed, he blushes if someone says "Intersection."
He only thinks about sex when he gets too drunk to go deer
hunting, and then he gets up his courage and goes downtown
and spends the night in a warehouse. Not good at spelling,
or arithmetic. He was trying to count up to twenty-one,
and they arrested him for indecent exposure. He was a
counterfeiter who made two-dollar bills by erasing the zeros
on twenties. And then he won the Norwegian lottery. That's
the one where you get a dollar a year for a million years.
To celebrate, he went to New York City. He called home,
all excited, and said, "I went down these stairs in the street,
down to some guy's basement, and you ought to see the
trains he's got down there."

Late one hot morning, two tourists driving through
Louisiana saw on the map that the next logical stop for
lunch would be at a town called Natchitoches. They
wondered about the pronunciation, one favoring NATCH-
ee-toe-cheese and the other saying it made more sense as
Natch-eye-TOTT-chez. They stopped at a franchise burger
place and went inside; a fresh-faced girl took their order.
One said: "We need somebody local to settle an argument
for us. Could you please pronounce where we are...very
slowly?" The girl leaned over the counter so they could watch
her lips and said as distinctly as she could, "Brrrrrrrr, grrrrrrr,
Kiiiiinngg."

What's the difference between a Yankee Stadium hotdog and a Fenway Park hotdog?

You can buy a Yankee Stadium hotdog in October.

New York is a place where all the girls are looking for husbands and all the husbands are looking for girls.

New York is a place where you spend more than you make, on things you don't need, to impress people you don't like.

New York is where you can get the best cheap meal and the lousiest expensive meal in the country.

In New York, if you don't have a shrink, you gotta be crazy.

The difference between the Upper West Side and the Upper East Side is that on the Upper East Side, the Salvation Army bands have a harp and a string section.

If you live in Green Bay, Wisconsin, how do you keep bears out of your backyard?

Put up goalposts.

Why does the Boston rowing team beat the New York rowing team?

Because the Boston team has one guy yelling, and eight guys rowing.

Why are Yankee fans like laxatives?

Because they irritate the crap out of you.

Rules for driving in New York City:
- Keep to the right on a one-way street.
- Take the first parking space you see. There will not be another.
- Don't get in the way of a car that needs extensive bodywork.
- Always look both ways when running a red light.
- Never signal a lane change. It only gives other drivers a chance to speed up and not let you in.
- Making eye contact revokes your right of way.

An old Irishman was coming home late one night from the pub. As he passed the old graveyard, he thought of all his friends in there, and then he saw a stone beside the road. He thought, "The poor man, buried out here by the highway. And he lived to the ripe old age of 145. A fine man. Let's see, his name was Miles, from Dublin."

When the Irish say that St. Patrick chased the snakes out of Ireland, what they don't tell you is that he was the only one who SAW any snakes!

Did you hear about the Irish attempt on Mount Everest?
    They ran out of scaffolding.

Why don't Italians like Jehovah's Witnesses?
    We don't like any witnesses.

What would you call it when an Italian breaks his arm?
    A speech impediment.

A German tourist was driving 140 miles an hour in his BMW, and the highway patrol pulled him over. The patrolman said, "I'm going to have to search your car."

"Okay, javohl," said the German. The patrolman looked inside the trunk, and there was a piece of raw, bloody meat. When he questioned the German, he said, "Oh ja, that is mine spare veal!"

"Excuse me, Kate, may I come in? I've somethin' to tell ya."

"Of course you can come in, you're always welcome. But where's my husband?"

"That's what I'm here to be tellin' ya, Kate. There was an accident down at the Guinness brewery…"

"Oh, God, no!" cries Kate. "Please don't tell me…"

"I must, Kate. Your husband Patrick is dead and gone. I'm sorry."

Finally, she looked up. "How did it happen?"

"It was terrible, Kate. He fell into a vat of Guinness Stout and drowned."

"Oh, my dear Jesus! But you must tell me true, did he at least go quickly?"

"Well, no, Kate, no. Not really. Fact is, he got out three times to pee."

What do rednecks call duct tape?
Chrome.

You know why it's so hard to solve a redneck's murder?
Because the DNA is all the same, and there are no dental records.

The difference between good ol' boys and rednecks is that good ol' boys may raise livestock, but rednecks get emotionally involved.

The Alabama Highway Patrol turns on the red flashers and pulls the pickup over to the side of the road. The officer walks up to the driver's window and asks, "You got any I.D.?"
"'Bout whut?"

The Alabama football coach walked into the locker room before a game, looked over to his star player, and said, "I'm not supposed to let you play since you're failing math, but we need you in there. So what I have to do is ask you a question, and if you get it right, you can play."
The player agreed, and the coach looked intently into his eyes, and said, "Okay, now concentrate hard and tell me the answer to this. What is two plus two?"
The player thought for a moment and then said, "Four?"
All the other players yelled, "Come on, Coach, give him another chance!"

The University of Alabama football team played Harvard. At a party after the game, an Alabama player approached a girl and asked, "What school do you go to?"
"Yale," the girl replied.
"Okay. WHAT SCHOOL DO YOU GO TO?"

What's the difference between a southern zoo and a northern zoo?
A southern zoo has a description of the animal on the front of the cage, along with a recipe.

They've passed a law in Texas that says a woman has to wait to inherit her husband's estate until she's fourteen.

An Alaskan was on trial in Anchorage. The judge turned to him and asked, "Where were you on the night of October to April?"

A Brit, a Frenchman and a Russian were viewing a painting of Adam and Eve frolicking in the Garden of Eden. The Brit said, "They look so calm. They must be British." The Frenchman said, "Nonsense. They're naked, and so beautiful. Clearly, these are French people." The Russian disagreed, "I don't think so. They have no clothes, no shelter, they have only an apple to eat, and they're being told this is paradise. They are Russian."

A Czech man went to the eye doctor to have his vision checked. The eye chart said: CVKPMWXFCZ. The doctor said, "Can you read that?" The man said, "Can I read it? I dated her once."

When NASA started sending up astronauts, they discovered that ballpoint pens don't work in zero gravity. So they spent twelve million dollars and more than a decade developing a pen that writes under any condition, on almost every surface. The Russians used a pencil.

The difference between comedy and tragedy in Russian drama is that in a tragedy, everybody dies; but in a comedy, they die happy.

An American went to live in the Shetland Islands. He bought a house in the middle of nowhere and lived there for three months and saw no one. One day there was a knock on the door. He opened the door and there was a howling gale outside and there stood a six-foot-four Shetlander with a dirty old sweater and a huge beard and he said, "I'm here to welcome you to the Shetland Islands."

"Hi! It's really nice to see you," the American said.

"I'm here to invite you to a party."

"I've been here for three months on my own, and I haven't seen a soul," said the American. "I'd be delighted to come to a party."

"But I have to warn you, it will be a wild Shetland party," said the Shetlander. "There's going to be drinking."

"Well, I like a little drop of Scotch now and again. I can hold my own with the best of them for drinking," said the American.

"And there's going to be wild Shetland dancing."

"Well, when I was in college, I was considered very light on my feet."

"There's going to be a fight. There's always a fight."

"Well, actually, when I was in the military, I was the unit boxing champion, so I can hold my own."

"And then," said the Shetlander, "there's going to be sex. Wild Shetland sex."

"Well, I've been here for three months, and I haven't seen a soul. A little bit of that wouldn't be out of the question either. So, what should I wear?"

"Just you come as you are. It's just going to be you and me."

SENIOR MOMENTS

For their 10th anniversary, the couple had dinner at the Ocean View restaurant because the wine selection was good. For the 25th, they had dinner at the Ocean View because it was quiet.

For the 50th, they went to the Ocean View because it was wheelchair accessible. And for their 60th anniversary, they went to the Ocean View because they'd never been there before.

A reporter interviewing a 104-year-old woman asked, "What do you think is the best thing about being 104?" She said, "No peer pressure."

The old man died while he was making love with his old wife. They made love every Sunday morning to the rhythm of the church bells, nice and slow, and then that ice cream truck came along.

There is one big advantage in turning 70. You don't get a lot of calls from life insurance salesmen.

An elderly Floridian called 911 on her cell phone to report that her car has been broken into. She was hysterical as she explained her situation to the dispatcher: "They've stolen the stereo, the steering wheel, the brake pedal and even the accelerator!" she cried. The dispatcher said, "Stay calm, ma'am, an officer is on the way." A few minutes later, the officer radioed in. "Disregard," he said. "She got into the back seat by mistake."

The nice thing about Alzheimer's is, you can enjoy the same jokes again and again.

One day, two old folks were playing cards when one looked at the other and said, "Now don't get mad at me. I know we've been friends for a long time...but I just can't think of your name! I've thought and thought, but I can't remember it. Please tell me what your name is."

Her friend glared at her. For at least three minutes she just stared and glared at her. Finally she said, "How soon do you need to know?"

A man in Phoenix calls his son in New York the day before Thanksgiving and says, "I hate to ruin your day, but I have to tell you that your mother and I are divorcing; forty-five years of misery is enough." "Pop, what are you talking about?" the son screams. "We can't stand the sight of each other any longer," the father says. "We're sick of each other, and I'm sick of talking about this, so you call your sister in Chicago and tell her."

Frantic, the son calls his sister, who explodes on the phone. "Like heck they're getting divorced," she shouts, "I'll take care of this." She calls Phoenix immediately, and screams at her father, "You are NOT getting divorced. Don't do a single thing until I get there. I'm calling my brother back, and we'll both be there tomorrow. Until then, don't do a thing, DO YOU HEAR ME?" and hangs up.

The old man hangs up his phone and turns to his wife. "Okay," he says, "they're coming for Thanksgiving and paying their own way."

Old woman: Why, when I was your age, we never thought of doing the things you girls do today.
Young woman: That's why you didn't do them.

My grandfather is hard of hearing. He needs to read lips. I don't mind him reading lips, but he uses a yellow highlighter.

You know they are developing a new wine for older men. It's called Pino More.

What is forty feet long and smells like urine?
Line dancing at the nursing home.

I'm at that stage in life where your options are slim or none. It's like elephants and fleas. I used to be an elephant and now I'm a flea. An elephant can have fleas but a flea can't have elephants.

The old man signed up for a senior aerobics class. He showed up, and twisted, and gyrated and jumped up and down, and sweated and bent and pulled. And by the time he got his shorts on, the hour was over.

Old lady: Anyone who can guess what's in my hand can have sex with me tonight!
Old man: An elephant?
Old lady: Close enough.

Old woman: I found a lump in my breast. Lucky for me it was just my belt buckle.

An undertaker comes up to the elderly widow after the funeral and asks, "How old was your husband?"

"Ninety-eight. Two years older than me."

"So you're ninety-six."

"Hardly worth going home, is it?"

First old man: You want to go for a walk?

Second old man: Isn't it windy?

First old man: No, it's Thursday.

Second old man: Me, too. Let's go get a beer.

Old lady: Do you remember when we were first married and you used to take my hand and kiss me on the cheek and then you'd kind of nibble on my ear?

Old man: You bet. Let me go get my teeth.

Old lady: Do you remember if we ever had mutual orgasm?

Old man: Mutual orgasm? No, we always had Allstate.

Mildred was a ninety-three-year-old woman who was particularly despondent over the recent death of her husband, Earl. She decided to kill herself and join him in death. Thinking that it would be best to get it over with quickly, she took out Earl's old army pistol and made the decision to shoot herself in the heart, since it was so badly broken in the first place. Not wanting to miss this vital organ and become a vegetable and a burden to someone, she called her doctor's office to inquire just exactly where the heart would be. "On a woman," the doctor said, "your heart would be just below your left breast." Later that night, Mildred was admitted to the hospital with a bullet wound to her left knee.

An old man is sitting on a park bench, sobbing, and a young man walks by and asks him what's wrong. The old man says, "I'm married to a beautiful twenty-two-year-old woman."

The young man says, "What's wrong with that?"

And the old man says, "I forgot where I live!"

Why do they give old men in the nursing home Viagra before they go to sleep?

To keep them from rolling out of bed.

It was Mr. Ryan's funeral and the pallbearers were carrying the casket out from the church. When they bumped into a pillar, one of them heard a moan from inside the casket. They opened the casket and found that Mr. Ryan was still alive. God be praised. He lived for ten more years before he finally died. Another funeral was held for him and, as the pallbearers were carrying out the casket, Mrs. Ryan said, "Watch out for that pillar!"

This old guy goes to the doctor for a checkup.

Doctor: You're in great shape for a sixty-year-old.

Guy: Who says I'm sixty years old?

Doctor: You're not sixty? How old are you?

Guy: I turn eighty next month.

Doctor: Gosh, eighty! Do you mind if I ask you at what age your father died?

Guy: Who says my father's dead?

Doctor: He's not dead?

Guy: Nope, he'll be 104 this year.

Doctor: With such a good family medical history your grandfather must have been pretty old when he died.

Guy: Who says my grandfather's dead?

Doctor: He's not dead?!

Guy: Nope, he'll be 129 this year, and he's getting married next week.

Doctor: Gee-whiz! Why at his age would he want to get married?

Guy: Who says he wants to?

An eighty-year-old couple is having problems remembering things, so they go to the doctor to get checked out. They describe for the doctor the problems they are each having with their memory. After checking the couple out, the doctor tells them that they are physically okay, but that they might want to start writing things down to help them remember. The couple thanks the doctor and leaves. Later that night while watching TV, the old man gets up from his chair. His wife asks, "Where are you going?"

He replies, "To the kitchen." She asks him for a bowl of ice cream and he replies, "Sure."

She then asks him, "Don't you think you should write it down so you can remember?"

He says, "No, I can remember that."

"Well," she then says, "I also would like some strawberries on top. You had better write that down 'cause I know you'll forget."

He says, "I can remember that you want a bowl of ice cream with strawberries."

"Well," she replies, "I also would like whipped cream on top. I know you will forget that, so you better write it down."

With irritation in his voice, he says, "I don't need to write that down. I can remember that."

He fumes off into the kitchen. When he returns twenty minutes later he hands her a plate of bacon and eggs. She stares at the plate for a moment and says, "You forgot my toast."

The old lady walks up to the old man at the retirement home and says, "If you drop your pants, I'll bet I can tell your age." So, the man drops his pants, and she says, "You're eighty-three."

"You're right! How could you tell?"

"You told me yesterday."

Sitting on the side of the highway waiting to catch speeding drivers, a state police officer sees a car puttering along at twenty-two miles per hour. He thinks to himself, "This driver is just as dangerous as a speeder!" So he turns on his lights and pulls the driver over. Approaching the car, he notices that there are five old ladies—two in the front seat and three in the back—wide-eyed and white as ghosts.

The driver, confused, says to him, "Officer, I don't understand. I was doing exactly the speed limit! What seems to be the problem?"

"Ma'am," the officer replies, "you weren't speeding, but you should know that driving slower than the speed limit can also be a danger to other drivers."

"Slower than the speed limit? No sir, I was doing the speed limit exactly—twenty-two miles an hour!" the old woman proudly replies.

The officer explains to her that twenty-two was the route number, not the speed limit. A bit embarrassed, the woman grins and thanks the officer for pointing out the error.

"Before I let you go, ma'am, I have to ask: Is everyone in this car okay? These women seem awfully shaken."

"Oh, they'll be all right in a minute, officer. We just got off Route 212."

The old man thought his wife was going deaf, so he came up behind her and said, "Can you hear me, sweetheart?" No reply. He came closer and said it again. No reply. He spoke right into her ear and said, "Can you hear me now, honey?" His wife said, "For the third time, yes."

My grandmother started walking five miles a day when she was sixty.

She's ninety-seven today, and we don't know where the hell she is.

A man is celebrating his ninetieth birthday at the nursing home, and his friends decide to surprise him. They wheel in a big birthday cake and out pops a beautiful young woman who says, "Hi, I can give you some super sex!"

The old man says, "Well, I guess I'll take the soup."

"Grandma, I ate all the peanuts in the candy dish."

"That's okay. Since I lost my dentures, I can only suck the chocolate off them anyway."

"Man, that Mrs. Johnson. I got her husband all laid out in the casket in his black suit and she comes in and says she wants him buried in a blue suit."

"Oh boy."

"She insists that it has to be a blue suit."

"What'd you do?"

"Well, luckily, we got this body shipped out from Chicago and it came dressed in a blue suit."

"So you switched suits?"

"Naw. I just switched heads."

My teeth are gone, my digestion's a mess, my joints ache, but at least my mind is still there, knock on wood. (Knocks) Who's there?

First old man: So, tell me, how does an eighty-two-year-old man like yourself persuade a twenty-one-year-old beauty to be your bride?

Second old man: Easy. I lied about my age. I told her I was ninety-seven.

Celebrity: It's great to be here with you wonderful folks at the nursing home. Does anybody here know who I am? Huh?

Old woman: No, but don't worry. Go down to the front desk and they'll tell you.

Old woman: I can't believe it, doctor. Pregnant? It can't be. I'm seventy years old.

Doctor: I have your husband on the phone, ma'am. I know you'd like him to be the first to know.

Old woman: Gimme that phone—listen to me, you old goat, you've gone and knocked me up!

Old man: And to whom am I speaking?

MEN AND WOMEN

Mrs. Cohen is attending a performance of *The Book of Mormon*, and there is an empty seat next to her. An usher asks her why there's an empty seat and she says, "I bought these tickets for my husband and me, and he passed away." The usher says, "Couldn't you give the ticket to someone else?" She says, "They're all at the funeral."

A man goes to his rabbi and says, "Rabbi, my wife is poisoning me."
The rabbi says, "Let me talk to her."
The next day, the rabbi talks to the man and says, "I spoke to your wife for about four hours. You want my advice? Take the poison."

A little boy asked his mother how people came to exist. So his mother said, "Adam and Eve made babies, then their babies became adults and made their own babies, and so on." The child wanted a second opinion, so he went to his father and asked him the same question. The father sat the boy down and said, "It's like this, son: we were monkeys, and then we evolved over time to become like we are now." The boy went to his mother and said, "You lied to me!" His mother replied, "No, your father was just talking about his side of the family."

A man was an only child and his billionaire father was breathing his last. Since he was a soon-to-be billionaire it only made sense that he should have a woman with whom to share his riches. He approached a beautiful woman. "I may

317

look like a regular guy, but I'm soon going to be a billionaire! Do you want to come home with me?" "Sure thing," she replied. "I would love to come home with you." The next day she became his stepmother.

Marriage is like a deck of cards. In the beginning, all you need is two hearts and a diamond. By the end, you are wishing you had a club and a spade.

"I love you."
"Is that you or the wine talking?"
"It's me, talking to the wine."

"Dad, I just heard that in some countries a groom doesn't know the bride until after he is married."
   "That's true in all countries, son."

What is the recipe for Honeymoon Salad? Lettuce alone without dressing.

Marriage is the process of finding out what kind of man your wife would have preferred.

God gave men a penis and a brain, just not enough blood supply to run both at the same time.

Men don't go through menopause because they're still in adolescence.

What do you get when you cross GPS with PMS? A crazy woman who will find you.

"Honey, I have good news and bad news about the car."
"Give me the good news first."
"The airbags work."

The man approached a very beautiful woman in a large supermarket and asked, "You know, I've lost my wife here in the supermarket. Would you mind talking to me for a couple of minutes?"
"Why?"
"Because every time I talk to a beautiful woman, my wife appears out of nowhere."

"Oh, my goodness, get your clothes on, my husband is driving in the driveway!"
"I gotta get out of here. Where's your back door?"
"We don't have a back door."
"Well, where would you like one?"

1st man: My wife's taking a trip to the Caribbean.
2nd man: Jamaica?
1st man: Not at all. She wanted to go.

Woman: Did you know that women are smarter than men?
Man: No, I didn't.
Woman: See what I mean?

How can a woman rid her apartment of cockroaches?
Ask them for a commitment.

A cop sees two kids parked in a car late Saturday night on the edge of town and he walks over with his flashlight and shines it in the window. The boy is listening to the radio and the girl is knitting a scarf. The cop says, "What are you doing here?" "Just listening to music and she's knitting." "How old are you?" The boy says, "I'm 22." The cop says, "And is she 18?" The boy says, "She will be in about fifteen minutes."

How is a singles bar different from the circus?
   At the circus the clowns don't talk.

Finnegan's wife had been killed in an accident and the police were questioning him about the incident. "Did she say anything before she died?" asked the sergeant. "She spoke without interruption for about forty years," said Finnegan.

A wife was making a breakfast of fried eggs for her husband. Suddenly, her husband burst into the kitchen. "Careful," he said, "CAREFUL! Put in some more butter! Oh my GOD! You're cooking too many at once. TOO MANY! Turn them! TURN THEM NOW! We need more butter. Oh my GOD! WHERE are we going to get MORE BUTTER? They're going to STICK! Careful. CAREFUL! I said be CAREFUL! You NEVER listen to me when you're cooking! Never! Turn them! Hurry up! Are you CRAZY? Have you LOST your mind? Don't forget to salt them. You know you always forget to salt them. Use the salt. USE THE SALT! THE SALT!" The wife stared at him. "What in the world is wrong with you? You think I don't know how to fry a couple of eggs?" The husband calmly replied, "I just wanted to show you what it feels like when I'm driving."

"You married?"

"I am."

"Happily?"

"Yes, of course."

"You and your wife both happy?"

"Sure. Every week we go out to a romantic restaurant, have a candlelight dinner, some wine—she goes on Fridays, I go on Tuesdays."

Marriage is like a three-ring circus—engagement ring, wedding ring, and suffering.

Three men were hiking through a forest when they came upon a large, raging river. Needing to get on the other side, the first man prayed, "God, please give me the strength to cross the river." Poof! God gave him big arms and strong legs and he was able to swim across in about two hours, having almost drowned twice.

After witnessing that, the second man prayed, "God, please give me the strength and the tools to cross the river." Poof! God gave him a rowboat and strong arms and strong legs and he was able to row across in about an hour after almost capsizing once.

Seeing what happened to the first two men, the third man prayed, "God, please give me the strength, the tools and the intelligence to cross this river." Poof! He was turned into a woman. She checked the map, hiked one hundred yards up stream and walked across the bridge.

How do you keep your husband from reading your e-mail?

Put it in a file labeled "Instruction Manual."

A man's wife was in labor with their first child and suddenly she began to shout, "Shouldn't, couldn't, wouldn't, didn't, can't!" He asked the nurse what was wrong with her.

The nurse said, "She's having contractions."

My wife says I spend too much money on beer and liquor, and I tell her that the more I spend on beer and liquor, the better she looks to me, and the more she can save on makeup and hair products.

A man and his wife are sitting in the living room and he says to her, "Just so you know, I never want to live in a vegetative state dependent on some machine. If that ever happens, just pull the plug." His wife gets up and unplugs the TV.

There once were two people of taste
Who were beautiful down to the waist.
So they limited love
To the regions above,
And thus remained perfectly chaste.

How do you know that a dog is man's best friend?

Try this experiment. Lock your dog and your wife in the trunk of your car and drive around for a while. Come back home and open it up, and see which one of them is glad to see you.

A married couple in their late nineties went to a divorce lawyer after seventy years of marriage. They had never got along but they wanted to wait until the children were dead.

322

What do you call the feeling that your husband's computer is better than yours?

PC-ness envy.

A man and his wife were celebrating their sixtieth birthdays and their thirty-fifth wedding anniversary. He opened her gift to him, a green vase, and rubbed it and a genie jumped up and granted him a wish. The man whispered, "I'd like to have a woman twenty years younger than I." So the genie made him eighty.

Why don't cannibals eat divorced women?

Because they're bitter.

"Honey, will you love me when I'm old and overweight?"

"Yes, I do."

Ben invited his mother over for dinner. During the meal, his mother couldn't help noticing how beautiful Ben's roommate was. She had long been suspicious of a relationship between Ben and his roommate and this only made her more curious. Over the course of the evening, while watching the two interact, she started to wonder if there was more between Ben and the roommate than met the eye. Reading his mom's thoughts, Ben volunteered, "I know what you must be thinking, but I assure you, Allison and I are just roommates." About a week later, Allison came to Ben and said, "Ever since your mother came to dinner, I've been unable to find the beautiful silver gravy ladle. You don't suppose she took it, do you?" Ben said, "Well, I doubt it, but I'll e-mail her just to be sure." So he sat down and wrote: "Dear Mother, I'm not saying you 'did' take a gravy ladle from my house, and I'm not saying you 'did not' take a gravy ladle. But the fact remains that one has been missing ever since you were here for dinner."

Several days later, Ben received a response from his mother that read: "Dear Son, I'm not saying that you 'do' sleep with Allison, and I'm not saying that you 'do not' sleep with Allison. But the fact remains that if she were sleeping in her own bed, she would have found the gravy ladle by now. Love, Mom."

A woman was in bed with her husband's best friend when the phone rang. After hanging up, she turned to her lover and said: "That was Jim, but don't worry, he won't be home for a while. He's playing cards with you."

A skinhead and his girlfriend are walking down the street. She sees a ring in a store window and says, "I'd really like that ring." The skinhead says, "No problem." He throws a brick through the window and grabs the ring. A couple blocks later, the girlfriend spots a leather jacket in another store window. The skinhead says, "No problem." He picks up another brick, throws it through the window, grabs the jacket, and they walk on. Later, they pass a Mercedes showroom, and she says, "I would love that car." He says to her, "Do you think I'm made of bricks?"

A man and woman are standing at the altar, about to be married, when the bride-to-be looks at her prospective groom and sees that he has a set of golf clubs with him.

"What on earth are you doing with those golf clubs in church?" she whispered.

He replied, "This isn't going to take all afternoon, is it?"

"Somebody stole my wife's credit card."

"That's terrible."

"Not really. Whoever took it is spending a lot less than she did."

"What do you mean by coming home half-drunk?"

"I ran out of money."

Why are married women heavier than single women?

Single women come home, see what's in the fridge, and go to bed. Married women come home, see what's in bed, and go to the fridge.

Woman's Prayer: Dear Lord, I pray for wisdom, to understand a man; love, to forgive him; and patience, for his moods. Because, Lord, if I pray for strength I'll just beat him to death.

My friend is engaged in a major custody battle. His wife doesn't want him and his mother won't take him back.

Why is psychoanalysis quicker for men than for women?

When it's time to go back to childhood, they're already there.

My husband is on a new diet. He's losing five pounds a week. In a year and a half, I'll be rid of him completely.

"Do you take off your glasses because you think it makes you look better?"

"No, because it makes you look better."

Man: Did you know that women use about 30,000 words a day and a man uses only about 15,000?

Woman: That's because we have to repeat everything.

How many men does it take to open a beer?

None. It should be open by the time she brings it.

What is the difference between men and women?

A woman wants one man to satisfy her every need. A man wants every woman to satisfy his one need.

What's the difference between a dog and a fox?

About eight beers.

"Aren't you wearing that wedding ring on the wrong hand?"

"Yes, I married the wrong man."

"I look in the mirror, and it's so depressing. My face is all wrinkled, my legs are fat, my arms are flabby and my butt is hanging out."

"Well, there's nothing wrong with your eyesight."

Have you heard about the new *Playboy* for married men?

The centerfold is the same every month.

I heard about this new morning-after pill for men. It changes your blood type.

"Swami, tell me: What does the future hold?"
"My child, you must prepare yourself for widowhood. Your husband will die soon."
"Swami, tell me: Will I be acquitted?"

"Grandpa, can you make a noise like a frog?"
"Why would I want to do a thing like that?"
"Well, Grandma says when you croak, we're all going to Hawaii."

Marriage is nature's way of preventing people from fighting with strangers.

What do you call a man who's lost 75 percent of his intelligence?
Divorced.

My wife is such a bad cook that the flies took up a collection to fix the screen door.

My wife is such a bad cook that last week *Gourmet* tried to buy her magazine subscription back.

Why do men like BMWs?
They can spell it.

How many men does it take to change a toilet-paper roll?
Who knows, it's never happened.

What do you call a man with half a brain?
Gifted.

What's the difference between government bonds and men?
Bonds mature.

Why is it so hard for women to find men who are sensitive,
caring, and good looking?
Because those men already have boyfriends.

Why are women's brains cheaper than men's brains?
Because women's are used.

How do you get a man to do sit-ups?
Put the remote control between his toes.

Husband: I haven't spoken to my wife for eighteen
months—I don't like to interrupt her.

Women like silent men; they think we're listening.

"Did you know there are female hormones in beer?"
"Female hormones in beer? Impossible."
"There are. You drink a lot of beer and you get fat, you
talk too much and don't make sense, you cry, and you can't
drive a car."

Waitress: So, what'll it be, mister?
Customer: Tell you what. I want my eggs hard and burned
around the edges, I want my bacon burnt to a crisp, and I
want my toast blackened and hard. I want my coffee bitter,
and when you bring me my food, I want you to yell at me.
Waitress: What, are you crazy?
Customer: No, I'm homesick.

Why are men like blenders?
You need one, but you're not quite sure why.

Do you know why women fake orgasms?
Because men fake foreplay.

"I want to buy a shotgun for my husband."
"Yes ma'am, does he know what gauge he wants?"
"No, he doesn't even know I'm going to shoot him."

I've never understood why women love cats. Cats are independent, they don't listen, they don't come in when you call, they like to stay out all night, and when they do come home they expect to be fed and stroked and then left alone to sleep. Everything that women hate in men, they love in cats.

So, a husband and wife are in bed watching *Who Wants to be a Millionaire?* and the husband says, "Would you like to make love?"
The wife says, "No."
The husband says, "Is that your final answer?"
The wife says, "Yes."
The husband says, "Then I'd like to call a friend."

If a man is in the forest, talking to himself, with no woman around, is he still wrong?

If a woman is in the forest, talking to herself, with no man around, is she still complaining?

One good thing about having a woman for president—we wouldn't have to pay her as much.

What's the fastest way to a man's heart?
Through the chest wall with a sharp knife.

You and your husband don't seem to have an awful lot in common. Why did you get married?
I suppose it was the old business of "opposites attract." He wasn't pregnant and I was.

Scientists have discovered a new food that lowers the female sex drive: wedding cake.

I never knew what real happiness was until I got married—then it was too late.

Why do female black widow spiders kill the males after mating?
To stop the snoring before it starts.

Wife: If I died, would you marry again?
Husband: Yes, I would.
Wife: And would you let her come into my house?
Husband: Yes.
Wife: Would she sleep in my bed?
Husband: Probably, yes.
Wife: Would she use my golf clubs?
Husband: Definitely not.
Wife: Oh, why not?
Husband: Because she's left-handed.

"Did you know that the shortest sentence in the English language is, 'I am'?"

"Really. What's the longest sentence?"

"'I do.'"

"I decided that instead of getting married I'd just buy a dog."

"Why?"

"Because after the first year, a dog is still excited to see you."

Very few things upset my wife and it makes me feel special to be one of them.

Men pass gas more often than women because women never close their mouths long enough to let the pressure build up.

A woman comes home shouting, "Honey, pack your bags! I won the lottery!"

The husband exclaims, "Wow! That's great! Should I pack for the ocean, or for the mountains, or what?"

And she says, "I don't care. Just get the hell out."

Why were men given larger brains than dogs?

So they won't hump your leg at a cocktail party.

A man exercises by sucking his stomach in every time he sees a beautiful woman.

A young lady came home from a date looking sad. She told her mother, "Jeff proposed to me an hour ago."

"Then why are you so sad?" her mother asked.

"Because he also told me he was an atheist. Mom, he doesn't even believe there's a hell!"

Her mother replied, "Marry him anyway. Between the two of us, we'll show him how wrong he is."

A man walked into a supermarket and bought a loaf of bread, a pint of milk, and a frozen dinner for one. The woman at the checkout said, "You're single, aren't you?"

The man said, "Yeah, how did you guess?"

She said, "Because you're ugly."

Wife: Let's go out and have some fun tonight.

Husband: Okay, but if you get home before I do, leave the hall light on.

Why did God make man before woman?

You need a rough draft before you make the final copy.

Son: Dad! I got a part in the school play! I play the husband.

Dad: Too bad they didn't give you a speaking role.

A wife wakes up in the middle of the night and finds her husband sitting on the bed crying. She asks, "What's wrong?"

He says, "Remember when your daddy caught us in your room when you were sixteen and told me I'd have to marry you or he was gonna send me to jail for thirty years?"

She says, "Yeah, but why are you thinking about that?"

He says, "I'd be a free man today."

After twelve years in prison, a man finally escapes. When he gets home, filthy and exhausted, his wife says, "Where have you been? You escaped eight hours ago!"

Man: Hey. Nice earring. How long have you been wearing an earring?
Second man: Ever since my wife found it in the car.

A man took his wife to the livestock show and they looked at the champion breeding bulls. The wife said, "Look here. It says that this bull mated over 150 times last year. Isn't that something!"
And the husband replied, "Yes, but it wasn't all with the same cow."

And God created woman. And she was good. She had two arms, two legs, and three breasts. And God asked woman what she would like to have changed about herself, and she asked for her middle breast to be removed. And it was good. She stood with her third breast in her hand and asked God what should be done with the useless boob. And God created man.

A woman was going through her husband's desk drawer and discovered three soybeans in an envelope containing thirty dollars in cash. So she asked him about it.
And the husband said, "Well, I have to confess. Over the years, I haven't been completely faithful to you. But every time I cheated, I put a soybean in the drawer to remind myself."
"So where did the thirty dollars come from?" she asked.

"Well, when soybeans hit ten dollars a bushel, I decided to sell."

"Honey, would you like a BMW for your birthday?"
"No, I don't think so."
"How about a mink coat?"
"No, thanks."
"How about a diamond necklace?"
"No. I want a divorce."
"Oh. I wasn't planning on spending that much."

"Ma'am, I think your husband has had enough to drink. He just slid under the table."
"No, my husband just walked in the door."

Dying man: You know, honey, you've always been with me through all my troubles. Through all my bad times, you've been there. When I got fired, you were there. When my business went down the toilet, you were there. When I had the heart attack, you were there, and when we lost the house, and then when I got liver cancer, you were always by my side. You know something?
Woman: What?
Dying man: I think you're bad luck.

A man's idea of planning for the future means that he buys two cases of beer instead of one.

Sex is hereditary. If your parents didn't have it, chances are you won't either.

Wife: Do you love me?

Husband: Of course I love you. If I didn't love you, we wouldn't have all this damn furniture. I mean, maybe there's no chemistry left between us, but there's still archaeology.

My wife has been great. In just three years of marriage, she's gotten me to stop drinking and stop smoking, taught me how to dress well, how to enjoy music and painting and fine literature, how to cook gourmet meals, and how to have confidence in myself. So I'm getting a divorce. Frankly, she just isn't good enough for me.

A woman sends her husband out to buy some escargot for a dinner party that night. Instead of going straight to the store, the husband decides to stop at the local bar. He has a few beers, and then some more, and pretty soon he looks at his watch and finds he's over an hour late for the dinner party. He dashes to the store, picks up the escargot, and frantically drives home. When he walks in the door he can hear his wife coming from the kitchen. So he takes the bag of snails and quickly throws them all over the floor. When his wife walks into the room, he says, "Come on, guys, we're almost there!"

Why did Dorothy get lost in Oz?

She had three men giving her directions.

"Mr. Johnson, I have reviewed this case carefully and I've decided to give your wife $800 a week alimony."

"That's very generous, your honor. And believe me, I'll try to help out a little myself now and then."

"Honey, am I the first man you ever made love with?"
"Why does everyone ask me that?"

How do girls get minks?
The same way minks get minks.

Men are like fine wine. They all start out like grapes, and it's our job to stomp on them and keep them in the dark until they mature into something we'd like to have dinner with.

Why do women have smaller feet than men?
So they can stand closer to the sink.

The most difficult thing for a man after a divorce is learning how to express himself.

"Can I have your number?"
"It's in the phone book."
"But I don't even know your name."
"That's in the phone book, too."

I wanted to be a flight attendant because it's a chance to meet men. When they're strapped down.

"What would you do if you caught another woman with your husband?"
"Well, I guess I'd break her cane and send her back to whatever institution she escaped from."

Wife: You know, that young couple next door are so sweet. Every morning, when he leaves the house, he kisses her

goodbye, and every evening when he comes homes, he brings her a dozen roses. Now, why can't you do that?
Husband: I don't even know her.

"Hey, gorgeous, where have you been all my life?"
"For most of it, I wasn't born yet."

"Your body is like a temple."
"Sorry, no services today."

"I would go to the end of the world for you."
"Yes, but would you stay there?"

"I want you to be the mother of my children."
"How many you got?"

Man: I have a magic watch that tells me you aren't wearing any underwear.
Woman: But I am wearing underwear.
Man: Well, it's about an hour fast. So how do you like your eggs in the morning?
Woman: Unfertilized.

Old man: So how was your date with Edgar last night?
Old woman: Well, I had to slap his face.
Old man: He tried to go too far?
Old woman: No, I thought he was dead.

The CIA was accepting applications for an assassin. They narrowed the finalists to two men and one woman, and they gave them the final test. They gave each of them a gun and brought the first man in and pointed to the big wooden door and said, "Right in there is your wife. Go in and kill her." The man dropped the gun. He said, "I can't do it."

They brought in the second man and said, "Your wife is behind that door. Go kill her." The second man walked to the door and put his hand on the knob but he couldn't do it either.

Finally, they brought in the woman and told her, "Behind that door is your husband. Go and kill him." So she went through the door and they heard the gun start firing, one shot after another for thirteen shots. Then they heard screaming, crashing, and banging on the walls. Then everything was quiet. The door opened slowly, and the woman came out, wiping the sweat from her brow, and she said, "Some idiot loaded the gun with blanks. So I had to strangle him."

Priest: I'm so sorry to hear of Jim's passing, Mary. My deepest condolences.
    Widow: Oh thank you, Father.
    Priest: It's a hard time.
    Widow: Yes, Father. It is.
    Priest: And did he have any last requests?
    Widow: Yes, Father. He did.
    Priest: And what was his last request, Mary?
    Widow: Well, he asked me to please put the gun down.

Three gents in a bar are discussing a female acquaintance who is trying without success to have a family. The first says, "I believe she is impregnable."

The second says, "I think she is inconceivable."

The third disagrees, saying, "You're both off the mark. She is obviously unbearable."

"Honey, something's always bugged me about the children. I can't help noticing that out of our eight kids, Ben looks different from all the others. I know it's a terrible thing to ask, but does he have a different father?"
"Yes, it's true. He does."
"Please tell me. Who is Ben's father?"
"You."

I almost fell in love with a psychic but she left me before we met.

"I saw two houseflies in the kitchen today. Both females."
"How did you know they were females?"
"They were on the phone."

Wife: If you had to do it all over again, would you still marry me?
Husband: I guess so. If I had to.

Husband: Before I die, darling, I have to confess something to you.
Wife: I know all about it, darling. That's why I poisoned you.

Why does an archeologist make a good husband?
Because the older you get, the more interested he is in you.

The wife smacks her husband upside the head. He says, "Hey! What was that for?"

"That's for the piece of paper in your pants pocket with the name Marylou on it."

He explains, "That's from two weeks ago. I went to the races, and Marylou was the name of one of the horses I bet on."

She hits him again. He says, "Now what was that for?"

"Your horse called on the phone today."

The secret of our marriage is that my wife worries about the little things, like what we should spend money on and what we should do on weekends, and I worry about the big things, like…energy policy and…Canada and…NATO.

My wife came home the other night and told me to take off her blouse. Then she told me to take off her skirt. Then she told me never to wear her clothes again.

My husband gives himself bubble baths by eating beans for dinner.

The only thing I have in common with my husband is that we were married on the same day.

A man and his wife weren't speaking to each other and one night the man left a note for her saying, "Please wake me at 5:00 a.m. I have to be at work for an early meeting." The next morning the man woke up at 9:00 a.m., and noticed a piece of paper by his pillow. It said, "This is your 5:00 a.m. wake up."

PICK-UP LINES, RESPONSORIAL

Man: Haven't I seen you someplace before?
Woman: Yes, that's why I don't go there anymore.

Man: Can I buy you a drink?
Woman: I think I'd rather have the money!

Man: Will you go out with me this Saturday?
Woman: Sorry, I'm having a headache this weekend.

Man: So what do you do for a living?
Woman: I'm a female impersonator.

BLONDE JOKES

So a blonde texts her husband on a cold winter's morning: "Windows frozen, won't open." Husband texts back: "Gently pour some lukewarm water over it." Wife texts back five minutes later: "Computer is really screwed up now."

What did the blonde name her zebra? Spot.

Why can't blondes be cattle ranchers? They can't keep their calves together.

A blonde walks into a shoe store to try on a pair of shoes. After trying on a pair she complained that they were a bit tight. The sales clerk says, "Try pulling the tongue out." "Nath theyth sthill feelth a bith tighth."

Last year I replaced all the windows in my house with that expensive double-paned energy-efficient kind. Today I got a call from the contractor who installed them. He was complaining that the work had been completed a whole year ago, and I still hadn't paid for them. Hello! Just because I'm blonde doesn't mean I'm stupid. His salesman told me last year. These windows would pay for themselves in a year. Hello! It's been a year."

A blonde went in the store to buy pink curtains for her computer monitor. The salesman said, "But computers don't need curtains!" She said, "Helllloooooooooo! I've got Windows!"

Blonde: I'm having a problem with my computer. When I type in my password, all it shows are those little stars.
Computer Tech: Right. Little asterisks. That's for your protection. So if someone were standing behind you, they couldn't see what your password is.
Blonde: Okay, but they show up even when nobody is standing behind me.

The blonde got a present from her boyfriend, a cell phone, and the next day, while she was shopping, the phone rang and it was him. He said, "How do you like your new cell phone?" She said, "I just love it. It fits in my purse, and your voice is so clear. But how did you know I was at Walmart?"

A car was driving down the street when suddenly it started swerving. A police officer pulled the car over. A blonde rolls down the window and says, "Officer, I'm so glad you are here. I saw a tree in the road, and then I saw another. So I had to swerve to keep from hitting it!" The officer looks at her, and then says, "Ma'am, that's your air freshener."

What is it called when a blonde blows in another blonde's ear?
Data transfer.

A blonde, a brunette and a redhead escaped from prison. The cops were chasing them when they stopped at a dock. On the dock were three gunnysacks. The redhead said they should get in them to hide, and they did. A cop kicked the one with the redhead in it, and she said, "Ruff, ruff, ruff!" The cop says, "It's only a dog." Then he kicked the one with the brunette in it and she said, "Meow, meow, meow!" The cop said, "It's only a cat." Then he kicked the one with the blonde in it, and she said, "Potatoes, potatoes, potatoes!"

One day, a blonde girl was running out to check her mail and a neighbor was watching. Five minutes later, she checked it again. This happened all through the day until the neighbor went outside and stopped her and asked her why she kept looking in her mail box and her reply was: "My computer keeps telling me I have mail!"

Once there was a blonde cowboy walking naked down the Main Street of Dodge. The sheriff said, "What happened, Blonde Cowboy?" The blonde cowboy said, "Well, I was with this cheap floozy and she took off her clothes and I took off my clothes and she said, 'Now go to town cowboy...' So here I am."

What did Paris Hilton say when someone blew in her bra?
Thanks for the refill.

How do you make Paris Hilton laugh on Saturday?
Tell her a joke on Wednesday.

How did Paris Hilton try to kill a bird?
She threw it off a cliff.

Paris Hilton took her Jaguar to the garage because it was running rough. The mechanic looked under the hood and then he said, "Just crap in the carburetor." Paris said, "How often do I have to do that?"

What do you see when you look into Paris Hilton's eyes?
   The inside of the back of her head.

Why did Paris Hilton cross the road?
   I don't know.
   Neither does she.

Why did Paris Hilton climb over the chain-link fence?
   To see what was on the other side.

Paris Hilton is walking down the street with a pig under her arm. Somebody asked, "Where did you get that?" The pig says, "I won her in a raffle!"

Paris Hilton orders a pizza and the clerk asks if he should cut it in six or twelve pieces. Paris says, "Six. I could never eat twelve pieces."

The blonde got pregnant and had a maternity test to make sure it was hers.

Did you hear that a piece of gum once chewed by Jessica Simpson is up for bid on eBay? Now that she doesn't have anything to chew, she will be able to walk again.

Why did the blonde have square boobs?
   She forgot to take the tissues out of the box.

How are blondes like cowpies?
   The older they get, the easier they are to pick up.

Why does a blonde nurse always carry a red pen?
To draw blood.

Why do blondes need transparent lunchboxes?
So they can tell if they're coming home or going to work.

Why does it take blondes so long to drive to Florida?
Every time they see a sign that says, "clean restrooms," they stop and do it.

The blonde was so proud because she finished a puzzle in 52 days that was labeled "2 to 3 years."

A blonde is bragging about her knowledge of state capitals. She proudly says, "Go ahead, ask me. I know all of them."
A friend says, "O.K., Wisconsin?"
The blonde replies, "Oh, that's easy, W."

How do you sink a submarine full of blondes?
Knock on the hatch.

A blonde arrived at the emergency room with her finger all mangled. The ER doctor asked her how it happened.
"Well," she said, "I wanted to commit suicide so I took a gun and I put it to my chest and then I thought, I don't want to ruin that $10,000 breast-enhancement surgery! So I put the gun in my mouth and I thought, I don't want to ruin the $12,000 of dental work that gave me this beautiful smile! So I decided to stick the gun in my ear. Then I thought, you know, this is going to be really loud."

Employer: I see you left some blanks on your job application, ma'am. Hair color. I see you're a blonde.
Blonde: Oh. Right.
Employer: How old are you?
Blonde: (counting quickly under her breath) 22.
Employer: What is your name?
Blonde: (under her breath) Happy birthday to you, happy birthday to you, happy birthday dear—Mandy!

The blonde looked at the other blonde who was wearing a nametag and she said, "'Debbie'—that's cute. What did you name the other one?"

Why do so many blondes move to L.A.?
It's easy to spell.

How do you keep a blonde occupied for hours?
Write "Please turn over" on both sides of a piece of paper.

Why don't blondes breastfeed?
Because it's so painful to boil your nipples.

A blonde walks into the hair salon with a pair of headphones on. The stylist asks her to take them off for the haircut, so she does, and a moment later she faints. The stylist picks up the headphones and there's a little voice saying, "Breathe in…breathe out…in…out…in."

A blonde walks down the street and sees a banana peel ahead, and she says: "Here we go again."

347

A blonde decided to kidnap a kid so she went to the playground, grabbed a kid, and wrote a note saying, "I've kidnapped your kid. Tomorrow morning, put $10,000 in a paper bag and put it under the tree next to the slide on the playground. Signed, A Blonde." The blonde pinned the note to the kid's shirt and sent him home.

The next morning the blonde checked, and sure enough, a paper bag was sitting under the tree. The blonde opened up the bag and found the $10,000 with a note that said, "How could you do this to a fellow blonde?"

A blonde wanted to buy personalized license plates but she couldn't afford them. So she changed her name to JKM345.

A blonde and her father are walking down a street when the father says, "Look, a dead bird."

And the blonde looks up and says, "Where?"

Did you hear about the blonde couple who were found frozen to death in their car at a drive-in movie theater?

They went to see "Closed for the Winter."

JOKES FROM THE NEWS

TURN-OF-THE-CENTURY EDITION

Martha Stewart has a new recipe for tuna casserole that serves six to eight.

Martha Stewart has a new recipe for chicken casserole. You boil the chicken and dump the stock.

There was a pro–Martha Stewart rally. Only four people showed up, and three of them were made out of crepe paper.

Martha Stewart says each spice has its secret. The key to thyme is how it is served.

Kobe Bryant's teammates don't believe the stories about him because he's never made a pass before.

They gave Kobe a vocabulary test and he thinks harass is two words.

Kobe Bryant added an "O" to his bracelet so now it stands for "What Would O.J. Do?"

The police pulled Janet Jackson over because her right headlight was out.

Victoria's Secret is having a Janet Jackson sale. Bras are half off.

The problem with CEOs is that the 90 percent who are crooked give the rest a bad name.

The convicts were in the exercise yard at the federal prison in Danbury and one of them said, "You know, this is the first time that our entire board of directors has been together at one time."

What do you call 50,000 geeks playing Monopoly?
    Microsoft.

Communism: You have two cows. You take care of them, but the government takes all the milk.
    Capitalism: You have two cows. You sell one and buy a bull. Your herd multiplies, and the economy grows. You sell them and retire on the income.
    Enron Capitalism: You have two cows. You sell three of them to your brother-in-law, who then sells you all four cows back, which gives you five cows in the annual report which gives you a tax exemption for eight cows. But you're not aware of it at the time.

What's the difference between God and Bill Gates?
    God doesn't think he's Bill Gates.

Bill Gates built a new house for himself and it's great, except that sometimes when you flush the toilet it won't stop. When that happens you need to exit the house, walk around the block, re-enter the house, and usually it's better.

If you see Bill Gates on a bicycle, should you swerve to hit him?

No. It might be your bicycle.

Why should Bill Gates be buried 100 feet deep?

Because deep down, he's a really good man.

After Bill Gates and his wife returned from their honeymoon, she said to him, "Now I know why you named it Microsoft!"

A little boy and a little girl were talking on the playground, and the little boy said, "My daddy's an accountant. What does your daddy do for a living?"

She said, "My daddy's Bill Gates."

"Honest?"

"No, I didn't say that."

You know something? If Bill Gates had a nickel for every time Windows crashed…. Oh wait, he does.

A man gets to make a wish, and he wishes he could wake up in bed with three women. When he wakes up, there are Lorena Bobbitt, Tonya Harding, and Hillary Clinton. And his penis is gone, his leg is broken, and he has no health insurance.

Did you hear about the new pill? It makes you feel good but has the side effect of making you dull. It's called Prosaic.

Did you hear that after she broke her leg, Picabo Street, the Olympic skier, donated money for a very special hospital wing?

It's going to be called the Picabo ICU.

A man and his wife are watching the news about gay marriage. The man says, "Haven't they suffered enough already?"

POLITICAL JOKES

If con is the opposite of pro, is congress the opposite of progress?

What's the difference between democracy and feudalism? In democracy, your vote counts. In feudalism, your Count votes.

The candidate was giving a speech at the Indian reservation, and he thought it was going well. Every so often, the Indians would all yell, "OONGAH, OONGAH." Just as the candidate came down off the podium, the tribal representative said, "Thanks for coming—oh, and as you walk to your car, be careful not to step in the oongah."

Why do we call it politics?
    Because poly means many and ticks mean blood-sucking parasites.

Philip Morris said today that the tobacco settlement is costing so much money that they may have to lay off two Republican senators.

They finally drafted a constitution for Iraq. We should've given them ours. We're not using it anymore.

Why do Republicans wear earmuffs? To avoid the draft.

There's a Republican dating service, but it's not working that great.
    Neither date wants to pay.

The real reason you can't have the Ten Commandments in a courthouse is that you cannot post "Thou Shalt Not Steal," "Thou Shalt Not Commit Adultery" and "Thou Shall Not Lie" in a building full of politicians. It creates a hostile work environment.

A cannibal was walking through the jungle and came upon a restaurant opened by a fellow cannibal. Feeling somewhat hungry, he sat down and looked over the menu: Broiled Missionary $10—Fried Explorer $15—Baked Politician $100. The cannibal called the waiter over and asked, "Why such a price difference for the politician?" The waiter replied, "Have you ever tried to clean one?"

I'm tired of hearing critics say that Democrats don't stand for anything. That's really unfair. They DO stand for anything.

So the Republican was riding in his limousine when he saw all these poor people on their hands and knees eating grass by the roadside. He stopped and asked them why they were eating grass and they said, "Because we don't have any money for food."

He said, "Well, come along with me then. I'll take care of you. The grass at my house is almost half a foot high."

A man goes into a shop to buy a car radio, and the salesman says, "This is the latest model. It's a voice-activated car radio. You just tell it what you want to listen to and the station changes. No need to take your hands off the wheel."

So the man has it installed and takes off down the road. He says, "Classical!" and a public radio station comes on with a Mozart symphony. Then he says, "Country!" and a Garth Brooks song comes on, and he listens to that. Then a guy drives by really fast and cuts in front of him, so he yells, "Stupid!" and the radio changes to Rush Limbaugh.

Republicans and Democrats have a lot in common.
Republicans wear $1,000 suits, and Democrats drive $1,000 cars.

Once upon a time, there were six little kittens, all of them Democrats. They were born Republican but then their eyes opened.

"My father was a Democrat and my grandfather was a Democrat and that's why I'm a Democrat."
"Well, that's no argument at all. If your father was a swindler and your grandfather was a swindler, would that make you a swindler also?"
"No, that would make me a Republican."

THE BILL CLINTON YEARS

They took a poll of American women, and they asked, "Would you have an affair with Bill Clinton?"
Seventy percent said, "Never again!"

They had a Presidents' Day Sale at Macy's—all men's pants were half off.

The Pope met with President Clinton. The good news was that they agreed on 80 percent of what they discussed.

The bad news was that they were discussing the Ten Commandments.

You know why Bill Clinton is so reluctant to deal with this young Cuban boy in Miami?

It's because the last time he decided where to put a Cuban he was impeached.

President Clinton looks up from his desk in the Oval Office to see one of his aides nervously approaching him. "What is it?" the president asks.

"It's the abortion bill, Mr. President. What do you want to do about it?" the aide asks.

"Just go ahead and pay it," responds the president.

We always knew you could get AIDS from sex, and now President Clinton has shown us you can get sex from aides.

Bill Clinton liked Monica Lewinsky's dress from the first time he spotted it.

Why did Monica Lewinsky have sex with the president in the Oval Office?

Because she didn't have $50,000 for the Lincoln Bedroom.

Monica walks into her dry cleaning store and says to the clerk, who is hard of hearing, "I've got another dress for you to clean." The clerk replies, "I'm sorry, come again?" "No," says Monica. "This time it's mustard."

He never told Monica Lewinsky to lie. He told her to lie down.

"Run Hillary Run!" bumper stickers are selling like hotcakes in New York.

Democrats put them on their rear bumpers; Republicans put them on the front.

Dan Quayle, Newt Gingrich, and Bill Clinton went to the Emerald City to see the Wizard of Oz. And Dan Quayle says, "I'm going to ask the wizard for a brain."

And Newt Gingrich says, "I'm going to ask him for a heart."

And Clinton says, "I wonder where Dorothy is?"

What do you call it when the vice president plays the drums?

Algorithm.

THE GEORGE W. BUSH YEARS

What's the difference between George W. Bush, Bill Clinton and Jane Fonda?

Jane Fonda went to Vietnam.

President Bush was sitting in the Oval Office when a young man walked in the door and said, "Hey, you turkey."

The president said, "Do you know who I am? I'm the president of the United States. You can't say that to me."

The young man said, "Do you know who I am?"

The president said, "No."

The young man said, "Good."

What's the difference between the Vietnam War and the Iraq War?

George W. Bush had a plan to get out of the Vietnam War.

A woman driving down the freeway in an SUV got so mad at the man in front of her who was driving the speed limit that she pulled up alongside him, honked her horn, screamed obscenities at him, gave him the finger, and waved a pistol. And then the blue lights behind her flashed and the police pulled her over and arrested her and took her to the station, fingerprinted her, and put her in a cell. After a couple hours, the policeman came and apologized. He said, "I'm very sorry. You see, when I saw you do that, I noticed the Bush-Cheney bumper sticker and the 'What Would Jesus Do' bumper sticker and the chrome-plated fish emblem, and I assumed you had stolen the car."

After the Swift Boat Veterans who served with John Kerry in Vietnam claimed that Kerry lied about his heroism, the Democrats wanted to make a similar ad attacking Bush, but they couldn't find anyone who served with him.

John Kerry was running behind, but thanks to the fact that he's married to Teresa Heinz, he was able to ketchup.

What were George W. Bush's three hardest years?
Second grade.

John Kerry has two problems. People outside the Northeast don't know who he is, and people inside the Northeast do.

The reporter asked Colin Powell, "What proof do you have that Iraq has weapons of mass destruction?"

He replied, "We kept the receipts."

George W. Bush died and went to the pearly gates and met St. Peter, who said, "Welcome to the afterlife. Would you like to go to heaven or to hell?" So Mr. Bush took a look at hell and there was a beautiful country club with an 18-hole golf course and a fine residential neighborhood with lovely lawns and a shopping mall, and then he looked around heaven and found a lot of serious people talking about ethics and mathematics and history and playing their harps and praising God.

"Well," he said, "I never thought I'd say this, but frankly, I'd rather go to hell." So he went and there were people chained to red-hot rocks and screaming. "What happened to the golf course?" said Mr. Bush.

"Oh, that was just campaigning," the Devil said. "Now you've voted for us."

A speechwriter for President Bush felt unappreciated by the president and so when the president came to give his next speech, he looked at the teleprompter and it said:

"Some say that this war against Iraq is all about oil. It isn't, and I'll tell you why."

"Some say that a tax cut will lead to even worse federal deficits. It won't, and I'll tell you why."

"Some say that my policies favor the wealthy over the middle class. They don't, and I'll tell you why."

And then there was a blank space on the teleprompter. And then the words:

"Okay, George, you take it from here."

After the Super Bowl, President Bush called the Patriots to congratulate them on their victory and Al Gore called the Panthers to say he thought they'd been robbed, and Bill Clinton called Janet Jackson.

What do you call someone in the White House who is honest, caring, and well-read?
A tourist.

Mrs. Bush is opposed to same-sex marriage. She's been trying to get George to do something different for years.

There was a contentious staff meeting at the White House about the health of Dick Cheney. When someone mentioned that Cheney had acute angina, Bush angrily interrupted and said, "Men do not have anginas."

George W. Bush in the White House is like a turtle on a post. You know he didn't get there by himself, he doesn't belong there, he can't get anything done while he's up there, and you just want to help him get down.

They're taking out all the K-Marts in Iraq and putting in Targets.

"Surgeon General, what are the results of my brain scan?"
"Mr. President, your brain has a left side and a right side."
"Well, everyone has two sides to their brain, don't they?"
"Yes, but in your brain, on the left side there isn't anything right, and on the right side there isn't anything left."

Pentagon officials now believe they have found Osama bin Laden because he has found a place in which to hide where you can buy your way in, no one will remember you were there, and you have no obligations: the Texas Air National Guard.

They sent the Iowa National Guard out to find bin Laden and they came back with bed linen.

Did you know the U.S. has already converted to the metric system?
We have a half liter in charge of the country.

Three Texas surgeons were boasting about their talent, and the first said, "I reattached all five fingers on a man's right hand and he resumed his career as a concert pianist."
And the second said, "I reattached both arms and both legs to a man who went on to become an Olympic champion."
And the third said, "I operated on a cowboy who had a terrible accident on his horse, and all I had to work with was the horse's rear end and a ten-gallon hat, and right now he's the president of the United States."

I've decided to do some volunteer work. I'm joining the Committee to Re-defeat the President.

The reason America is running low on oil is that most of it is in Alaska and most of the dipsticks are in Washington.

The main thing that separates George H.W. Bush and George W. Bush is eight years of prosperity.

You should always invite two Republicans to a party, because if you invite only one he'll smoke all your pot.

President Bush is really worried about the Iraq situation. It's cost him a lot of sleepless afternoons.

Why do all Iraqi soldiers carry a piece of sandpaper?
   For a map.

How do you play Taliban bingo?
   B-52...F-16...B-1...

Osama bin Laden came to the pearly gates, and there were George Washington, Patrick Henry, James Madison, John Randolph, and Thomas Jefferson, and they picked him up and threw him into hell. And he yelled at the angel and said, "This isn't what I was promised!"
   And the angel said, "I told you there would be Virginians waiting for you. What did you think I said?"

It appears Bush has a new plan for solving the Social Security crisis: Influenza.

Nancy Pelosi is the Speaker of the House. That's the farthest anyone who wears a dress has gotten since J. Edgar Hoover.

In his State of the Union address President Bush said the economy is on the move. It's moving to India.

In 2004, the Center for Disease Control issued a warning about a new form of gonorrhea called gonorrhea lectim.

Nancy Pelosi was visiting Iraq. President Bush said he was against setting any timetables for her to return. He said to bring her back prematurely would send the wrong message.

Thousands of people are expected for the 15th annual Burning Man festival this year in Black Rock Desert north of Reno, Nevada. This is the big hippie festival, where people run around naked, drink and get stoned, or as George W. Bush might think of it, get ready to run for president.

President Bush's State of the Union speech got higher ratings than *American Idol*. Millions of people tuned in thinking they could vote him off.

The states of Texas and Louisiana have decided to build an airport on the border they share. They wanted to honor Tom Delay of Texas and Huey Long of Louisiana, so they're calling it Long Delay International Airport.

What's the difference between "Congress" and the "Library of Congress"? In the Library of Congress you can't mess with the pages.

What is the Iraqi national bird?
  Duck.

Thirty-three percent of the American people think Bush is doing a good job. The same thirty-three percent who think Adam and Eve rode dinosaurs to church. That's what happens when you mix the New Testament with the Old Milwaukee.

George W. Bush walked into Burger King.
"Welcome to Burger King."
"Let's see," he says. "It's tough to decide, but I'm the Decider. I'll have two Whoppers."
"Okay. You're an intellectual genius, and you're the best president we ever had."

Saddam Hussein tells his jailer that he wants to write his memoirs, and he needs a stenographer. The jailer returns with a laptop computer. Saddam says, "I cannot write my own memoirs! I AM A DICTATOR!"

The Nobel committee could have stopped global warming if, instead of giving the prize to Al Gore, they had given it to George W. Bush. Then hell would have frozen over.

Why can't Dick Cheney play hockey?
You know he'd blow the face off.

For years, Democrats have been shooting themselves in the foot. Dick Cheney taught them a lesson: aim higher.

THE BARACK OBAMA YEARS

Did you hear about the new Obama Happy Meal? Order anything you like. The guy behind you has to pay for it.

What's the difference between Obama's dog and the Affordable Care Act?
Obama's dog is fixed.

SPORTING JOKES

How do you keep bacon from curling in the pan? You take away its tiny brooms.

The great Bronco Nagurski retired from the NFL and went back to International Falls and opened up a gas station. Everyone in the Falls went there for gas, because when Bronco put on your gas cap, only Bronco could unscrew your gas cap.

A kid was ice fishing, but wasn't having much luck. He saw a guy across the way who was hauling in a bounty of fish, one after another. So the kid went over to the guy and said, "What are you doing to get all these fish? I'm just a few feet away from you, and I'm not catching anything."
　　The guy answered in a muffled voice, "Ee yer erms orm." The kid didn't understand, and the guy tried to speak again, "Ee yer erms orm." The kid still couldn't understand him, so the guy said, spitting off to the side, "Spfffff…I said: 'Keep your worms warm!'"

A man phones home from his office and tells his wife, "I have a chance of a lifetime to go fishing for a week, but I have to leave right away. So pack my clothes, my fishing equipment, and my blue silk pajamas. I'll be home in about an hour to pick them up." He goes home, grabs everything, and rushes off. He returns a week later and his wife asks if he had a good time. He says, "Oh yes, great! But you forgot to pack my blue pajamas!"
　　His wife smiles and says, "Oh no, I didn't. I put them in your tackle box!"

What do Billy Graham and the Minnesota Vikings have in common?

They both can get 65,000 people on their knees screaming "Jesus Christ!"

A man went out hunting, and he tripped over a log with his rifle cocked. He was survived by his wife, his two children, and one deer.

Two backpackers see a bear about to charge them. One backpacker takes off his hiking boots and puts on running shoes. His companion says, "You'll never outrun the bear—why are you putting those on?"

The guy with the running shoes responds, "I don't have to outrun the bear. I just have to outrun you."

Two guys out hunting find a hole in the woods that's about three feet across but so deep that when they drop a small rock in it, they hear no sound. They drop a bigger rock in it, and still no sound. So they go looking for something larger, and they find a railroad tie. They haul it over to the hole, heave it in, and it disappears without a sound. Then a goat comes running up at about sixty miles an hour and dives head first into the hole. And there's still no sound. Nothing.

Suddenly a farmer appears from the woods and says, "Hey! You fellas seen my goat around here?" And they say, "Well, there was a goat just ran by here real fast and dove into this hole here."

"Naw," says the farmer, "that wasn't my goat—my goat was tied up to a railroad tie."

A guy takes his boy tiger hunting. They're creeping through the weeds and the man says, "Son, this hunt marks your passage into manhood. Do you have any questions?"

And the boy says, "Yes, if the tiger kills you, how do I get home?"

Alaska's Department of Fish and Game is advising hikers, hunters, and fishermen to take extra precautions and be observant. They advise that outdoor enthusiasts wear bells on their clothing and carry pepper spray. They also recommend watching out for fresh signs of bear activity, and learning the difference between black bear and grizzly bear dung: Black bear dung is smaller and contains lots of berries and squirrel fur. Grizzly bear dung has little bells in it and smells like pepper spray.

A woman went on vacation with her husband to a fishing resort. While he was taking a nap, she took the boat out so she could sunbathe. She anchored in the bay, and along came the sheriff in his boat and said, "Ma'am, there's no fishing here. I'm going to have to take you in."

She said, "But officer, I'm not fishing."

"But you have all the equipment, ma'am. I'll have to take you in."

At which point she said, "If you do that, I will charge you with rape."

"But I didn't even touch you," said the sheriff.

"Yes, that's true, but you have all the equipment."

Five doctors went duck hunting one day: a GP, a pediatrician, a psychiatrist, a surgeon, and a pathologist.

After a while a bird came winging overhead. The GP raised his shotgun but didn't shoot because he wasn't sure if it was a duck or not. The pediatrician also raised his gun, but then he wasn't sure if it was a male or female duck, so he didn't shoot. The psychiatrist raised his gun and then thought, "I know that's a duck, but does the duck know it's a duck?" The surgeon was the only one who shot. BOOM! He blew it away. Then he turned to the pathologist and said, "Go see if that was a duck."

First football player: Hey, Tiny. Gimme the answer to that third one on page two. The fill in the blank, Old MacDonald had a what?

Second football player: Farm, you dummy.

First football player: Oh, right. Farm. How do you spell it?

Second football player: E-I-E-I-O.

A huge college freshman decided to try out for the football team. "Can you tackle?" asked the coach.

"Watch this," said the freshman, who proceeded to run smack into a telephone pole, and knocked it completely over.

"Wow," said the coach. "I'm impressed. Can you run?"

"Of course I can run," said the freshman. He was off like a shot, and in just over nine seconds, ran a hundred-yard dash.

"Great!" enthused the coach. "But can you pass a football?"

The freshman hesitated for a few seconds. "Well, sir," he said, "if I can swallow it, I can probably pass it."

A Scotsman went to a baseball game and enjoyed it, but when one batter got a walk and tossed the bat aside and strolled to first base, the Scotsman stood up and yelled, "Rrrrrun, man! Rrrrun!"

The fan next to him said, "He doesn't have to run. He's got four balls."

And the Scotsman yelled, "Walk with pr-r-ride, man! Walk with pr-r-ride!"

Why was the team called a Cinderella team?

They kept running away from the ball.

Our team finished in last place because our batters never got to hit against our pitchers.

Baseball is 90 percent mental. The other half is physical.

A Little League team had just been whipped, and the coach told them, "Boys, don't get down on yourselves. You did your best and you shouldn't take the loss personally. Keep your chins up. Your parents are just as proud of you boys as the parents of the girls' team that beat you."

Stevie Wonder and Tiger Woods were talking and Stevie said, "Tiger, I've been having trouble with my putting."

Tiger said, "You play golf? But you're blind."

Stevie said, "I know, but I just have my caddy put a beeper in the hole and I do pretty well. In fact, I'm usually under par."

Tiger said, "Hey, we should play a round sometime."

Stevie said, "Sure. Anytime. Pick a night."

Our shortstop is having such a terrible season, he tried to kill himself the other day by jumping in front of a bus, but it went right through his legs.

A golfer was sitting in the clubhouse after playing a round. He looked upset, so his friend went over and asked what was wrong. The golfer said, "It was terrible. On the 16th hole I sliced one out onto the freeway and it went through the windshield of a bus, and there was a horrible accident. The bus went out of control and hit a car head-on. There were dead people all over the place."

His friend said, "That's awful. What did you do?"

"Well, I closed up my stance and shortened my backswing a little."

A guy takes a gorilla out golfing. They come up to the first tee, and the gorilla asks, "What am I supposed to do?"

The guy says, "You see that little round green spot about 400 yards from here? You're supposed to hit the ball onto that." So the gorilla hauls off and whacks the ball, and it goes screaming down the fairway and lands on the green. The man drives his ball and it goes about 150 yards, and he hits an iron shot and a second iron shot and finally lands on the green, the gorilla following along behind him.

They come to the green, and the gorilla says, "What do I do now?"

The man says, "Now you hit it into that cup."

The gorilla says, "Why didn't you tell me that back there?"

A young man was playing this hole with a senior citizen. Just as the older man was about ready to hit his tee shot he noticed a funeral procession approaching. He took off his hat, put it over his heart, and stood silently and watched the procession go by until it disappeared.

The younger man said, "That's really nice of you. Do you always do that when a funeral goes by?"

"No," said the senior citizen, "not usually, but I was married to the woman for forty years!"

LAST-BUT-NOT-LEAST JOKES

A donkey had an IQ of 186. He had no friends at all, though. Because even in the animal kingdom, nobody likes a smart-ass.

What does IDK stand for?"
  "I don't know."
  "OMG, nobody does!"

"I'm sorry" and "I apologize" mean the same thing, but you shouldn't say, "I apologize" when you're at a funeral.

Why do Priuses have more accidents than any other cars?
  It's hard to drive while patting yourself on the back.

Did you hear about the ATM with an addiction problem? It suffered from withdrawals.

A star walks into a black hole but doesn't seem perturbed. The black hole says to the star, "I don't think you understand the gravity of this situation."

A teenage boy is getting ready to take his girlfriend to the prom. First he goes to rent a tux, but there's a long line at the tux shop and it takes forever. Next, he has to get some flowers, so he heads over to the florist and there's a huge line there too. He waits forever but eventually gets the flowers. Then he heads out to rent a limo. Unfortunately, there's a large line at the rental office, but he eventually rents a limo. Finally, the day of the prom comes. The two are dancing happily, and his girlfriend is having a great time. When the song is over, she asks him to get her some punch, so he heads over to the punch table and there was no punchline."

Once upon a time there was a prince who, through no fault of his own, was placed under a spell by an evil witch. The curse was that the prince could speak only one word each year. He could, however, save up credits, so if he did not speak at all in one year, he could speak two words the following year.

One day he met a beautiful princess and fell madly in love. He decided to refrain from speaking for two years so that he could look at her and say, "My darling." At the end of the two years, however, he wanted to also tell her he loved her, so he decided to wait three more years, for a total of five years of silence. At the end of the five years, though, he knew he had to ask her to marry him, so he needed to wait still another four years. Finally, as his ninth year of silence ended, he was understandably overjoyed.

He led the princess to the most romantic part of the royal garden, knelt before her, and said, "My darling, I love you. Will you marry me?" The princess replied, "Pardon?"

There are three guys in the waiting room of a hospital. A nurse comes out to the first and says, "Congratulations, you are the father of twins." He says, "What a coincidence. I work for Twin City Federal."

A while later, the nurse comes out to congratulate the second father: "You are the proud father of triplets." "What a coincidence!" says the father. "I work for AAA."

Hearing that, the third expectant father runs out of the waiting room. "Sir, where are you going?" calls out the nurse. He yells over his shoulder, "I work for 10,000 Auto Parts!"

A carpenter fell off the scaffolding at the building site and he was killed. One of the guys on the crew volunteered to go tell the carpenter's wife. He came back two hours later with a six-pack of beer. "Got it from his wife," he said. "When she answered the door, I asked her, 'Are you Steve's widow?' She said, 'No, no, I'm not a widow!' I said, 'I'll bet you a six-pack you ARE!'"

I bought these new boots. They are made from possum and deer hide and they feel great when I wear them. There is just one problem. When I see headlights in the dark, I get this uncontrollable urge to run into the middle of the road and just stand there.

A man with a compulsive winking problem applies for a job as a sales representative for a large firm. The interviewer looks over his application and says, "You're the best qualified candidate but I'm afraid that your constant winking will scare off potential customers."

The man says, "But wait! If I take two aspirin, I'll stop winking!" He reaches into his jacket pocket and pulls out all sorts of condoms: red condoms, blue condoms, ribbed condoms, flavored condoms; finally, a packet of aspirin. He tears it open, swallows the pills, and stops winking.

"Well," said the interviewer, "that's all well and good, but this is a respectable company, and we don't want our employees womanizing all over—what about those condoms?"

"Oh, that. Have you ever walked into a pharmacy, winking, and asked for aspirin?"

A wild rabbit was caught and taken to a National Institutes of Health laboratory. When he arrived, he was befriended by a rabbit that had been born and raised in the lab. One evening the wild rabbit noticed that his cage hadn't been properly closed and decided to make a break for freedom. He invited the lab rabbit to join him. The lab rabbit was unsure, as he had never been outside the lab, but the wild rabbit finally convinced him to give it a try.

Once they were free, the wild rabbit said, "I'll show you the number-three best field," and took the lab rabbit to a field full of lettuce. After they had eaten their fill, the wild rabbit said, "Now I'll show you the number-two best field," and took the lab rabbit to a field full of carrots. After they had had their fill of carrots, the wild rabbit said, "Now I'll show you the number-one best field," and took the lab rabbit to a warren of female bunnies. It was heaven—nonstop lovemaking all night long.

As dawn was beginning to break, the lab rabbit announced that he would have to be getting back to the lab. "Why?" said the wild rabbit. "I've shown you the number-three best field with the lettuce, the number-two best field with the carrots, and the number-one best field with the ladies. Why do you want to go back to the lab?" The lab rabbit replied, "I can't help it. I'm dying for a cigarette!"

It's like the kid who never said a word for six years. His parents took him to speech therapists but the kid never spoke. And then one morning at breakfast, he looked up from his bowl of cereal and said, "The milk is sour." The parents were so happy. They said, "You talk perfectly. Why did you wait so long?" He said, "Up until now everything's been okay."

A woman answers her door, and a man is standing there. He says, "Lady, I'm sorry, but I think I just ran over your cat." The woman says, "Oh, no! I don't think so, he hardly ever gets out of the house. I don't think it could be my cat." He says, "Yeah, I'm afraid so. It came running right out of your yard. I tried to stop, but I couldn't stop." "Oh, surely not!" "What does it look like?" "Well, it's kind of flat and runny." "No, what did it look like before you hit it?" "Surprised."

A woman was walking to work one day, and she passed a pet shop. There was a parrot outside, and when she walked past, it said, "You're ugly. You're stupid." The next day, she walks by the parrot again, and again it says, "You're ugly. You're stupid." She can barely believe this, but she's late for work, so she keeps going. On the third day, she hears the same thing, "You're ugly. You're stupid." She can't stand it. She goes marching into the store and tells the owner how rude the parrot is. The store owner apologizes and tells her it will never happen again. The next day, she walks by the pet store, and the parrot is outside. She looks at the parrot as she walks by, and the parrot says, "Oh, you know."

A park ranger is explaining the difference between a raven and a crow. "A raven has six pinions on each wing, and a crow has five pinions on each wing. So really, it's just a matter of a pinion."

The father asked his son why he got poor grades in English. The son said, "I don't like to read."
    The father said, "What's wrong? Are you dyslexic?"
    The boy said, "On."

Obituary: The world champion crossword puzzler died today. In a quiet ceremony he was buried 6 down and 3 across.

Why don't Junior Leaguers go to orgies?
    Too many thank-you notes.

A beggar walked up to a well-dressed woman shopping on Rodeo Drive and said, "I haven't eaten anything in four days."
    She looked at him and said, "God, I wish I had your willpower."

A manic-depressive goes away on vacation and sends a postcard back to his psychiatrist:
    "Having a wonderful time…wish I were dead."

"These turkeys in your frozen-food section seem so small. Do they get any bigger?"
    "No, ma'am, they're dead."

One day the captain of the royal barge went down to address the slaves chained to the oars. "Men, the good news is that the queen will be joining us today for a trip up the river. The bad news is she wants to go water-skiing."

The man who wrote the "Hokey-Pokey" died peacefully at age 93. The most traumatic part for his family was getting him into his coffin. They put his left leg in. Then the trouble started.

"Boat number 99, come in, please. Your time is up. Return to the dock immediately or I'll have to charge you overtime."
"Boss, we only have 75 boats. There is no number 99."
"Boat number 66, are you in trouble?"

A police dog responds to an ad for work with the FBI. "Well," says the personnel director, "you'll have to meet some strict requirements. First, you must type at least 60 words per minute."
Sitting down at the typewriter, the dog types out 80 words per minute.
"Also," says the director, "you must pass a physical and complete the obstacle course."
This perfect canine specimen finishes the course in record time.
"There's one last requirement," the director continues. "You must be bilingual."
With confidence, the dog looks up at him and says, "Meow!"

There's been a falling-out between Madonna and Cher. Apparently they're no longer on a first-name basis.

Did you hear about the invisible man who married the invisible woman?

Yeah, their kids aren't much to look at either.

I have a stepladder. It's a very nice stepladder. But it's sad that I never knew my real ladder.

A man is lost in the desert. He walks for miles and he's dying of thirst when he sees a tent ahead and cries out, "Water! Please, water!"

A Bedouin comes out of the tent and says, "How'd you like to buy a jacket and tie?"

The man says, "No, I need water. Please."

The Bedouin says there's a tent about two kilometers south where the man can get water.

The man drags himself over the burning sands for two kilometers to the next tent, where he collapses and cries out, "Water!"

A Bedouin comes out in a tuxedo and says, "I'm sorry, but you'll need a jacket and tie."

Three samurai meet to decide which is the greatest swordsman. The judge approached the first samurai and opened a small box. Out flew a fly. The samurai's sword flashed through the air and the fly fell to the ground, sliced in half. "Very impressive," said the judge. Now the judge came to the second samurai and again opened a small box. The samurai's sword flashed twice and the fly fell neatly cut into four parts. "Superb!" exclaimed the judge. Finally it was the third samurai's turn. The judge opened a third small box and a third fly buzzed out. The samurai's sword flashed through the air and the fly continued to buzz away. The third samurai put up his sword with a satisfied grin on his face. "But the fly still lives," observed the judge. "True," replied the samurai, "but he will never have children."

Charles, the son of an ailing rich man, decided he was going to need a woman to enjoy life with when his dad died. He went to a singles' bar, saw a beautiful woman, and walked up to her and said, "I'm just an ordinary man, but in a week or two my father will die and I'll inherit twenty million dollars."

The woman went home with Charles, and the next day she became his stepmother.

Some turtles went on a picnic. It took them ten days to get there, and when they arrived they realized they'd forgotten the bottle opener. So they told the littlest one to go back for it. He said, "No, as soon as I go you'll eat the sandwiches." But they promised they wouldn't, and he left. They waited for him ten days, twenty days, and after thirty days they were so hungry they had to eat a sandwich. And as soon as they took a bite, the turtle came out from behind a rock and said, "See? That's why I'm not going!"

A waitress comes to the table where Jean-Paul Sartre is sitting.

"Can I get you something to drink, Monsieur Sartre?"

"Yes, I'd like a cup of coffee with sugar, but no cream."

"Ah. I am so sorry, Monsieur Sartre, but we are all out of cream. How about with no milk?"

Why not say "288" in polite conversation?

Because it's two gross.

A nearsighted whale was following the submarine. Every time it shot a torpedo, the whale passed out cigars.

A young guy from Texas moves to California and goes to a big department store looking for a job. The manager says, "Do you have any sales experience?"

The kid says, "Yeah, I was a salesman back home in Texas."

Well, the boss liked the kid so he gave him the job. "You start tomorrow. I'll come down after we close and see how you did."

His first day on the job was rough but he got through it. After the store was locked up, the boss came down. "How many sales did you make today?"

Kid says, "One."

The boss says, "Just one? Our sales people average twenty or thirty sales a day. How much was the sale for?"

The kid says "$101,237.64"

The boss says "$101,237.64? What did you sell?"

The kid says, "First I sold him a small fishhook. Then I sold him a medium fishhook. Then I sold him a larger fishhook. Then I sold him a new fishing rod. Then I asked him where he was going fishing and he said down at the coast so I told him he was gonna need a boat, so we went down to the boat department and I sold him that twin engine Chris Craft. Then he said he didn't think his Honda Civic would pull it so I took him down to the automotive department and sold him that 4x4 Blazer."

The boss said, "A guy came in here to buy a fishhook and you sold him a boat and truck?"

The kid says, "No, he came in here to buy a box of tampons for his wife and I said, 'Well, your weekend's shot. You might as well go fishing.'"

An old blind man was standing on the corner when his dog cocked its leg and pissed all over the man's trousers. The man reached into his pocket and pulled out a dog biscuit. "You shouldn't reward him for doing something like that," said a passerby. "He'll never learn."

"I'm not rewarding him," replied the blind man. "I'm just trying to find his mouth so I can kick him in the ass!"

A guy was driving down the road and ran over a rooster, and he felt guilty, so he stopped and went up to the farmhouse and said to the farmer, "I'd like to replace your rooster," and the farmer said, "Okay. The chickens are out back."

A guy in a restaurant yells to the waiter, "Hey, there's a fly in my soup." The waiter replies, "It's possible. The cook used to be a tailor."

A guy is driving down the road and sees a farmer lifting a pig up under an apple tree. Each time the farmer lifts the pig up, it bites off an apple. The guy in the car stops and asks what's going on. The farmer says, "I'm feeding my pig." The guy in the car says, "If you shook the apples down on the ground and let the pig eat them that way, wouldn't that save a lot of time?" And the farmer says, "What's time to a pig?"

If you could have a conversation with someone, living or dead, who would it be?

I'd choose the one who's living.

So this frog goes to a psychic and the psychic tells him, "You are going to meet a beautiful young woman who will want to know intimate things about you."

The frog says, "That's great! Will I meet her at a party?"

The psychic says, "No, next week in her biology class."

A family decided to go into cattle ranching and bought some land out west and a hundred head of cattle. The father wanted to call the ranch the Bar-J and his wife liked the name Suzy-Q, and their son thought it should be the Flying-W, and their daughter wanted to call it Lazy-Y. So they compromised and called it the Bar-J-Suzy-Q-Flying-W-Lazy-Y, and unfortunately none of the cattle survived the branding.

"Would you like a cup of coffee?"

"No, thanks. When I drink coffee, I can't sleep."

"Huhh. In my case it's the other way around. When I sleep, I can't drink coffee."

"Hello? Is this the fire department?"

"Yes."

"Listen, my house is on fire! You've got to come right away! It's terrible!"

"Okay, how do we get to your house?"

"You don't have those big red trucks anymore?"

"Sadie, I–I tink I svallowed a bone."

"Are you choking, Hyman?"

"No, I'm serious!"

A horse is tied up at a hitching post. A little dog comes along and starts playing around the horse. The horse gets annoyed and starts pawing the ground.

The dog looks up and asks, "What are you doing that for?"

The horse looks down and says, "Well, I'll be damned, a talking dog."

"Mr. Johnson, I want to speak with you about your son. I discovered him playing doctor with my daughter!"

"Well, it's only natural for children that age to explore their sexuality in the form of play."

"Sexuality?! He took out her appendix!"

"Miss Francis, I ain't got no crayons."

"Young man, you mean, I don't have any crayons. You don't have any crayons. We don't have any crayons. They don't have any crayons. Do you see what I'm getting at?"

"I think so. What happened to all the crayons?"

One night, a caveman comes running into his cave and says, "Whew! There was a tiger chasing me all the way across the savannah!"

His wife says, "Why?"

The caveman says, "I didn't stop to ask!"

I've got a dining room set that goes back to Louis the Fourteenth. That is, unless I pay Louis by the thirteenth.

Two cows are lying in a field. One of them says to the other, "So, what do you think about this mad cow disease?"

The other says, "What do I care? I'm a helicopter."

I was driving to work the other day when I hit a pig. I was just gonna drive away when I thought better of it and called the police to tell them.

The dispatcher said, "Thanks for calling us, but don't you go anywhere. It's illegal to hit livestock in this state. That's a $300 fine."

So I hung up, got in the car, and drove off. When I got to work there was a cop waiting for me. He gave me a ticket for $300. When I asked him how he found me he said, "The pig squealed."

I was walking down the street and saw two guys trying to steal an old lady's handbag. She was putting up quite a fight, and I didn't know if I should get involved or not. Finally I decided to help, and it didn't take the three of us very long to get it away from her.

The baby snake says to the mommy snake, "Mommy, are we poisonous?"

The mommy snake says, "Why do you ask?"

And the baby snake says, "Because I just bit my tongue."

Two penguins are standing on an iceberg. One penguin says to the other, "You look like you're wearing a tuxedo."

The other penguin replies, "Who says I'm not?"

A male and female pigeon made a date to meet on the ledge outside the fiftieth floor of the Chrysler Building. The female was there on time, but the male arrived an hour late.

"Where were you? I was worried sick."

"It was such a nice day, I decided to walk."

A girl brought her new boyfriend home to meet her parents and they were horrified by his greasy hair, tattoos, dirty language, and air of hostility. After he left, the mother said, "Dear, he doesn't seem like a very nice person."

And the daughter said, "Mother, if he wasn't a nice person, why would he be doing 500 hours of community service?"

One day a guy answers his door and finds a snail at his doorstep. The guy picks it up and tosses it into the garden.

Two years later, he hears a knock on his door. He opens the door and finds the same snail. And the snail says, "Hey, what was that all about?"

This man buys a pet parrot and brings him home. But the parrot starts cursing him and using terrible language and insulting his wife, so finally the man picks up the parrot and throws him in the freezer to teach him a lesson.

He hears the parrot squawking and screaming in there for a while, and then all of a sudden the parrot is quiet. So the man opens the freezer door, and the parrot walks out, looks up at him, and says, "I apologize for offending you, and I humbly ask your forgiveness."

The man says, "Well, thank you. I forgive you."

And the parrot says, "If you don't mind my asking, what did the chicken do?"

In the middle of a show, a guy stands up and yells at the ventriloquist, "Hey! You've been making enough jokes about us Polish people! Cut it out!"

The ventriloquist says, "Take it easy. They're only jokes!"

And the guy says, "I'm not talking to you. I'm talking to that little guy sitting on your knee!"

Two ladies are sitting next to each other on the plane, one from the North and one from the South. The lady from the South turns to the lady from the North and says, "Where y'all from?"

The lady from the North says, "We are from a place where we do not end our sentences with prepositions."

The flight continues for an hour or so, and finally the lady from the South says, "So where y'all from, bitch?"

Woman running for garbage truck: Am I too late for the garbage?

Garbage man: No, no. Hop right in.

Hotel clerk: Would you like the sixty-dollar room or the eighty-dollar room?

Guest: What's the difference?

Clerk: The eighty-dollar room has free TV.

When I was a kid, we were so poor that when my little brother broke his arm we had to take him out to the airport for X-rays.

We were so poor, my dad would eat Cheerios with a fork so he could pass the milk around the table.

We were so poor, we'd lick stamps for dinner.

We were so poor, we didn't even use the "O" and "R."

What's the birth rate in your town?
    Same as everywhere: one per person.

A dog owner takes his sick dog to the vet. The vet examines the dog and pronounces it terminally ill. The pet owner requests a second opinion. So the vet brings his own kitten in, and the kitten examines the sick dog and shakes his head. The pet owner requests another opinion. This time the vet brings in his Labrador retriever, who jumps up on the examining table with the sick dog, sniffs and licks it, and then also shakes his head. The pet owner, now convinced, asks how much he owes the doctor. The doctor says he owes $650. The pet owner, surprised, asks why the bill is so high. The doctor replies that the exam was only $50; the additional $600 was for the cat scan and the lab test.

What do you get when you use LSD along with birth control pills?
    A trip without the kids.

"We went to this wonderful restaurant today and I can't remember the name of it. What's that flower with the sharp thorns that can be red, white, or pink?"
    "Rose?"
    "Yeah. Hey, Rose, what's the name of that restaurant?"

My father decided that I should learn how to swim. We went to one of the lakes in the area, and my father put a boat in the water. He rowed me out a little way from shore and threw me overboard. I swam back to shore. He took me out farther and threw me overboard again. Again, I swam back to shore. He took me out still farther, to the deepest part of the lake, and threw me overboard once more. I swam back to shore again. That's how I learned to swim. Actually, learning to swim wasn't the hard part—it was getting out of that burlap bag.

A visitor to a dude ranch is walking around the corral one day and sees one of the older hands feeding the horses. He walks over and strikes up a conversation.

"How long have you worked here?" he asks.

"Twenty-five years," the ranch hand says.

"Ever had any accidents?"

"Nope," says the ranch hand, "none at all."

"Really?" says the visitor. "Twenty-five years, and not a single problem?"

"Well," says the ranch hand, "I did get bit on the hand by a horse once."

"Well, isn't that an accident?" asks the visitor.

"Nope," says the ranch hand. "He bit me on purpose."

Ticket seller: Excuse me, ma'am. Your son is traveling on a child's ticket?! How old is he?

Mother: He's four years old.

Ticket seller: He looks at least twelve to me.

Mother: Can I help it if he worries?

"So I came into town around midnight, but there was only one hotel and the clerk said every room was taken."

"So what did you do?"

"I begged. I got down on my knees. I said, 'You've got to have a room. Anything. Please.'"

"And?"

"Finally, she said, 'Well, I do have a double room with only one occupant, and probably he wouldn't mind splitting the cost, but to tell you the truth, he snores so loud that people down the hall complain about it. You won't get a minute of sleep.'"

"So what'd you do?"

"I took the room."

"How'd you sleep?"

"No problem."

"Didn't the other guy snore?"

"No. I got dressed for bed, went over, gave him a kiss on the cheek, said, 'Goodnight, beautiful,' and he sat up all night watching me."

Sad man: Lady, I wonder if you wouldn't give a few bucks to help out a poor family here in the neighborhood. The father is dead, the mother is too sick to work, the nine children are hungry, and they're about to be thrown out into the street unless they can pay their rent.

Woman: How terrible! Are you a friend of theirs?

Sad man: I'm their landlord.

My computer has a virus called the PBS virus. Every hour it freezes up and asks for money.

Did you hear about the robbery at the public radio station? The thieves got away with $25,000 in pledges.

A group from Chicago spent a weekend gambling in Las Vegas. One of the men on that trip won $100,000. He didn't want anyone to know about it, so he decided not to return with the others. He took a later plane home, arriving back at 3 a.m. He immediately went out to the backyard of his house, dug a hole, and planted the money in it. The following morning he walked outside and found only an empty hole. He noticed footsteps leading from the hole to the house next door, which was owned by a deaf-mute. On the same street lived a professor who understood sign language and was a friend of the deaf man. Grabbing his pistol, the enraged man went to awaken the professor, and he dragged him over to the deaf man's house.

"You tell this guy that if he doesn't give me back my $100,000, I'm going to kill him!" he screamed at the professor. The professor conveyed the message to his friend, and his friend replied in sign language, "I hid it in my backyard, underneath the cherry tree."

The professor turned to the man with the gun and said, "He's not going to tell you. He said he'd rather die first."

What's big and gray and wrote gloomy poetry? T. S. Elephant.

Did you hear about the dyslexic devil worshipper? He sold his soul to Santa.

When it comes right down to it, dyslexics have more nuf.

What do the letters DNA stand for?
National Dyslexics' Association.

A man was walking down the street with two suitcases when a stranger came up and asked, "Have you got the time?"

The man put down the suitcases, looked at his wristwatch, and said, "It's exactly five forty-six and fifty-point-six seconds, and the barometric pressure is 30.06 and rising, and if you'd like to see where we are by satellite positioning, I can show you that, too, or get onto the Internet, check your e-mail, make a long-distance call, or send a fax. It's also a pager, it plays recorded books, and it receives FM."

The stranger said, "That's amazing. I've got to have that watch. I'll pay you."

The guy said, "Oh, no, it's not ready for sale yet. I'm the inventor. I'm still working out the bugs."

The stranger offered him ten thousand, fifteen, twenty—finally the guy sold it for twenty-five thousand. He took the watch off his wrist, and the stranger walked away with it. The guy held up the suitcases and called, "Don't you want the batteries?"

Painter: What's your opinion of my painting?
Critic: It's worthless.
Painter: I know, but I'd like to hear it anyway.

"You lied to me. You told me your father was dead, when in fact he's been in prison all these years."
"Well, I don't call that living."
"And he shot a priest."
"It was a white collar crime."

392

Man: I hate this modern art. What a piece of crap that is.

Woman: No, that's a Picasso.

Man: What about this one with all these crazy squiggles?

Woman: That's a Kandinsky.

Man: Okay, how about this one where the guy's got a pencil neck, his nose is upside down, and his eyes are on the same side of his head?

Woman: That's a mirror.

"Hey, Bob, remember when you and I went fishing up north nine months ago and the car broke down in that thunderstorm and we wound up spending the night at that farm owned by that gorgeous widow—you remember?"

"Yeah."

"You remember the gorgeous widow?"

"Yeah."

"And she had that big fabulous house and we slept in the guest wing and she was over in her wing and the next morning we got in our car and headed north and went fishing—you remember?"

"Yeah."

"Well, nine months later, I get a letter from her attorney."

"Oh?"

"Did you happen to get up in the middle of the night and go pay her a visit?"

"I did. Yes."

"And did you happen to use my name instead of telling her your name?"

"I'm sorry. I did. Why do you ask?"

"She just died and left me everything."

A businessman in New York called his mother on Long Island. "Mom, it's me."

"Don't worry about not calling. If I had a stroke, it probably wouldn't be that bad."

"I'm sorry."

"Don't worry about not visiting me. If I were on the floor I could probably drag myself over to the phone and call for help."

"Mom, I've been terribly busy. I'm awfully sorry. But we're coming this weekend, the whole family. Me and Doris and the kids."

"Doris?"

"My wife, Doris."

"Your wife's name is Hannah!"

"Is this 516-555-9312?"

"9313."

"Oh, I'm terribly sorry, madam."

"You mean you're not coming?"

I was having an asthma attack when I got an obscene phone call and after a couple minutes the guy said, "Wait. Did I call you or did you call me?"

Waitress: What can I get you?
Customer: Couple of eggs.
Waitress: How would you like those eggs cooked?
Customer: Yeah, I would.